VÁCLAV HAVEL

20th Century Political Thinkers
Series Editors: Kenneth L. Deutsch and Jean Bethke Elshtain

Raymond Aron: The Recovery of the Political
　by Brian C. Anderson
Jacques Maritain: The Philosopher in Society
　by James V. Schall
Martin Buber: The Hidden Dialogue
　by Dan Avnon
John Dewey: America's Philosopher of Democracy
　by David Fott
Simone Weil: The Way of Justice as Compassion
　by Richard H. Bell
Gandhi: Struggling for Autonomy
　by Ronald J. Terchek
Paul Ricoeur: The Promise and Risk of Politics
　by Bernard P. Dauenhauer
Carl Schmitt: The End of Law
　by William E. Scheuerman
Eric Voegelin: In Quest of Reality
　by Thomas W. Heilke
Yves R. Simon: Real Democracy
　by Vukan Kuic
Jürgen Habermas: A Philosophical-Political Profile
　by Martin J. Beck Matuštík
Aleksandr Solzenhenitsyn: The Ascent from Ideology
　by Daniel J. Mahoney
Charles Taylor: Thinking and Living Deep Diversity
　by Mark Redhead
Václav Havel: Civic Responsibility in the Postmodern Age
　by James F. Pontuso

VÁCLAV HAVEL

Civic Responsibility in the Postmodern Age

JAMES F. PONTUSO

ROWMAN & LITTLEFIELD PUBLISHERS, INC.
Lanham • Boulder • New York • Toronto • Oxford

ROWMAN & LITTLEFIELD PUBLISHERS, INC.

Published in the United States of America
by Rowman & Littlefield Publishers, Inc.
A wholly owned subsidiary of The Rowman & Littlefield Publishing Group, Inc.
4501 Forbes Boulevard, Suite 200, Lanham, Maryland 20706
www.rowmanlittlefield.com

PO Box 317
Oxford
OX2 9RU, UK

Copyright © 2004 by Rowman & Littlefield Publishers, Inc.

All rights reserved. No part of this publication may be reproduced,
stored in a retrieval system, or transmitted in any form or by any
means, electronic, mechanical, photocopying, recording, or otherwise,
without the prior permission of the publisher.

British Library Cataloguing in Publication Information Available

Library of Congress Cataloging-in-Publication Data

Pontuso, James F.
  Václav Havel : civic responsibility in the postmodern age / James F. Pontuso.
    p. cm. — (20th century political thinkers)
  Includes bibliographical references and index.
  ISBN 0-7425-2255-5 (cloth : alk. paper) — ISBN 0-7425-2256-3 (pbk. : alk. paper)
  1. Havel, Václav—Contributions in political science. 2. Political science—Philosophy.
  3. Responsibility. 4. Havel, Václav. 5. Czech Republic—Politics and government—
  1993–
  I. Title. II. Series.
  JC273.H37P66 2004
  943.7105′092—dc22   2004003265

Printed in the United States of America

∞™ The paper used in this publication meets the minimum requirements of
American National Standard for Information Sciences—Permanence of Paper for
Printed Library Materials, ANSI/NISO Z39.48-1992.

For Rosalind, a dear friend

CONTENTS

Preface		ix
1	A Life like a Work of Art	1
2	A Hesitant Philosopher	15
3	A Dissident in an "Unnatural" World	55
4	An Ironic Playwright	69
5	Free Markets and Civil Society: Citizen in the Global Economy	123
6	An "Untactical" President	152
Index		171
About the Author		175

PREFACE

In 1993 I was on a Fulbright grant in Prague lecturing to Charles University students about the American presidency. One student asked me to name the best president I had ever lived under. I gave a flippant answer, hoping for a laugh—Václav Havel, I said. Later I thought about it and decided that I had been right. This book is an effort to prove my claim.

Of course, Václav Havel cannot be counted as a great *political* leader. The opportunities for him to shape world events were limited by the institutional weakness of the Czech presidency and the size of the Czech Republic. But despite these handicaps, Havel cast a long shadow, partly because of the multidimensional character of his life. He has been at various times a playwright, a dissident, a philosopher, and a president. In all those roles, he has exhibited extraordinary determination, originality, irony, and humor. What was perhaps even more impressive was Havel's dedication to the principle of individual responsibility. Havel's greatness resides in his being a spokesman for, and an exemplar of, the highest and therefore the most difficult kind of moral behavior.

This book is primarily about Havel's ideas and his lifelong effort to defend and promote the principles of morally responsible action. But Havel is not only a thinker; he is also a man of action. Therefore, the book explores some of the events and issues that have shaped his life and tested his principles. I was attracted to this topic because I consider political science to be the study of how normative judgments relate to practical affairs.

As a teacher, I am sometimes bemused by the "half-life" of knowledge, how current events—about which almost everyone is aware—quickly disappear into the mists of history. Thus, I must remind those who have forgotten and inform those who never knew that I wrote an overly brief and admittedly superficial biographical sketch of Václav Havel. I trust that those who remember what was one of the hottest "current events" of the early 1990s—Havel's biography—will forgive me for trying to find "the middle of the class."

Portions of this book were previously published as "Transformation Politics: The Debate between Václav Havel and Václav Klaus on the Free Market and Civil Society," *Studies in East European Thought*, 54 (September 2002): 153–177; "Review Essay, *Václav Havel: A Political Tragedy in Six Acts*, by John Keane," *Society* 39 (July/August 2002): 80, 81–87; "The Political Philosophy of Václav Havel," *Critical Review of International Social and Political Philosophy* 5 (Spring 2002): 43–81; and "Havel's Vanek Plays: Disobedience and Responsibility," *Perspectives on Political Science* 34. I appreciate the permission to reprint them in this book.

I have selfish reasons for being grateful that the Cold War is over: I have been fortunate to meet and learn from a wonderfully literate group of Central Europeans. I extend my gratitude to all of them for putting up with what must have seemed like an unending series of questions. My appreciation goes to Slavenka Drakulic, Dan Draghici, Valária Hegyi, Hedi Hegyi, Paul Anghel, Mihaela Mihailescu, Krysztof Jasiewicz, Pavel Mertlík, Irena Sklenar, Jiri Sklenar, Pavla Cejnkova, Petr Kadlec, Milos Calda, Jakub Franek, Pavel Ripka, Jan Skaloud, Rudolph Kučera, and Jan Sokol. Special thanks to Viktor Janis for translating much-needed materials. Hanka Ripková, director of the Czech Fulbright Commission, honored me twice by selecting me to teach in her elegant city. Alena Hromádková, former spokesperson for Charter 77, offered an insider's view of the life of a dissident and introduced me to many interesting people.

The Committee for Professional Development at Hampden-Sydney College provided generous financial support. I would also like to thank the late Steva Freiden for first piquing my interest in Central Europe. James Angresano, former educational director of the Civic Education Project, helped acclimate me to the post-Communist world. Tobias Wolny, former foreign policy advisor to President Havel, provided firsthand recollections of his boss's intellect, integrity, and wit. Mary Carpenter at Rowman & Littlefield encouraged me to undertake this project. Aviezer Tucker, with whose interpretation of Havel I occasionally disagree, generously corrected some of my more egregious errors. Rosalind Warfield-Brown went above and beyond the responsibilities of a friend to edit the manuscript. Marie Balestra and Carolyn Moscatel gave me moral support, as they have done all their lives.

I would most especially like to thank Anne M. Pontuso, who, both in her professional role as a nurse and in her private life with her family, has pursued the highest ideals of responsibility detailed in this book.

1

A LIFE LIKE A WORK OF ART

> I have always been especially allergic to the remark attributed (wrongly, I think) to Goethe: "a life should resemble a work of art." It is because life is formless and does not resemble a work of art that man needs art. Yet in these great days for my old homeland, Central Europe, I learned with enormous joy that Václav Havel would soon become president of the Czechoslovak Republic. I think about him and say to myself: there are cases (very rare) where comparing a life to a work of art is justified.
>
> —Milan Kundera[1]

Imagine that you woke up one morning and found that almost everyone around you was lying. Government leaders, the police, judges, and journalists lied all the time. Many ordinary people seemed to believe the lies, and those who did not kept to themselves. The lies were so obvious that you had only to use the evidence of your senses to know that what people were saying was untrue. It was claimed that apartment buildings were grand, when they were uniform, gray, and ugly. It was said that material conditions in the country were improving, when in reality most people were worse off than their parents had been. Government officials maintained that the government was made up of laborers and was dedicated to the welfare of workers, yet few officials had ever held manual jobs, and most ordinary people toiled at low-paying, tedious work. The environment was contaminated; the educational system attempted to indoctrinate as much as it tried to teach; churches were subverted; and people's morale was low. If you looked at the media, however, you would not have thought that these problems existed.

When you described the reality that you saw around you, instead of reciting official linguistic formulas, you discovered that although the government declared that people could freely express their views, it vigorously suppressed those who did. Your penchant for telling the truth brought you no end of misery. You were ridiculed, threatened, and followed; and you were labeled an enemy of your country. You were not allowed to pursue a career. You could find employment only in the most menial jobs. You were sent to jail for signing a document that asked the government to obey its treaty obligations by granting its citizens natural rights. You stuck to telling the truth, even in prison—where your spirit was nearly broken—despite there being little hope that your actions would effect a positive political change. The only reward for your integrity was the principle of integrity itself.

Then one day, a short while after one of your stays in prison, everyone stopped lying. You and some of your friends stood before a huge crowd in a beautiful and historic square and swept away the government of lies by jingling your keys (signaling the death knell of the regime). Everyone now realized that *you* had been telling the truth all along. They decided to make you leader of the country. You took the oath of office, looking a bit uncomfortable in your newly tailored suit. You eschewed the customary optimistic rhetoric spoken by politicians on taking office and spoke the simple truth to your fellow citizens:

> For forty years you heard from my predecessors on this day different variations on the same theme: how our country was flourishing, how many million tons of steel we produced, how happy we all were, how we trusted our government, and what bright perspectives were unfolding in front of us. I assume you did not propose me for this office so that I, too, would lie to you. Our country is not flourishing.[2]

This little vignette might have been written by a surrealist playwright. In fact, it was written *about* a man whom playwright Arthur Miller has called the first surrealist president.[3]

Václav Havel's life has been full of contradictions, ironies, and strange twists and turns. His character comprises the most extreme incongruities. In 1936 he was born into a successful entrepreneurial family who had built and owned Lucerna Palace, a multiuse entertainment and shopping complex just off Wenceslas Square that was the first steel and concrete structure erected in Prague. His father added to the family fortune by constructing restaurant and housing complexes. The Havels owned an attractive house on the banks of the Vltava River, with a lovely view of the magnificent Hradčany—the

Prague Castle and the seat of the Czech government—as well as vacation homes in Moravia and in eastern Bohemia. The family fortune was substantial enough to support a staff of domestics, including a cook, gardener, governess, maid, and chauffeur. Young Václav Havel was embarrassed by the advantages of wealth. He felt somehow different from other children. He was also overweight, which was taken by his playmates as a symbol of his privileged life. The children teased him, making him self-conscious and introspective. It was not until he started dating Olga Šplíchalová, whom he married in 1964, that he gained confidence about his physical appearance and began to develop a sense of self-worth.[4]

Havel suffered twice from his wealth. He was not comfortable with the material benefits that affluence provided, and when the Communists took power in 1948, he was suspect as a consequence of his bourgeois background. Because of the Communist policy of disenfranchising members of the bourgeoisie, the family fortune was confiscated. Václav Havel was initially denied admission to higher education and excluded from studying humanities. Although he was not allowed to enroll in the Academy of Performing Arts, he was able to attend evening school at the Czech University of Technology, where he studied economics and worked as a laboratory technician to support his education. The discrimination he suffered was the genesis of his artistic genre: absurd theater.

> My childhood feeling of exclusion, or of the instability of my place in the world (later, after the victory of communism, it was augmented by the experience of being the constant target of the "class struggle," which once more evoked the experience of exclusion through no fault of my own), could not but have an influence on the way I viewed the world—a view which is in fact a key to my plays. It is a view "from below," a view from the "outside," a view that has grown out of the experience of absurdity. What else but a profound feeling of being excluded can enable a person better to see the absurdity of the world and his own existence or, to put it more soberly, the absurd dimensions of the world and his own existence?[5]

The Havel family's inheritance was not all bad. Family relations were affectionate, and both parents' loving acceptance created a strong sense of discipline, independence, and responsibility in Václav and his brother Ivan.[6] What informed the children's education was Masarykian humanism, a highly cultured and tolerant tradition of learning in the arts, philosophy, and literature. (Tomáš Garrigue Masaryk was Czechoslovakia's first president.)

Václav Havel began reading philosophy at an early age. Through his father's connections, Václav met many of the leading cultural figures of his day.

Havel seemed to have a knack for associating with talented people. When he was a young man, his circle of friends included writer Milan Kundera and eventual Oscar-winner Milos Forman. In spite of his shyness, he had the nerve (perhaps effrontery!) to introduce himself to Jaroslav Seifert, later winner of a Nobel Prize for literature, and the great Czech philosopher Jan Patočka. In his twenties and thirties, Havel was a member of a "table" at Café Slavia—just across from the National Theater and Magic Lantern entertainment complex—a favorite hangout of intellectuals, dissidents, and theater people.

Havel spent two years in the army fulfilling his compulsory duty, although he seemed more interested in writing and acting in plays than in acquiring military discipline. His professional life began in 1959, when he found work as a stagehand at the ABC Theatre of Prague. He moved on to the Theatre on the Balustrade, where he eventually rose to dramaturge. The early 1960s were a hopeful time in Prague. The Stalinist era had ended, ushering in by an awakening of personal and artistic freedom. That period was a particularly creative time in Havel's life, during which he wrote and directed *The Garden Party* (1963), *The Memorandum* (1965), and *The Increased Difficulty of Concentration* (1968), winner of an off-Broadway Obie Award.[7]

His predilection for telling the truth often landed Havel in trouble. While attending the University of Technology in 1956, he was invited to a Writers' Union conference for young artists. It was to be his first public address, and he found himself among writers of "socialist realism," the artificial and hagiographic style developed during Stalin's reign. Barely in his twenties and with no reputation to protect him, Havel promptly attacked socialist realism, the Writers' Union, the continued oppression of literature, and the blackballing of poets and artists who refused to copy the accepted styles. Edá Kriseová comments that "they looked at the blond young man, a little chubby, with clear blue eyes. He looked like an angel, and he spoke the truth." But it was a truth "they were reluctant to accept."[8]

Havel was equally undiplomatic and just as truthful at his second appearance at the Writers' Union.

> In 1965 there was a conference of the Writers' Union on the occasion of the twentieth anniversary of the liberation [from Nazi occupation].
> . . . I decided that the best defense was attack. I wrote an incendiary speech in which I said many harsh things about the Writers' Union, and particularly that this anniversary could best be marked by the Union's

taking a critical look at itself. I pointed out the rampant bureaucratism and inflexibility, the intolerance, the number of wonderful authors who were senselessly excluded from literature and whom the Union was incapable of pardoning.[9]

Havel's protesting picked up steam after the remarkable events of 1968. Under the reform-minded Communist Party leader Alexander Dubček, Czechoslovakia became, for a brief period at least, an open society. Havel used the opportunity to push the envelope of change, calling for a multiparty democracy. But, Leonid Brezhnev and the rest of the Communist establishment in the Kremlin were frightened that Dubček's brand of "Socialism with a human face" might lead exactly to the kind of liberal democracy that Havel advocated, resulting in the disintegration of the Soviet empire in Central Europe and the eventual collapse of the Soviet Union. In August, Soviet leaders sent the Red Army into Czechoslovakia in an act of "socialist fraternity" aimed at protecting a member of the Warsaw Pact from counterrevolution.

At the time, Havel was in Liberec, a city in northeastern Bohemia. He holed up with a friend at the local radio station, broadcasting news of events, commenting on what should be done, and offering strategies for resisting the occupation. Only after Dubček appeared on television in what appeared to be a capitulation did the Liberec resistance crumble.[10] In a desperate effort to rally his fellow citizens through a symbolic protest, a Charles University student named Jan Palach lit himself afire at Wenceslas Square. But the Soviets prevailed.

What followed was the "era of normalization," a dull, depressing period in which the Communist government sought to maintain order by squelching spontaneity, personal initiative, and anything that deviated from the Soviet model. It was an "era of apathy and widespread demoralization . . . an era of gray, everyday totalitarian consumerism. Society was atomized, small islands of resistance were destroyed, and a disappointed and exhausted public pretended not to notice."[11] Havel's avant-garde plays were banned, and he was eventually prohibited from working in the theater altogether. Although Havel's "career as a world-class playwright would disappear," his biographer John Keane writes that, "ironically," this would leave "him free to become a serious political essayist and to fight his way into political life."[12]

Havel reacted to the monotony in a number of ways. He moved out of Prague to his country cottage. He invited friends. They talked, conspired, and freed themselves from the oppression, if only in their minds. He cooked, although he never used the same recipe twice, in protest to the standardized menus in Czech restaurants. Havel's public defiance came in 1975, when he sent an open letter to Dr. Gustav Husák, general secretary of the Czechoslovak Communist Party. "Dear Dr. Husák" was a bitter indictment of the "post-totalitarian" system, whose major goal was to keep the nation calm, as "calm as a morgue or a grave," Havel wrote.[13] After sending the letter, Havel took to carrying around an "emergency packet" of toothpaste, a toothbrush, soap, cigarettes, and a change of underwear, just in case he was arrested.[14]

Havel helped form Charter 77, a human rights group that grew out of the trial and conviction of the Plastic People of the Universe, a rock-and-roll band whose antiestablishment lyrics infuriated the staid Communist rulers.[15] Havel enlisted his philosophic mentor, Jan Patočka, as spokesman for the group. When Charter 77's activities were noticed in the West, the Communist government reacted. Arrests were made, and Chartists were interrogated. During a week-long interrogation in which he attempted to engage StB (state security police) investigators in philosophic discussion, the sixty-nine-year-old Patočka died of a stroke.[16] Including family members, friends, and students, about one thousand mourners attended his funeral, all under the watchful eye of the StB. Those brave enough to take part in the ceremony were harassed and branded as enemies of the state. Careers were lost. Havel penned a poignant homage to Patočka in which the philosopher's last words were about the immortality of the soul; it reads not unlike *Crito* or *Phaedo*, Plato's tributes to his mentor.[17]

Havel also dedicated his most famous dissident essay, "The Power of the Powerless," to Patočka. Widely distributed in *samizdat* (the underground publishing network composed of little more than a typewriter and carbon paper), "The Power of the Powerless" quickly became the intellectual rallying call for the dissident movement. Zbygniew Bujak, a member of the Polish Solidarity movement, reports that Havel's article reached him just as Solidarity was about to give up.

> Then came the essay by Havel. Reading it gave us the theoretical underpinnings for our activity. It maintained our spirits; we did not give up, and a year later—in August 1980—it became clear that the party apparatus and the factory management were afraid of us. We mattered. And the rank and file saw us as leaders of the movement. When I look at the victories of Solidarity, and of Charter 77, I see in them an astonishing fulfillment of the prophecies and knowledge contained in Havel's essay.[18]

But Havel's troubles had just begun. He was arrested, and, without knowing what his Chartist colleagues were doing and in order to protect them, he signed a kind of agreement with his interrogators. The StB released the letter to the press as a capitulation. Havel was devastated and blamed himself for years thereafter for an act of cowardice.[19] He later turned his despair over the incident into creative energy, writing *Temptation* and *Largo Desolato,* based on the themes of entrapment, self-deception, and betrayal.

By 1979, the authorities had had enough. Havel and fifteen members of the Committee to Defend the Unjustly Prosecuted (known by its Czech acronym VONS) were arrested and charged with subversion, a crime carrying a ten-year prison sentence. The trial was a mockery of justice reminiscent of the show trials of the earlier Communist era. One defendant's state-appointed lawyer congratulated the prosecutor on the indictment and apologized for having to plead his client innocent. Although no evidence surfaced at the trial that any member of VONS had done anything but petition the government (a right nominally guaranteed under the constitution), Havel was sentenced to four-and-a-half years of hard labor.

Again Havel turned his setback into creativity, writing letters to his wife—which were later turned into the book-length *Letters to Olga,* one of the strangest "philosophic" works ever published. Along with lengthy theoretic reflections, Havel used the letters to bare his soul: he exhibited extraordinary courage and steadfastness yet at times showed himself to be frightened, self-absorbed, petty, and demanding. When he became seriously ill in prison, after serving more than three years of his term, Olga, always his anchor in life, raised such a stir that Havel was released.

The 1980s were a time of turmoil within the Communist world. China began to reform its economy; the Soviet Union under Mikhail Gorbachev loosened its grip on its citizens; and Solidarity showed itself to be a formidable movement by enlisting millions of Poles into its ranks. But the Czech Communists refused to change. In February of 1989 Havel was again arrested, this time for being present at a rally in honor of Jan Palach. He received a nine-month sentence but was released in May. During the summer, as European Communism began to disintegrate, strikes and antigovernment demonstrations became almost daily occurrences. Opposition groups in Poland and then Hungary negotiated power-sharing deals with Communists. Hungary opened its borders with Austria. Since East Germans could travel to a fraternal socialist state without a visa, many used the opportunity to escape to the West. For a time, so many East Germans fled that it seemed the country would be depopulated. But still the Czech leaders failed to move.

On November 17, 1989, some students decided to push. During a sanctioned demonstration in honor of Jan Opletal, a victim of the Nazi occupation, the students deviated from the approved route, marching along the Vltava past Havel's flat, some shouting "Long live Havel." When protesters neared Národní Street, they were met by police who were determined to keep them from reaching Wenceslas Square. A melee ensued, and about one hundred were arrested and dozens hurt. Although it did not commence all that gently, the Velvet Revolution had begun.[20]

As word spread, Havel, who had purposely been out of Prague and at his country home, rushed back and began to organize Civic Forum, a loosely knit group of activists, writers, and theater people who opposed the government. Larger and larger demonstrations took place, including a national strike that undermined the legitimacy of the Communist government. Negotiations took place between the authorities and Civic Forum, with Havel usually in the middle of the talks. On November 24 the entire politburo of the Communist Party resigned. The Communists attempted to salvage power by appointing Ladislav Adamec prime minister, but when he began to speak to a large crowd using standard Communist jargon, platitudes, and false promises, the mood turned ugly. "Too late, too late!" rang out. Adamec plunged ahead, not accustomed to heeding public opinion. The crowd booed him off stage.

With Adamec's political career over, Havel's began. He and Alexander Dubček were the most respected people in the country. But, the fondness for Dubček was part nostalgia; he was a symbol of the past. Havel, who had never been politically tainted by association with Communism—quite the reverse—spoke the open language of the future. Signs reading *Havel Na Hrad* (Havel to the Castle) popped up everywhere. (Prague Castle is the seat of the government.)

As his prestige grew, his ironic and self-effacing humor came to light. On December 7, Havel agreed to be interviewed. Dressed in his customary blue jeans and sweater, and chain-smoking as usual, he said, "I have called this conference because of the many requests from the press for interviews which I have been unable to grant. If I did so, I would be spending all my time commenting on the revolution and have no time for participating in the revolution." *The New Republic* reported:

> One journalist kept wanting to know whether Havel was a candidate for Czechoslovakia's presidency. "Many Civic Forum supporters are wearing Havel for President buttons today," he asked. "Are you running for president?" Havel replied, "My profession is that of playwright. The more democracy and normal conditions come to the country, the less will be my role in political life."

"Do you support those who produced the Havel for President buttons?"

"I understand the buttons come from Hungary. My influence does not yet extend that far."

Frustrated, the reporter shouted at Havel, "You are ducking my question. I asked whether you support those who produced the buttons. Answer my question."

"I've answered your question in a roundabout way, which it seems to me is very presidential. I've watched President Bush's press conferences on television, and he answers questions in the same fashion."

Three days later, on December 10, Havel formally declared his candidacy. On December 19, the new prime minister, Marian Calfa, told Parliament it had "no alternative" but to elect Havel president of Czechoslovakia.[21]

During another interview, Havel dodged a question about his personal life. The immediate follow-up asked Havel, the very creator of the concept of *living in truth*, when he had last told a lie. A grinning Havel just as quickly referred the reporter to his last answer.

Later, as president, when international acclaim began to pour in, he traveled to the Hebrew University in Jerusalem and gave a speech on Franz Kafka. In a roundabout way he stated that if Kafka did not exist, Havel would have had to create him. The new president considered his own existence something akin to a Kafka story.

> You may well ask how someone who thinks of himself this way can be the president of a country. It's a paradox, but I must admit that if I am a better president than many others would be in my place, then it is precisely because somewhere in the deepest substratum of my work lies this constant doubt about myself and my right to hold office. I am the kind of person who would not be in the least surprised if, in the very middle of my presidency, I were to be summoned and led off to stand trial before some shadowy tribunal, or taken straight to a quarry to break rocks. Nor would I be surprised if I were to suddenly hear the reveille and wake up in my prison cell, and then, with great bemusement, proceed to tell my fellow prisoners everything that had happened to me in the past six months.[22]

When an American company reneged on its contract to refurbish Café Slavia, leaving the famous dissident pub boarded up and the locals grumbling about the broken promises of Western capitalists, President Havel staged his own theatrical protest. Appearing on television in 1994, ostensibly to introduce one of his newly published books, he was interviewed on a stage set resembling Café Slavia, behind him a mock National Theater. While the interview was taking place, a suspicious character looking remarkably like one of Havel's former StB shadows began listening in on the conversation and taking notes. An adoring young woman approached, with Havel's book in hand, but was too shy to ask for an autograph. After a bit of circling, the young woman sat down next to the secret policeman, who promptly autographed her book. When the question-and-answer session ended, Havel, seemingly oblivious to the goings-on around him, thanked the interviewer as the National Theater became engulfed in flames behind them.

There was, of course, serious business. Havel oversaw the creation of democratic institutions protecting citizen rights and, much against his wishes, guided the peaceful dissolution of the country. He supported the difficult transition to a free-market economy, although, as we shall see in chapter 6, he had his reservations about the process. He dismantled the StB and reformed the army. The international press adored the poet-president, who rode a scooter through the long halls of the Czech Castle.

But no fairy tale lasts. Olga died of cancer. In 1996, the long years of smoking and stress caught up with Havel, and complications from the removal of a cancerous lung left him so ill that he was not expected to survive. John Keane's biography of Havel, written during the worst of one of Havel's health crises, reads in part like an obituary. Havel's remarriage—while in his sickbed—within a year of his first wife's death sparked a great deal of public disapproval. At the same time, the highly touted Czech economic miracle floundered, and Prime Minister Václav Klaus's political party was implicated in an election-finance scandal. Havel's popularity plummeted.

Against all odds, Havel survived, physically and politically. Thirteen years after taking office as leader of Czechoslovakia, Havel retired from the presidency of the Czech Republic. Although he was blamed by some in 1993 for the breakup of the country (the "Velvet Divorce") a week before the end of his term, Slovakia awarded him its highest civilian medal. At one of the ceremonies at the Prague Castle to mark his departure, supporters jingled their keys in remembrance of his central role in the Velvet Revolution. At another gala, Havel expressed great pleasure at the performance of Karel Gott, the popular but uninventive Czech pop singer who had signed the Communist government's "anti-Charter 77" document and whom Havel had ridiculed in his plays *Audience* and *The Unveiling*. Havel's ability to forgive should not be mistaken for a proclivity to forget the oppressed. He traveled to Miami to deliver his last major foreign address and presented what, for the normally understated Havel, can only be described as a fiery speech against Fidel Castro's dictatorship.[23]

Although many Czechs were disappointed that President Havel had not brought about change more quickly and perhaps less painfully, a week after his retirement, national polls revealed the ex-president to be the most trusted politician in the Czech Republic as "three out of five respondents gave him high trustworthiness ratings."[24] In much of the rest of the world, especially in intellectual circles, Havel was considered to be among the most respected and surely the most thoughtful statesmen on Earth. In his final presidential speech, Havel took time to apologize to his critics. "To all of you whom I have disappointed in any way, who have not agreed with my actions, or who have simply found me hateful, I sincerely apologize and trust that you will forgive me,"[25] he said. Havel was the surrealist president to the very end.

What are we to make of this complicated man? He wrote about nonpolitical politics but ended up becoming a politician. He was a chain-smoker who fretted about the environmental and health effects of air pollution. While always feeling out of place, he nonetheless perpetually seemed to be in the center of things. He was shy, polite, even reticent; yet, he could be charming, resolute, and forceful—a man of peace who nevertheless called for intervention in Bosnia and Kosovo. He was a tolerant person who in retirement used his international acclaim to seek regime change in Cuba. He exhibited enormous personal integrity and loyalty but admitted committing sins against his wife, so much so that a friend called him a "chaste centaur."[26] How is it that the same writer could foresee precisely how Communism would be overthrown yet consider John Lennon's death the most important assassination of the twentieth century?[27] How can we square his whimsical fascination with rock stars with his serious study of philosophy? What is it that led Havel, who accepts many of the same moral precepts as the religious Aleksandr Solzhenitsyn, to seriously consider appointing the avant-garde musician Frank Zappa to a government post?[28]

Perhaps the key to understanding Havel lies in his sense of being an outsider, of always feeling as if he did not belong, and of relentlessly having to prove his worth. He admits that he suffers from

> a profound, basal, and therefore utterly vague sensation of culpability, as though my very existence were a kind of sin. Then there is a powerful feeling of general alienation, both my own and relating to everything around me, which helps to create such feelings; an experience of

> unbearable oppressiveness, a need constantly to explain myself to someone, to defend myself, a longing for an unattainable order of things, a longing that increases as the terrain I walk through becomes more muddled and confusing. . . . Everything I encounter displays to me its absurd aspect first. I feel as though I am constantly lagging behind powerful, self-confident men whom I can never overtake, let alone emulate. I find myself essentially hateful, deserving only mockery.
>
> I can already hear your objections that I style myself in these Kafkaesque outlines only because in reality I'm entirely different: someone who quietly and persistently fights for something, someone whose idealism has carried him to the head of his nation. . . .
>
> I would only add that, in my opinion, the hidden motor driving all my dogged efforts is precisely this innermost feeling of mine of being excluded, of belonging nowhere, a state of disinheritance, as it were, of fundamental non-belonging. Moreover, I would say that it's precisely my desperate longing for order that keeps plunging me into the most improbable adventures. I would even venture to say that everything worthwhile I've ever accomplished I have done to conceal my almost metaphysical feeling of guilt. The real reason I am always creating something, organizing something, it would seem, is to defend my permanently questionable right to exist.[29]

Havel's alienation gave him a sense of the absurd, as if he were looking at everything from a distance. It also was the basis of his sense of humor: from his far-off vantage point he looked like a minor actor in a much grander production, and he never could take his role too seriously. Havel was unsure of his own identity, so the question of human identity became central to his philosophy, plays, political ideals, and life. Because he was never able to fully characterize his existence, he realized that the quest of Western culture since the Enlightenment—to fully know human nature the way scientific truths are comprehended—was an erroneous and perhaps dangerous endeavor. The human soul is complicated, and numerous and diverse paths shed light on its nature—hence, Havel's eclectic tastes. At the same time, he sought some stable point, some immutable principle by which to define his personality. That search led him to believe that there is a transcendent standard of human conduct at work in the universe that imperceptibly influences all human behavior. But if such a ground exists, then human beings have a responsibility to follow its dictates. Havel's efforts to discover the extent and scope of those responsibilities can best be considered if we turn to his philosophy.

NOTES

1. Milan Kundera, "A Life like a Work of Art: Homage to Václav Havel," *New Republic*, January 29, 1990, 16.
2. Václav Havel, "New Year's Address to the Nation," Prague, January 1, 1990. Unless otherwise indicated, all references to speeches were found at the (now defunct) website of former Czech President Havel.
3. Andrew Nagorski, "Parallel with a Prison," interview with Václav Havel, *Newsweek*, July 22, 1991, 31.
4. Václav Havel, *Disturbing the Peace: A Conversation with Karel Hvížala*, trans. and intro. Paul Wilson (New York: Knopf, 1990), 3–33.
5. Havel, *Disturbing the Peace*, 6.
6. James Q. Wilson suggests that people with a well-developed sense of responsibility have grown up in warm and loving families where one or both of the parents had a strong moral awareness (*The Moral Sense* [New York: Free Press, 1993], 39).
7. Havel, *Disturbing the Peace*, 51.
8. Edá Kriseová, *Václav Havel: The Authorized Biography*, trans. Caleb Crain (New York: St. Martin's Press, 1993), 15.
9. Havel, *Disturbing the Peace*, 81.
10. Havel, *Disturbing the Peace*, 110–112.
11. Havel, *Disturbing the Peace*, 119–120.
12. John Keane, *Václav Havel: A Political Tragedy in Six Acts* (New York: Basic Books, 2000), 208.
13. Václav Havel, "Dear Dr. Husák," *Open Letters: Selected Writings 1965–1990*, ed. Paul Wilson (New York: Knopf, 1991), 72.
14. Havel, "It Always Makes Sense to Tell the Truth," *Open Letters*, 87.
15. Havel, "The Trial," *Open Letters*, 102–108; *Disturbing the Peace*, 125–145.
16. The circumstances of Patočka's death were told to me by his son-in-law Jan Sokol, February 14, 2003.
17. Václav Havel, "The Last Conversation," in *Charter 77 and Human Rights in Czechoslovakia*, by H. Gordon Skilling (London: Allen & Unwin, 1981), 242–244.
18. Editor's introduction to Havel's "The Power of the Powerless," *Open Letters*, 126.
19. Václav Havel, *Letters to Olga: June 1979–September 1982*, trans. and intro. Paul Wilson (New York: Knopf, 1988), 347–349; Keane, *A Political Tragedy in Six Acts*, 255; Kriseová, *The Authorized Biography*, 134–137.
20. Timothy Garton Ash, *The Magic Lantern: The Revolution of '89 Witnessed in Warsaw, Budapest, Berlin, and Prague* (New York: Random House, 1990); Keane, *A Political Tragedy in Six Acts*, 339–347; Kriseová, *The Authorized Biography*, 245.
21. Stephen Cohen, "Roses in the Snow," *New Republic*, January 8, 1990, 13–14.
22. Václav Havel, "Speech at the Hebrew University," Jerusalem, April 26, 1990.
23. Václav Havel, "Speech at the Florida International University," Miami, September 23, 2002.

24. "Briefly Noted," *Prague Post*, February 12–18, 2003, A4.

25. Václav Havel, "Farewell Address to Czech Citizens," Prague, February 2, 2003.

26. Pavel Kohout, "The Chaste Centaur," trans. Milan Pomichalek and Anna Mozga in *The Vanek Plays: Four Authors, One Character,* ed. Marketa Goetz-Stankiewicz, (Vancouver: University of British Columbia Press, 1987) 241–246.

27. Havel, *Letters to Olga*, 149.

28. Havel wrote an obituary for Zappa ("Revolutionary: Musician Frank Zappa," *New Yorker* 69 [December 20, 1993]: 116).

29. Havel, "Speech at the Hebrew University," Jerusalem, April 26, 1990.

2

A HESITANT PHILOSOPHER

HAVEL AND MODERN PHILOSOPHY

This chapter presents Havel's philosophic views, although there is some doubt whether Havel's reflections deserve to be called "philosophy." For instance, although Edward F. Findlay acknowledges that Havel uses the language of philosophic discourse, he claims that Havel is confused, inconsistent, and poetic rather than rigorous and rational. Findlay explains,

> Unlike the philosophers whom he emulates, however, Havel makes use of metaphysical language without appending to it a rigorous definition or conceptual analysis, and the result is a distinct tension between traditional, moral language and postmodern critique. In contrast, for example, to his rejection of ideology and of a single truth, Havel often speaks of God, or of a transcendent "memory of Being" or "absolute horizon" encompassing reality. . . . The problem here is with Havel himself. The Czech president does not provide his readers with an analytical explication and philosophical defense of his stance. Philosophically, Havel stands on tenuous ground. His writings are not essentially philosophical. Rather, the technical language of twentieth-century philosophy is used in a literary fashion, often helping to engender confusion rather than resolve it.[1]

Havel seems to agree with Findlay's assessment, insisting that he is "not a philosopher" and that it is not his ambition "to construct conceptually fixed systems." Havel even confesses to "perpetually contradicting" himself and to using terms and concepts differently at different times.[2] In a 1986 interview he states that his most "philosophic" work, *Letters to Olga*, is not philosophy and that "there are many passages that I simply don't understand myself anymore." He maintains that "the world—in the West at least—is flooded with . . . far more readable and probably more penetrating books written by real philosophers."³

It is true, as Findlay claims, that Havel is neither a systematic thinker nor a professional philosopher. Yet, one needs to be careful of Havel's habitual humility and diffidence. Havel claimed that *Audience*, his most successful play, was written only for a few friends. Moreover, for those who have read the books of contemporary academic philosophers, Havel's "search" for himself is not probably but surely more penetrating than any "systematic" philosophic text.

Havel's philosophic principles were formed under the most inauspicious conditions, while he was serving a five-year prison sentence for criticizing the Czechoslovak state. Havel was singled out for harassment by a malicious prison warden, an admirer of Adolf Hitler who was never quite reconciled to the closing of Stalin's labor camps. Despite the distractions and hardships, Havel dedicated himself to writing letters that attempt to work out the nature of human responsibility and personal meaning. Havel also claims that he was "visited" by the spirit of philosophy in prison and that the letters to his wife especially are an expression of the experience of our time.⁴ "All week long," he explains, "I would develop my essays in my head—at work, during exercises, before going to bed—and then on Saturday . . . I would write them out in a kind of wild trance."⁵ Because of the censorship and persecution, Havel had to write carefully and disguise his ideas, making them too difficult for prison censors to understand. Perhaps because he was compelled to be obscure, his prison letters seem to lack coherence—as such, the most consistent letters were not allowed to be mailed. But to say that Havel's ruminations are neither a philosophy nor an attempt to understand the most important questions about life is somewhat like claiming that Socrates was not a philosopher because he often changed the subject during his discussions, thereby making his views seem confused and inconsistent.

Havel argues that life is too complex and diverse for a single philosophic system to encompass the fullness of existence, hence the lack of consistency. Yet Havel does make philosophic judgments, sometimes presented in the form of essays but often presented, as we shall see in chapter 4, in his absurd plays. Havel's meditations cannot be fully grasped unless his essays are interpreted in light of his philosophic poetry. Havel says that his plays—like his philosophy—are meant to be "of general interest and concern to everyone."⁶ Havel is best compared to Plato, who had a poetic skill and was clearly able to articulate philosophic issues. Peter Majer best explains the relationship between Havel's art and philosophy.

Havel is not just a playwright dealing with philosophical questions, but a philosopher in his own right. His plays, which started as jolly and absurd comedies, Ionesco style, gradually turned into modern Socratic philosophical dialogues. In them, however, wisdom is not imparted by a teacher to a student, but discovered in the course of a lonely character's conflict with a world whose reality does not match its established description.[7]

Many commentators accept Havel's philosophic credentials but differ widely on how to interpret his principles. Caroline Bayard focuses on Havel's openness to diversity and on his antipathy to closed systems of thought that make people self-righteous and perhaps oppressive. She compares Havel to one of the heroes of postmodern thought, Jean François Lyotard, arguing that, for both, "no discourse may receive absolute privileges over another" since there is an "unresolvable heterogeneity" in life.[8]

Dean C. Hammer disputes Bayard's claim that Havel belongs in the postmodern camp. Hammer argues that although Havel opposes ideological doctrines that claim to offer a full account of human action, the former Czech leader bases his rejection of ideology on transcendent moral considerations with a "metaphysical grounding." Moreover, Hammer insists that Havel is not open to every political discourse but rather clearly "privileges" a practical approach to life that depends on building stable political institutions that support not only citizens' participation but also their respect for responsible—and therefore limited—political actions.[9]

In a book-length study of Havel and his mentor, Czech philosopher Jan Patočka, Aviezer Tucker traces the origin of the Czech dissidents' political philosophy to the ideas of Martin Heidegger. Tucker claims that the dissident Havel was served well by Heidegger's existential doctrines, which include the principle of independent thought and choice. However, Tucker maintains that President Havel was a failure because he did not involve himself in the day-to-day politics of post-Communist transition, expecting instead that his country's difficulties would be solved by an "existential revolution" that would fundamentally reorder human society. Since no new revelation of Being took place, Tucker concludes that Havel squandered his political capital by adhering to his philosophic reflections.[10]

Richard Rorty takes a postmodern approach to Havel, celebrating Havel's openness but lamenting the Czech president's reliance on a metaphysical basis for moral obligation. According to Rorty, Havel's "philosophy" is irrelevant—at least to the English-speaking world—because the Anglo-American community derives its morals from a pragmatic application of tradition, not on abstract ideas. What are valuable to "English-speaking intellectuals" who are "baffled" by Havel's philosophic formulations are not his arguments but his moral example in resisting tyranny.[11]

Edward E. Ericson Jr. praises Havel exactly because Havel relies on a transcendent explanation of human morals. Ericson argues that Havel's views are "remarkably similar" to those of the Russian dissident Aleksandr Solzhenitsyn. Both dissidents reject atheism, especially its virulent Communist manifestation, and trace the catastrophes of the twentieth century to "anthropocentricity," which arrogantly sees man as "the center of all." Ericson claims that Havel's principles are shaped by a religious horizon, despite the Czech's reluctance to commit himself to a personal God.[12]

In a 1993 review of Havel's writings, Peter Augustine Lawler agrees with Ericson that Havel is fundamentally, although not overtly, a religious thinker. Lawler sees Havel's openness to the mystery of Being, his acceptance of a moral imperative beyond that dictated by the conventions of society, and his attack on anthropocentric humanism as evidence of the Czech dissident's acknowledgment of the existence of a transcendental realm. Lawler disputes Rorty's claim that morality—even in the English-speaking world—is based on chance, arguing instead that Havel is right about "the dependence of political life on philosophy." Lawler elaborates Havel's critique of modern philosophy, claiming that humanity has been led astray by successive manifestations of the Enlightenment belief that human choice and will are the center of the universe. The effect of these ideas has been, first and foremost, to raise the possibility of controlling human destiny to an unrealistically high level of expectation, thereby making adherents of these principles tyrannical in practice; however, Enlightenment principles have led to the more benign, but no less dispiriting, idea that humans are free to "play," to deny their mortality, and to live a superficial life dedicated to little more than material comfort.

Lawler argues that Havel properly grounds his philosophy in the experience of the "natural world," which accepts the existence of a metaphysical foundation for moral judgments. The acknowledgment of a precept higher than human will begins with the realization that we are not free to ignore our awareness of death without denying our humanness. For Lawler, Havel's brave stand against totalitarian domination is not a mark of pragmatism but an indication that our choices matter because our souls long to be responsible to what is true, good, and eternal. Had Havel desired to be pragmatic, Lawler indicates, he could have submitted and kept quiet. But since Havel understands that we are finite creatures who contemplate the infinite, his actions are based on a belief in a permanent spiritual order.[13]

Lawler reassesses his position on Havel in a 1997 article in *Perspectives on Political Science*. There Lawler argues that Havel's attempt to supply scientific or phenomenological evidence for the "order of Being" results in the collapse of the distinction between matter and spirit as well as between "man and God." By anchoring humans too fully in the material world, Lawler alleges, Havel obliterates "the experience of separateness or alienation, the one rooted in one's awareness of one's own death." Lawler states that only belief in a personal God can fully satisfy the human longing for the eternal and can supply an adequate foundation for the exercise of the responsible practice of morality. Lawler accuses Havel of pantheism for adopting the "anthropic cosmological principle and the Gaia hypothesis," which purport to explain the spiritual order of the universe in scientific terms. Lawler calls Havel's endeavor to make a spiritual home for human beings in the visible world a "self-deception" that may result in people throwing themselves ever more eagerly into "everydayness," the inane hope of satisfying human yearnings through consumerism, pop culture, and therapeutic drugs.[14]

Jean Bethke Elshtain attempts to show that Havel grounds his principles in both an acceptance of "the absolute" and a rejection of "fixed categories" of belief. Rather than criticize this seeming inconsistency, Elshtain endorses the paradox of existence that Havel identifies. We are in need of permanent principles if we are not to be victims of popular fashions that derive definitions of morality from the whims of popular culture. But life is mysterious, and even those who act in accordance with the "order of Being" are never certain that their choices are in accord with the transcendent principles they espouse.[15]

James W. Sire traces Havel's intellectual debt to philosopher Martin Heidegger. Sire argues that the validity of Havel's "notion of Being" rests, in part, on "the whole system within which the system of Being fits." Sire then excuses himself from the intellectual task of analyzing that system by admitting that he is "not prepared to comment" on Heidegger, who is "notoriously difficult to understand." Instead, Sire quotes Roger Scruton's ironic remark that Heidegger's philosophy "may be unintelligible."[16]

Sire is surely correct that Havel has been profoundly affected by Heidegger. Havel calls Heidegger "the greatest philosopher of our time," a "great genius who lent such modern and penetrating meaning to words like '*Sein*,' '*Dasein*,' and '*Existenz*.'" Havel claims that existentialism and phenomenology, the intellectual milieu of Heidegger, "stimulated and attracted" him most. He labels the letters to Olga his "Heideggerean meditations."[17] In fact, as we shall see, much of Havel's intellectual life, including his artistic work, has been shaped by both a fundamental agreement with Heidegger's critique of contemporary life and an even more profound disagreement with Heidegger's exploration of the character of Being. Therefore, to understand Havel, we cannot avoid a confrontation with Heidegger.

THE CHALLENGE OF HEIDEGGER

Any attempt to clarify Heidegger's complex philosophy is daunting because the questions he raises are difficult and because he raises them in language at once poetic and idiosyncratic. Moreover, he claims that his way of thinking has "no result" and "no effect"; that is, he presents questions but few answers.[18] Adding to the confusion is what he calls the "turn," a major reassessment and transformation of his ideas that took place after World War II. Finally—and perhaps of primary importance—is Heidegger's attack on metaphysics and with it his abandonment of the customary rules of logic. Thus, if one were to ask, "What is Heidegger's final position on whether a certain proposition is true or false?" the answer might be, "Yes, no, neither, and both." The problematical character of Heidegger's philosophy has given rise to a plethora of often contradictory interpretations. The intensity of that debate has been fueled by the so-called *l'affaire* Heidegger, his association with the Nazi movement in the 1930s, and his refusal to disavow Nazism for the rest of his life.

What then can be said of Heidegger's views? He seems to be most interested in the problem raised by Friedrich Nietzsche—nihilism—which Heidegger believes arose as the result of Western culture's misinterpretation of existence.[19] The principles of the West, Heidegger maintains, are founded on the belief that humans can direct their lives by comprehending the objects around them; they can know how best to live by cataloging, characterizing, and controlling phenomena—the "beings," he calls them. According to Heidegger, Plato is responsible for the endeavor to establish a transcendent explanation for the experiences of everyday life. Plato transforms Socrates' "What is?" questions (What is justice? What is love? What is friendship? etc.) into the theory of the forms. Plato seems to claim that although justice, truth, and morality cannot be understood quite in the same way as tables and chairs can, they are nevertheless kinds of phenomena that can be described and classified. Aristotle calls the study and indexing of such nonvisible phenomena "metaphysics."

Heidegger argues that all philosophers after Plato have accepted the principle of metaphysical certainty. Although later philosophers may have disagreed with Plato's concepts, they all reasoned that it makes sense to consider phenomena the result of overarching metaphysical truths that elucidate and order experiences. The consummation of the quest to comprehend existence through the application of human reason is found in the philosophy of René Descartes, who claimed that science is the only true form of human understanding. Descartes attempted to ground philosophic speculation not in the transcendent realm, as Plato did, but in the certainty of scientific experiments and mathematical formulas. Descartes believed that scientific inquiry and discovery could liberate people from ignorance, superstition, disease, poverty, and sectarian violence. Once the secrets of nature were revealed, he theorized, the human race could use them to satisfy its needs and desires. Knowledge of nature's secrets we now call "technology," the instrument by which the discoveries of science are put to the service of the human species.[20]

For Heidegger, the problem with technology is not so much that we become its slave, as Karl Marx argues, but that technology liberates us from all restraints and limits. In place of a moral or spiritual order, through which people of the past had been inspired to dedicate their lives to some purpose beyond themselves, the ascendance of technology results either in an assertion of the will that directs our activity or in a bureaucracy that attempts to limit the caprice of our will. Technology robs our experience of mystery and uproots our sense of belonging. Heidegger gives the famous example of how the Rhine, whose myths once helped define the German people, has been abased in the modern world.

> The hydroelectric plant is set into the current of the Rhine . . . to dispatch electricity. In [this] context, even the Rhine itself appears to be something at our command. What the river is now, namely, a waterpower supplier, derives from the essence of the power station. In order that we may even remotely consider the monstrousness that reigns here, let us ponder for a moment the contrast that is spoken by the two titles: "The Rhine," as dammed up into the power works, and "The Rhine," as uttered by the art work, in Hölderlin's hymn by that name. But, it will be replied, the Rhine is still a river in the landscape, is it not? Perhaps. But how? In no other way than as an object on call for inspection by a tour group ordered there by the vacation industry.[21]

Technology has succeeded in bringing the physical world under human control. It has created wealth, long life spans, and comfortable existences. It has also liberated humans from the overriding concerns experienced by preindustrial people—that is, by providing for current humankind's bodily needs. Yet this new freedom has also brought a new awareness and a novel anxiety. Once the whole of existence is under humans' command, what should they do with it? The fruits of technology provided for people's physical needs, but they could not answer the more difficult questions, such as, Why am I alive? Where did I come from? What am I to do with my life? Why must I die?

Heidegger argues that, oddly, anxiety over the inability of science and technology to answer the fundamental questions about existence pushed the human race headlong into more and greater efforts to control the world through science. As the religious interpretation and significance of death receded, people feared death more than ever. They wanted to live longer, and they expended great efforts on techniques—medical science, for instance—to lengthen their life spans. This exertion succeeded only in making the entire material world into an object of use. All things became "standing reserve," to be used in whatever way people saw fit. Science and technology also provided the human race with a new power, a power that in the twentieth century was forcefully exercised over humans, who also became objects of use. Even the seemingly chaotic events of human history were systematized and made comprehensible in the philosophies of history put forward by Georg Hegel and Karl Marx. Marxism, especially, became a mechanism of oppression because it sought to base human societies on "scientific" models.[22]

Neither the philosophies of history nor the technological conquest of nature fully answer our questions about life and death or help us create a sense of personal identity. Heidegger argues that there can be two responses to our quest for meaning and the inevitability of death. The first is the "inauthentic" disposition to throw ourselves more deeply into everyday concerns, not to question the prevailing order of things, and avoid facing our anxiety over our death. The "authentic" response to the human predicament is to bravely confront extinction, an act that leads to the realization that neither the things of this world nor the metaphysical speculations of philosophers can adequately create meaning for human existence.

After all, Heidegger asks, what is Being? Being is the precondition of existence of the beings. It is what makes all things exist, but it is not one of the things. During his lectures, Heidegger performed a sort of exhibition of Being: He remained silent in front of the class for long stretches. When there are no things to distract us, we become bored. We say that there is nothing (no-thing) to do. It is then—when we put aside the everyday practical matters that fill up our time—that we achieve a glimpse of the mystery that is Being. Although Being gives substance to other things, Being is not one of the things. Therefore, it is unclear if Being has substance; Being is no-thing. From no-thing, human beings are "thrown" into life. We have no control over the past, and we have little power over each passing moment of our personal existence. We have no idea why Being is, and therefore we have no true sense of how best to live our lives. We are unsure of the meaning of our own existence. Most of all, we are a mystery to ourselves.

Heidegger speculates that there may be rare moments when a few human beings apprehend Being directly. He claims that it is possible to experience a "moment of *vision*" that "discloses the authentic 'there'" of existence.[23]

Heidegger calls our normal way of experiencing the world *Dasein*, which could be translated as "being there." Dasein does not exist like any of the other things in the universe. Everything else just *is*, but Dasein wonders why it is. Although there might be existence without Dasein, no one would really know or care. Hence, Being speaks through Dasein—or as Heidegger puts it, Dasein is "the lighting of Being."[24] Yet Dasein is hardly an explanation of our Being, since it too is a mystery and can be illustrated only by what it is not. He writes,

> But have we not confined ourselves to negative assertions in all our attempts to determine the nature of this state of Being? Though this Being-in is supposedly so fundamental, we always keep hearing about what it is *not*. Yes indeed. But there is nothing accidental about our characterizing it predominantly in so negative a manner. In doing so we have rather made known what is peculiar to this phenomenon, and our characterization is therefore positive in a genuine sense—a sense appropriate to the phenomenon itself.[25]

Our effort to comprehend and control the beings, according to Heidegger, makes it nearly impossible for us to grasp Being. "Man is not the lord of beings," he says. "Man is the shepherd of Being."[26] In fact, the very busyness of technological societies—the constant need to get things done—interferes with our ability to think about much of anything. Even the categorically based language inherited from Western metaphysics distorts our relationship to Being, making it necessary for Heidegger to create language anew.[27]

Without some awareness of Being, there can be no transcendent ordering principle. Without some grounding in a first principle, there can be no hierarchy of values. Absent a revelation of Being, the things and events we perceive can have no meaning. The long and complicated endeavor to structure the beings so as to enable humans to live worthwhile lives has been a failure, according to Heidegger. Or, as he puts it, the metaphysics of the

West, begun by Plato and deconstructed by Nietzsche, has not brought us to an understanding of the true and the false, the just and the unjust, the beautiful and the ugly, the courageous and the cowardly, or indeed of any other human virtues.[28] While it may be accurate to say that there is "truth," that truth changes from place to place and from age to age, Being reveals itself differently to different people and cultures. Heidegger writes,

> Before there was any Dasein, there was no truth; nor will there be any after Dasein is no more. For in such a case truth as disclosedness, uncovering, and uncoveredness, *cannot* be. Before Newton's laws were discovered, they were not 'true'; it does not follow that they were false, or even that they would become false if ontically no discoveredness were any longer possible. . . .
>
> To say that before Newton his laws were neither true nor false, cannot signify that before him there were no such entities as have been uncovered and pointed out by those laws. Through Newton the laws became true and with them, entities became accessible in themselves to Dasein. Once entities have been uncovered, they show themselves precisely as entities which beforehand already were. Such uncovering is the kind of Being which belongs to 'truth.'
>
> That there are 'eternal truths' will not be adequately proved until someone has succeeded in demonstrating that Dasein has been and will be for all eternity. As long as such a proof is still outstanding, this principle remains a fanciful contention which does not gain legitimacy from having philosophers commonly 'believe' it. . . . *Because the kind of Being that is essential to truth is of the character of Dasein, all truth is relative to Dasein's Being.*[29]

Heidegger's thought underwent a change as the result of his inability to control the intellectual currents of Nazism, its descent into totalitarianism, and Germany's defeat in World War II. Prior to this "turning," Heidegger expected that a new revelation of Being would bring about a more authentic relationship between human beings and their lives. Heidegger hoped that nihilism would open a space or an opportunity for a rethinking of metaphysics and with it a new attitude toward existence, one that did not expect technology to solve every human problem. After the turn, he abandoned his quest for a practical expression of authenticity and counseled "waiting"—openness to the mystery and wonder of Being. Waiting is the alternative to an active attempt to bring about a new revelation of Being and is necessary because technology "enframes" the world by conquering and using nature, just as Descartes had desired. When all of existence is at hand and able to be controlled, human life becomes bereft of meaning. Nothing stands above human power to provide guidance for human choice. But it is at this moment—when the nothingness of Being is revealed—that meaning may again show itself.

Heidegger says, "The coming to presence of Enframing is the danger. ... As the danger, Being ... turns away from coming to presence ... with *this* turning, the truth of the coming to presence of Being will expressly turn in—turn homeward—into whatever it is."[30] By clearly uncovering the essential no-thing of Being, technology makes possible a recovery of significance. Leslie Paul Thiele explains that "the primordial nothingness of Being ... is neither the emptiness of space, nor the negation of logic. Rather, the nothingness of Being is pure potentiality, that hiddenness that comes to presence in all things, in emptiness and negation no less than in being and affirmation."[31] Heidegger concludes that it is the absence of a ground that causes the ground to appear. He explains,

> Only when the strangeness of beings oppresses us does it arouse and evoke wonder. Only on the ground of wonder—the revelation of the nothing—does the 'why?' loom before us. Only because the 'why' is possible as such can we in a definite way inquire into grounds, and ground them.[32]

Heidegger does not fully explain where this waiting will lead, what we should learn from it, whether we are waiting for a new revelation of Being, or what we should do if Being reveals itself. When pressed on these issues, he answered cryptically, "Only a god will save us."[33]

Heidegger's philosophy helped spawn the existential and postmodern varieties of antifoundational thought. Antifoundationalists argue that morals are an effort to overcome the emptiness of Being. Morality provides people with standards to live by and with a purpose for living. Moral dictates are an attempt to order the chaos of existence by placing constraints on our utter free will. But since the core of Being is nothing (no-thing), there are no restraints on free will, and morality is no more than a salutary illusion. Followers of Heidegger, especially the existential movement, took the lack of a foundation to mean that we must construct our "self" as an act of will. Individuals must construct their own guideposts and their own identities; they must choose how to act and whether to act, despite there being no metaphysical support for any particular action.

It is not exactly clear what Heidegger thought of antifoundationalism. In "Letter on Humanism," he quotes Jean Paul Sartre's declaration that it is very distressing that God does not exist because with him vanishes every possibility of finding values in some intelligible heaven; we can no longer locate an *a priori* Good since there is no infinite and perfect consciousness to think it; it is nowhere written that the Good exists, that we must be honest, that we mustn't lie, precisely because we are in a situation where there are only human beings.[34]

Heidegger suggests that Sartre's antifoundational position misapplies his own views presented in *Being and Time*. Antifoundationalism rests on the logical claim that if we are unable to discover a foundation, then one must not exist. But Heidegger holds that logic itself is a metaphysical postulate that cannot be grounded in Being. "By continually appealing to the logical," he argues, "one conjures up the illusion that he is entering straightforwardly into thinking when in fact he has disavowed it." Thus, Heidegger's opposition to "'humanism' in no way implies a defense of the inhuman but rather opens up other vistas."[35]

Postmodern thinkers focus on Heidegger's understanding of language. Heidegger states that "language is at once the house of Being and the home of human beings. Only because language is the home of the essence of man can historical mankind and human beings not be at home in their language, so that for them language becomes a mere container for their sundry occupations."[36] Postmodernists interpret this statement to mean that language constructs our understanding. We learn about the world from our parents, our teachers, the media, and fellow humans—in short, our culture. Since culture is expressed primarily through the medium of language, language is, as Heidegger put it, "the house of Being."

Heidegger also claims that by attempting to make existence comprehensible, everyday language interferes with our appreciation of the incomprehensible—the ineffable quality of Being. Postmodernists take Heidegger's point further and reason that since language establishes our understanding, words play an independent role in establishing what we believe to be true and even influence how we perceive the world. They argue that much common language is loaded with an established content or meaning that supports the preexisting power structure. Postmodernists insist that language must be deconstructed in order to liberate it from its ideological bias. Words become weapons in the war for freedom and equality. No matter how precise, words cannot portray "truth." They are at best "narratives" about what a particular person or group of persons thinks is true. Postmodernists, to quote Jean-François Lyotard, react with "incredulity toward metanarratives."[37]

America's reluctant postmodernist Richard Rorty presents what is perhaps the most cogent account of the implications of Heidegger's teaching on language. If language constructs our understanding, and yet if there is no ground for morals, how did values come to be? As we know, every society enforces a moral code. Rorty maintains that morals are shaped by the community in which one lives. Rorty argues that human beings are "centerless networks of beliefs." Moral principles are nothing but "discourses," and none can lay claim to being conclusive. "What counts as a decent human being is relative to historical circumstances, a matter of transient consensus about what attitudes are normal and what practices are just or unjust."[38]

No belief, no practice, and no way of life is superior to any other. Rorty does hold that the relativism, multiculturalism, and eclecticism of postmodernism are most compatible with liberty and tolerance, but he makes no claim that liberty is better than servitude. One could ask why liberty and tolerance are good things. In the end, Rorty falls back on convention to defend his preferences. When "historical circumstance allows," it is possible to have an "agreement about political topics." In other words, for people who by chance are born and raised in a democratic culture, liberal democracy is a beneficial and worthy choice because other people of the same culture will have similar prejudices. As for those with "unusual views" who disagree with his democratic sentiments, Rorty indicates that "extensive attempts at an exchange of political views have made us realize we are not going to get anywhere."[39]

Other postmodernists are less sanguine about accepting the mores of their society. Michel Foucault, for instance, maintains that resistance to the established power relationships of society is a more dignified way to exert one's freedom. He seems more akin to Sartre's existential stance as he argues that freedom can best be expressed through individual "invention" of the self. Foucault takes his bearing from the most inventive of human activities, the arts, and asserts that we should "create ourselves as a work of art."[40]

Here again, Heidegger's own words seem to contradict the implications that postmodernists have drawn from them. For Heidegger the world is "there." Language does not "create" the world, as it does for postmodern thinkers; rather, language reveals the world. He argues that language mediates our understanding of the phenomena but does not simply construct our comprehension. He states, "Beings can be determined in their Being without the explicit concept of the meaning of Being having to be already available. If this were not so there could not have been as yet any ontological knowledge, and probably no one would deny the factual existence of such knowledge."[41] For Heidegger, even if no definitive ground exists—"Homelessness is the coming to be of the destiny of the world"—Dasein does encounter something.[42] It encounters a world that it did not create and cannot control by an act of will. He writes:

> Man does not decide whether and how beings appear, whether and how God and the gods or history and nature come forward into the lighting of Being, come to presence and depart. The advent of beings lies in the destiny of Being. But for man it is ever a question of finding what is fitting in his essence which corresponds to such destiny; for in accord with this destiny man as ek-sisting has to guard the truth of Being.[43]

Thiele argues that Heidegger would reject the principle of self-creation because "the postmodern attempt to mold the self into a work of art orients the individual to itself as a malleable object of production."[44] Self-creation is but another attempt to find metaphysical certainty, a goal that Heidegger rejects. Because Heidegger's work can be interpreted as being open to a variety of social models and individual predilections, Thiele and Fred Dallmayr make determined efforts to rescue Heidegger both from critics who accuse him of complicity in the Nazi regime and from disciples who insist that the deconstruction of society is necessary in order to secure human autonomy. Dallmayr claims that Heidegger is a "Friend of the World" who wants to preserve nature by protecting it from the ravages of technological mastery. Moreover, Dallmayr interprets Heidegger's statement "the spirit of home yearns itself for otherness from where alone a return home is possible" as a plea for an open, diverse, and tolerant world community.[45] Thiele also maintains that Heidegger's openness to "the other" is the key to applying his thought. For Thiele, the very uncertainty about Being that Heidegger conveys throughout his work is consistent with responsible democratic politics. In fact, Thiele argues that democracy rests on accepting the authority of the many to undertake a "continuous founding," a formless process in which "community, authority, and power" continually remake themselves in light of the changing principles of the people.[46]

Efforts to rescue Heidegger from his Nazi past create several problems, some of which are presented here in a general form but are related to the key difference between Heidegger and Havel. First, for Heidegger there is no ground: Being is no-thing. Without a metaphysical point of reference, it is never clear to an observer living in a particular historical moment—until perhaps after the fact—whether a strong and passionate social movement is the basis of a unique and authentic belief system or is merely the ravings of a demagogue able to bend masses of people to his will. Having no foundation for judgments makes it impossible to distinguish if a particular historical manifestation of Being is an affirmation or negation of humanity. This is the essence of *l'affaire* Heidegger, the debate over whether his philosophy is essentially connected to his Nazi sympathies during, and perhaps after, Hitler's ascendancy. If the revelation of Being establishes the truth, then Nazism might have been life affirming. There is no way on Heideggerean grounds to tell, because Heidegger denies that there is any basis for determining the worth of a thing until after Being reveals itself. In essence, both schools are correct: the critics argue that Heidegger's philosophy is essentially connected with Nazism, whereas his proponents maintain that Heidegger wanted to affirm the human good.

Second, having no foundation also makes it difficult for Heidegger to distinguish between what is authentic and what is characteristic of "everydayness"—that is, for the former, what is according to Being; and for the latter, the continual human concern for personal well-being that includes the desire for comfort and the pursuit of distraction from the confrontation or consideration of death. Dasein experiences the world as normal and "natural," for if it did not, children would be born anxious and alienated. Most children are not worried about existence, because anxiety—or "care," to use Heidegger's term—occurs only later in life with the almost visceral realization of one's sure and inevitable extinction. If the most normal way that Dasein encounters Being is through everydayness—and Heidegger admits that it has been true since the beginning of time—why is this not Being's authentic way of revealing itself?[47] Is not Heidegger's support for an authentic, rather than an inauthentic, life a metaphysical principle? Heidegger may wish to escape the metaphysical morass of logic, but his desire to do so does not ground his position in reality.

Third, Dasein is at home in everydayness. Dasein encounters reality through social life. It receives knowledge from its social and cultural milieu of what should be and how to perceive what is. Parents teach children right from wrong, and safe from unsafe. Teachers make students salute the flag and learn what a square root is. What Dasein sees is partly an observation of the world and partly a social construct. We often call this ability to comprehend and cope with life "common sense." Heidegger explains, "The dominance of the public way in which things have been interpreted has already been decisive even in the possibilities of having a mood—that is, for the basic way in which Dasein lets the world 'matter' to it. The 'they' prescribes one's state-of-mind, and determines what and how one 'sees.'"[48] If "they" really do determine how we see, then truth is relative to its culture. Even the greatest minds employing the most strenuous efforts to reach beyond the horizon of culture are doomed to failure. Heidegger does not exempt philosophy from historical determinism. He states that since "our human being is historical, it remains so in philosophizing, too."[49] Moreover, since Dasein is established by the particular perspective of our own culture, we cannot be sure whether the unfamiliar practices of another culture are merely everydayness or an authentic revelation of Being. Heidegger's account of Dasein does not make us open to "the other." Instead, it makes "the other" incomprehensible to us.

Finally, without something to ground it, Heidegger's early fascination with Nazism is not essentially different from his later inclination to patiently wait for a god to save him. He explains that "in regard to 1933, I expected from National Socialism a spiritual rejuvenation of all life, a reconciliation of social antagonisms, and a rescue of Western existence from the danger of communism."[50] After the turn, he was still expecting something important to happen, but he was no longer sure what. He comments that "in waiting we leave open what we are waiting for."[51] But what would replace the principles of Western rationalism once they were destroyed? What is Heidegger's cure for the challenge of nihilism? The answer, as always, was a new revelation of Being. Michael Allen Gillespie explains the difficulty of Heidegger's attitude toward existence:

> History, as Heidegger understands it, does not move forward gradually and regularly but spasmodically and unpredictably. Mankind is thus not gently turned toward a new future that is among the possibilities already present in its tradition, but is wrenched out of its historical world by the nothingness of Being and cast toward a new goal that is utterly alien to this tradition, a goal so alien that it requires the construction of a new tradition to make it comprehensible. It is a submission to this truly revolutionary reconstitution of the world in accord with the revelation of Being that Heidegger sees as necessary to the salvation of the earth and man's humanity. ... A concern for the mundane decisions of everyday life, with economic, political, and morality, not only is historically meaningless, but is detrimental to an authentic and resolute response to the revelation of Being.[52]

HAVEL'S RESPONSE TO HEIDEGGER

It is fair to say that Havel views Heidegger's work as both a blessing and a curse. On the one hand, Havel uses Heidegger's openness to metaphysical uncertainty to criticize the closed and absolutist metaphysical system of post-totalitarian societies; on the other, Havel parts company with Heidegger on the question of a moral or spiritual ground for human action.

Havel takes a great deal from Heidegger's analysis, including his views on the metaphysical uncertainty of modern life; the emptiness of postindustrial societies; the anxiety-riddled quest to discover one's identity; the profound shadow that death, or non-Being, casts over human life; the capacity of language and symbols to obscure reality; and the deadening effect of large bureaucratic organizations on the human psyche. Havel agrees with Heidegger that we must live authentic lives, make choices for ourselves, and refuse to accept things as they are. Living responsibly entails taking charge of our fates and refusing to accept that "they"—some distant, unknown others—control our destinies. Havel's existential attitude caused him to dissent from the monolithic regime of Communist Czechoslovakia. Havel dissented from Marxist ideology, which he argued was an effort to structure reality by forcing the complex and multifarious phenomena of life into a simple, comprehensible scientific structure. He labeled Communism the "order of death" because it killed all novelty and spontaneity.[53]

Havel maintains that the Communist totalitarian regimes of the East had the same goal as the huge multinational corporations of the West, the endeavor to understand and govern Being through technology. He argues that this quest to bend nature to our will's existence has created

> the crisis of contemporary technological society as a whole, the crisis that Heidegger describes as the ineptitude of humanity face to face with the planetary power of technology. Technology—that child of modern science, which in turn is a child of modern metaphysics—is out of humanity's control, has ceased to serve us, has enslaved us and compelled us to participate in the preparation of our own destruction. And humanity can find no way out: we have no idea and no faith, and even less do we have a political conception to help us bring things back under human control. We look on helplessly as that coldly functioning machine we have created inevitably engulfs us, tearing us away from our natural affiliations (for instance, from our habitat in the widest sense of that word, including our habitat in the biosphere) just as it removes us from the experience of Being and casts us into the world of "existences."[54]

For Heidegger, Being is an impenetrable mystery. As we have seen, he calls the awareness of that mystery Dasein. When Dasein entered the world, it marked the beginning of time, for although events occurred before Dasein, there was nothing to record their coming into being and passing away.

Havel's account of the human condition is strikingly similar to Heidegger's definition of Dasein. Havel states that "man is the only creature who is both part of Being (and thus a bearer of its mystery), and aware of that mystery as mystery."[55] Havel also agrees with Heidegger that "a kind of mystic co-operation" exists between Dasein and the material world. Havel explains, "Our need to discover our own meaning by touching 'absolute meaning' entices this meaning out of what surrounds us, and what surrounds us, on the contrary, entices from the deepest regions of our being our own veiled certitude that meaning exists." Moreover, Havel agrees with Heidegger that the human perception of time is associated with our desire for significance. We commemorate important events because we want to recall their meaning. We do not want all we do to be swallowed up and disappear in the passing away of all things.[56]

Like Heidegger, Havel believes that the atheistic anthropocentric principles of contemporary society make people too self-interested and rob the world of much of its charm, mystery, and beauty. Havel's "Rhine River" is the majestic St. Vitus Cathedral at the castle overlooking Prague. He says,

> Allow me ... to turn back to the Cathedral of which I spoke at the beginning. I think that the first people to whom it brings calculable financial gain are Prague hotel owners in the era of restoration of the market economy in the Czech Republic. Nowadays, this holds particularly true.
>
> Why, therefore, did someone, in long bygone times, engage in the construction of such a costly edifice which appears to be of so little use by today's standards?
>
> One possible explanation is that there were periods in history when immediate material gain was not the highest value in human life, and when humankind knew that there were mysteries that they would never understand, and before which they could only stand in humble amazement—and, perhaps, project that amazement into structures whose spires point upwards. Upwards, in order that they may be seen from far and wide, and that they highlight to everyone what is worth looking up to. Upwards, across the borders of ages. Upwards, to that which is beyond our sight—that which, by its mere silent existence, appears to preclude for humanity any right to treat the world as an endless source of short-term profit, and which calls for solidarity with all those who dwell under its mysterious vault.[57]

Havel does not follow Heidegger further, for Havel believes that there is both a foundation on which we can establish truth and a ground for making responsible moral choices. In fact, Havel's philosophic meditations are an effort to refute Heidegger's presentation of Being, for if Being is no-thing, there can be no moral principles guiding life. If morals are little more than human constructs, as the existentialists and postmodernists insist, then such morals lose their hold over us, for we are free to remake them at any moment. Even the awareness that Being created morals differently for different cultures at different times undermines our sense that morals have authority as standards of conduct, for we see the mutability of all moral action. Without moral principles by which to judge them, one political system is as good as another. But if Heidegger's position is accurate, then there are no legitimate grounds on which to oppose the evil of Communism. Indeed, absent moral principles, the very concept of evil is meaningless. Because Havel personally experienced the evil of Communism, he set out to discover a foundation for morality.

Havel's first and most obvious response to Heidegger's philosophy is the principle of *living in truth*. For Havel, it is not necessary to know Being before understanding the beings or making judgments about the things we experience. If food in restaurants is dull, uniform, and monotonous, as was the case when the Communist bureaucracy standardized menus throughout Czechoslovakia, we sensually experience the lack of variety and choice. When we look at gray, uniform, high-rise apartments, we see their brutal ugliness. When we listen to repetitious ideological speeches proclaiming the excellence of the country's restaurants or the beauty of its buildings, we know these statements are false. Living in truth has a phenomenological reality.

Havel sees the original awareness of the human condition as a spiritual awakening—not as an intellectual one, as in Heidegger. After all, almost every culture cherishes a creation myth, something that speaks to the human desire for meaning. While Heidegger recognizes these confrontations with Being as an important element of the human condition, he rejects the idea that any are true, simply or metaphysically. Havel, however, thinks that the cultures do not create, but rather discover, the spiritual order of the universe; and, true to the complexity and variety of life, they express their spiritual discovery differently. He explains that "the beginning of man's history as man, the history of culture" is "the history of the 'order of the spirit.'"[58]

Havel discounts Heidegger's presentation of Dasein. Havel complains that Heidegger viewed "human subjectivity ... too instrumentally ... something like a lighted passageway, containing nothing more than what passes through it—or rather, like something defined chiefly by what it is not." Havel argues that this entirely negative definition of our psyche is itself a "metaphysical" principle, since it claims to be an accurate or "true" account of the human condition. But to maintain that something is true is to admit that there is "truth" as such.

The antifoundationalist school that Heidegger's philosophy helped establish rests on a principle that denies everyday experience. We do not experience life as if there were no truth. Of course, we do perceive ourselves as distinct from others and the world. We are not "identical with Being." There is a sense in which we can understand what is happening around us only by being alienated from it, by not being a part of it—that is, by standing back and looking at it. But there is also a part of our lives in which we feel at home and comfortable with our surroundings. We feel a kind of certainty about our perceptions and recognize that others share the same perceptions. Therefore, we are not simply strangers without an ability to rationally conceive meaning. Havel claims that the ability to make sense of our lives, to fit in with others, and to feel at home in the world is the result of a ground common to all people. Although culture shapes our particular understanding of objects and events, we share the common experience of meaning, as expressed in our everyday experience of such attributes as love, friendship, courage, justice, and the like.[59]

Heidegger argues that human beings experience meaning historically, as part of a culture's belief system, its religion, art, myths, and general awareness of what is true and important. Truth reveals itself in different civilizations at different places and different times. Nazism's celebration of the German people against the technological and bureaucratic conformity of the West could have been one of those moments of Being revealing itself. There was no way for Heidegger to decide whether Nazism was true, because truth changes radically from one time to another, at least the truth as it presents itself in social life. Since there is no transhistorical ground for knowing what the reality of Being might be, Nazism really could have been a new revelation of Being. Although Havel hoped for improvement after the fall of Communism, he did not expect a new revelation of Being, as Tucker suggests.

Havel's philosophy is grounded in the transhistorical reality of what he calls the "natural world," which includes human virtue. It is therefore more moderate than Heidegger's, because one cannot remake human beings or human virtues anew, as Heidegger expected. There can be no all-embracing transformation of the human condition, because "the order of Being," the ground of human virtue, dictates both positive responsibilities and limitations on human action. Havel explains,

> I do not believe it is merely by chance or with no good reason that all cultures assume the existence of something that might be called the

"Memory of Being," in which everything is constantly recorded, and that they assume the related existence of supra-personal authorities or principles that not only transcend man but to which he constantly relates, and which are the sole, final explanation of . . . phenomenon [and] . . . human responsibility.[60]

Although Havel agrees with Heidegger that the awareness of death—the contemplation of the extinction of Being—is the most profound human experience, Havel does not believe that living an ordinary life rooted in everydayness is necessarily inauthentic. There is an order to everydayness, a rhythm established by the relationship of ordinary events and experiences to Being. For Havel, our experience is not constructed by Being's relationship to the beings, but rather "the order of Being" constructs a comprehensible and even acceptable existence for our everyday lives.[61] Put more simply, since there is an order to existence, not simply a mystery about Being, we are not inauthentic when we feel comfortable in our normal lives. It is possible to "enter and find a place in this order easily, authentically, and spontaneously and with supreme confidence." In fact, most people do not brood about "abysses"; rather, they "experience a kind of elementary sensation of meaningfulness." For them "the question of meaning is answered before it is asked." If we live responsibly, we are likely to feel that life has meaning, while irresponsible behavior often may cause us to "develop everything . . . that is base and distorted."[62]

The usual objection to such an argument is that people disagree about what they think is good. But even people who do evil justify their evil in some way. Why would people bother giving an account or defense of their actions if they did not want to show that they were good? People think that their actions are good because they recognize that good exists. All believe that life is meaningful. The problem is that there is no simple universal formula for what is good, as ideologues desire to bring into being. Life has no simple answers since moral choices are "infinitely diverse."[63]

Havel asks an obvious yet intriguing question: Why do people do good? If humans are always and everywhere self-interested, or if there is no true source or standard of proper human conduct, how can so many acts of virtue or good behavior be explained? Some individuals are antisocial and amoral. For them, force and threat of force might be the only means to subdue their aggressive behavior. But most people do not abuse their parents, beat their children, steal from their local grocery store, wantonly destroy public property, or kick their pets. Havel argues that in a normally functioning society, humans are more often good than bad and that honesty and civil obedience are the rule, not the exception. Havel speculates why this is so. He concludes that what is at work is something similar to what people call "conscience"; but for him, conscience is complicated. It could be argued, of course, that morality is merely a human construct passed down from one generation to the next. Morals are no more than conventions, whose origins have been lost in the mists of time, invented to meet the needs of social life. But this argument only serves to push Havel's question back further. Why have all societies established moral rules? Why has narrow self-interest, dishonesty, theft, and, cruelty—especially to the innocent—been proscribed in every culture known to us? Perhaps Being dictated these principles; and perhaps humans discovered, rather than invented, morality. We are not merely selfish or subjective. We act for the sake of others. Compassion, love, and "spontaneous help to our neighbors" are a part of "human subjectivity."[64]

In May of 1982, exactly three years into his prison sentence, Havel chronicles the following experience to his wife, Olga:

> Several days ago, during the weather report (it precedes the news on television each day, so I see it regularly), something went wrong in the studio and the sound cut out, though the picture continued as usual (there was neither an announcement "Do not adjust your sets" nor landscape photographs, as there usually is in such cases). The employee of the Meteorological Institute who was explaining the forecast quickly grasped what had happened, but because she was not a professional announcer, she did not know what to do. At this point a strange thing happened, the mantle of routine fell away and before us stood a confused, unhappy and terribly embarrassed woman: she stopped talking, looked in desperation at us, then somewhere off to the side, but there was no help from that direction. She could scarcely hold back her tears. Exposed to the view of millions, yet desperately alone, thrown into an unfamiliar, unexpected and unresolvable situation, incapable of conveying through mime that she was above it all (by shrugging her shoulders and smiling, for instance), drowning in embarrassment, she stood there in all the primordial nakedness of human helplessness, face-to-face with the big bad world and herself, with the absurdity of her position, and with the desperate question of what to do with herself, how to rescue her dignity, how to acquit herself, how to be. Exaggerated as it may seem, I suddenly saw in that event an image of the primal situation of humanity: a situation of separation, of being cast into an alien world and standing there before the question of the self. Moreover, I realized at once that with the woman, I was experiencing—briefly—an almost physical dread; with her, I was overwhelmed by a terrible sense of embarrassment; I blushed and felt her shame; I too felt like

crying. Irrespective of my will, I was flooded with an absurdly powerful compassion for this stranger (a surprising thing here, of all places, where in spite of yourself you share the general tendency of the prisoners to see everything related to television as a part of the hostile world that locked them up): I felt miserable because I had no way of helping her, of taking her place, or at least of stroking her hair.

Havel then begins to reflect on his own reaction to the experience. "Why," Havel asks himself, "did I suddenly—and quite irrationally—feel such an overwhelming sense of responsibility for someone whom I not only did not know, but whose misery was merely transmitted to me via television?"[65]

The answer he provides seems to be as follows. Human beings have a capacity to convey ideas, emotions, feelings, and experiences. The most fundamental of those experiences is our "throwness" into existence. We are all aware of one another's vulnerability and anxiety. The recognition of our own weakness in the situation of another is the experiential root of compassion. It is the source of our caring about anything outside ourselves. It is the reason why the harming of the innocent is so abhorred, for they are the most weak and vulnerable, the closest to the original condition of the human species. For Heidegger, our "throwness" into existence leads away from community and toward solipsism; however, Havel shows by his caring for a stranger that awareness of our "throwness" may lead to empathy, compassion, and responsibility toward others.[66]

Havel does one other thought experiment in an effort to establish a phenomenology of responsibility. Here, he puts himself on an all-but-empty night tram in Prague. With no one to see him, he could easily avoid paying the one-crown fare. Why then does he pay for the one-stop ride? Or, if he fails to pay, why does it bother him? We have, Havel maintains, a kind of "partner," another "I," not the same "I" who pays or fails to pay the crown. The "partner-I" surveys our behavior and judges it. This voice could be called "conscience," but it is deeper than the traditional account of conscience since it seems to address those who have no conscience. Havel explains that "a certain residue of moral awareness clings to every human tendency." Even a "thoroughly evil person" needs "to make excuses for his evil in some way or to lie to himself about it." Havel's position is similar to Adam Smith's. Smith argued that we can lie to others about our immoral actions, but it is far more difficult to fool ourselves since we know the motivation of our own behavior.[67] For Havel, it is as if there were a disinterested, impartial spectator surveying our behavior who can "understand the most subtle intricacies of our decisions and motives behind them."[68]

Where does this other "I" come from? It is a product of our being thrown into a world that we did not create but in which we must live. It is our alienation from ourselves that comes when we realize that our own personal concerns are not the only things that matter in the universe. This distance from ourselves makes it possible to see and judge our behavior as if it were committed by another. It makes it possible for us to ask, What would I think if someone else behaved this way? The inner workings of the human soul indicate to Havel that Being is constructed in such a way as to make morality possible. He argues that

> one thing is certain to me: that our "I"—to the extent that it has not been entirely successful in suppressing its orientation toward Being, and completely absorbed in its existence-in-the-world—has a sense of responsibility pure and simple . . . it hears within and around itself the "voice" in which Being addresses and calls out to it . . . and it takes this voice more seriously than anything.[69]

Havel considers whether responsibility is merely an opinion, a personal one perhaps created by his Masarykian humanist background. He admits that his upper-class background influenced him but that it does not fully explain his feelings of responsibility toward others. Just as have millions of people of different backgrounds who have lived and died, he worries not merely about what is good for him but about what is good generally. The "scientific" explanation of his experience, one based on a casual relationship, cannot account for what he, or anyone else, has experienced. The problem with the "positivistic" explanation of experience is that it "reduces human responsibility—as it does everything else—to a mere relationship." For example, even if Havel were influenced by Masarykian humanism, why did Masarykian humanism come to be? Where did this moral code come from? Can it be explained by Masaryk's upbringing? Why did that upbringing create a moral code? Positivism merely pushes the origins of morality back in time and posits them in a mysterious social process. It does not explain them.

Havel argues that the relativist argument "hides . . . what is most important," since even relativists "know" what is lacking. How can something that we know not exist? But how can something be "relative" to nothing? Havel argues that there cannot be "two relativities to each other." What makes it possible to "experience relativity as relativity" is an idea of an "absolute horizon" by which we comprehend what is lacking. Although the "absolute horizon" seems "super-abstract" and "super-imaginary," it has a concrete reality, since we use it in our everyday judgments, even when we make claims that all actions are relative. Havel explains that "the very categories of change, motion, relativity, impermanence, etc. would not exist, or rather could not be contemplated, if their polar opposites did not exist and were not always contemplated along with them."[70] He thus answers Heidegger's assertion that Being changes over time, for if Being does change over time, Heidegger would be incapable of articulating concepts such as permanence and change.

Havel argues that antifoundationalists make the same error as Marxists. Both want the meaning of life to be "data," knowable as a piece of information. Marxists think they possess the truth as a factual reality, while antifoundationalists claim that no such factual truth can explain life. Havel maintains that truth exists, but truth is always difficult to discern precisely because life cannot be reduced to information.[71]

Havel disagrees with Heidegger about the relationship between Being and nature. For Heidegger, our longing to comprehend and apply the virtues is just one more example of the endeavor to codify Being, to shape it into knowable metaphysical categories and thus place it under our command. Havel argues that the metaphysics of power applies only to science and the goal of science to dominate creation. For Havel another realm of human activity and practical knowledge exists, which he calls "the natural world," the place where individuals must make sometimes difficult choices using only their judgment and conscience. The natural world is where "categories like justice, honor, treason, friendship, infidelity, courage, or empathy have a wholly tangible content." We actually experience this natural world personally, for who among us has not felt the glow of friendship, the sting of betrayal, or the thrill of overcoming fear? The natural world is "pre-speculative": virtues exist before we reflect on them; in fact, they shape our speculation about how we should behave. The natural world is "the hidden source of all rules, customs, commandments, prohibitions, and norms" and is based on "the presupposition of the absolute which grounds, delimits, animates, and directs." Although the natural world is ubiquitous—so much so that we can easily forget that we constantly make value judgments based upon its rules—it is not simply a human construct, since human life without it would be "impersonal and inhuman." The natural world is the transcendent reason why we can make responsible choices.[72]

Havel also grapples with this problem: Even if people are aware of their responsibilities to do good, why should they obey the dictates of conscience? "To whom are we responsible?" he asks and then adds, "certainly not . . . to any of the transitory things of this world." There are two questions, then. Can we know the good? And once we know it, why should we follow it? On the latter point Havel attempts to show that "the memory of Being" records all our actions, both for good and evil. Havel justifies his own defiance of the established authorities of his nation by claiming that everything that one does matters. There is a "memory of Being" that records what was done and that cannot be changed. Just as we do not forget a friend's personality when he leaves the room, Havel argues, Being does not forget our choices; we made them.

This transcendent historical record of one's deeds is a bit odd, since no sentient being actually writes down what has happened and since no living person is ever rewarded or punished for one's own good or evil actions. The "memory of Being" does not mete out punishments or rewards. It simply reminds people that they are responsible for what they have done and that they can never change the choices they have made. People pay no price for thwarting the "memory of Being." It is at this point that Havel comes closest to admitting that his theory presupposes a knowing, caring God who actually is attentive to how people behave and who is responsible for judging their deeds. Yet, Havel cannot bring himself to profess belief in God because "God, after all, is one who rejoices, rages, loves, desires to be worshiped; in short, he behaves too much like a person for me." Havel's own religion is not based on traditional dogmas.

> I don't believe that any of the religions we have today, constituted as they are, as a sum of dogmas, prohibitions, and liturgical rubrics, and so on, will save civilization. I think that all religions are important, particularly in view of our multi-cultural world. Each of these religions has to lead its own life and respect the existence of all the others, but none of them will save us. You are familiar with Martin Heidegger's famous line: "Only a god can save us now." And I am convinced that indeed only a god can save us now, but it will not be the god of today's religions. It cannot be a god embedded in a concrete doctrine, in a concrete theology. It will be a sort of particular universal god that is completely unimaginable and, for me, of inconceivable greatness, without any sort of personal image; a god that will be more like the principle of all principles, but one that, at the same time, will be immanent within each one of us, from the rising to the setting of the sun; a god that awakes five minutes before we do, that is to say, a god that is already awake when we get up in the morning and that remains with us at all times. In other words, what I am talking about is conscience.[73]

Havel simply concludes that our "spiritual experience, or rather [our] experience of something supremely spiritual" is prevalent enough in the human race and felt strongly enough in individuals to make responsibility toward a moral life more fulfilling.[74] "Genuine conscience and genuine responsibility are always, in the end, explicable only as an expression of the silent assumption that we are observed 'from above,' that everything is visible, nothing is forgotten."[75]

But is there really an "order of Being"? We live with a sense that what we do matters, both for good and bad. Life would have little meaning if we thought that nothing we do counts. Havel struggled with this problem in prison because he was never sure that his opposition would bring a practical change in the regime.[76]

But Havel asks: Why do we all live as if life matters and is worth our efforts? It could be that we are merely interested in comfort and afraid of death. But it seems the issue is more complicated than that. We attempt to justify what we do. Havel argues that when we attempt to justify our actions, we end up "gradually overcoming all relative, apparent, changeable and transitory horizons, and seeking in oneself and one's experience of the world, 'the absolute horizon of Being.'"[77] Of course, it could be that we "create" meaning to justify our existence. Or, we could say that the absolute horizon constructs us in such a manner that we recognize that there is meaning and therefore think that existence matters. Havel argues that

> the meaning of any phenomena lies in its being anchored in something outside itself, and thus in its belonging to some higher or wider context, in its illumination by a more universal perspective; in its being "hung," like a picture, within a higher order, placed against the background of a horizon. As a consequence, the "higher context"—what is "outside it," is projected, as it were, "back" into the phenomena to which it lends meaning, so that it appears not only to permeate and animate it, but to provide an immediate foundation for its ... identity.[78]

Havel's view is something like Plato's theory of the Good, but in a way the former not only pays homage to Heidegger's account of existence but also points out its shortcomings. Havel agrees with Heidegger that we are "thrown" into existence, "for no living creature ever appeared in the world of his own free will." But why do we enjoy life? Why do we think that we should continue living? It could be that we just want to survive and that our life is guided by instinct. But since we can ask "the question 'to be or not to be,'" we indicate that we are able to oppose our instincts. Life must be more than simply the satisfaction of desires, since people can lead full lives without wealth and lead miserable ones with great wealth.

Why then do people have hope? Why do they continue to struggle? Why do we think pleasures are good? Why do we justify our pleasures? Why do we think life is good? What gave us that idea? Perhaps it was our relationship to the absolute horizon of goodness. Havel argues that because Being creates a meaningful universe, humans discover—that is, we live within the horizon of the Good. Havel's absolute horizon is similar to Plato's Good, in that it gives meaning to other things.[79]

Every philosopher who has ever written has attempted to explain the way in which the world works. In giving an account, philosophers assume that their own lives have meaning—or, that life in general has meaning. The very act of explication is proof that philosophers believe there is a knowable order to Being. Philosophers write because they believe that pointing out the truth to people matters, and it matters because knowledge of the truth will be good for people. Even Heidegger and his antifoundationalist followers act is if they can explain the meaning of life—even if for them that meaning is entirely negative. A person who truly believes that life has no meaning would not bother to explain, justify, and give an account.[80]

Havel wonders what life would be like if there really were no metaphysical ground and no meaning to life. He recognizes that the inexplicable character of existence, its throwness, can lead to "the temptation of Nothingness," in which people become embittered because they cannot discern a meaning in life. But those who vigorously argue that life has no meaning—be it Heidegger, the antifoundationalists, or the existentialists—actually have a kind of hope or inspiring principle. They attempt to give an account of the meaning of life—that is, that life has no meaning. People who have truly lost hope and succumbed to the "temptation of nothingness" exhibit signs of "resignation, indifference, the hardening of the heart and laziness." Havel explains, "The person who has completely lost all sense of the meaning of life is merely vegetating."[81]

If there were no higher or transcendent principles, people would have only themselves and their concerns to worry about. People who really think only of themselves, who are perpetually driven by motives of pure self-interest, are almost always unhappy. In fact, such people are often called self-absorbed. They have no higher perspective from which to look at themselves, and they do not see the absurdity or the humor of their situation. The horizon of self-concern makes them almost neurotic. Havel would say that they have lost a sense of responsibility to others. What they lack is an absolute horizon that gives them an awareness of their own situation, an ability to bear up under the absurdity of life—its throwness—and a sense of why they need to be responsible and committed to others for their own well-being.[82]

However, because we are separated from Being, because we feel alienation and confusion about our lives, we are tempted to adopt some material explanation of reality that answers all our questions. Perhaps because science can offer clear and unequivocal answers, there is a temptation to view it as the only source of truth. Natural science is an account of the nature of everyday existence and of physical life—although, of course, the explanation is more detailed and accurate than common sense. Natural science itself is not antithetical to openness to Being. Science becomes part of "the order of death" only when its advocates claim that science is the only explanation for life and when, acting on that principle, they attempt to use the scientific mode of thinking to control all of existence.[83]

Alternatively, we can be tempted to make spiritual concerns our single guiding principles and our answer to all life's mysteries, as do some fundamentalist religions. Havel argues to the contrary that life is neither totally material nor physical; thus, there are no simple answers to our perplexities. He writes, "Existence . . . is a kind of permanent balancing act between the unattainability of Being and succumbing to existence-in-the-world."[84]

PLATO AND PATOČKA

Edward F. Findlay's informative article explores Havel's intellectual debt to his mentor, Jan Patočka.[85] Findlay contends that Havel is a devotee of Patočka's notion of "Negative Platonism." For Patočka, negative Platonism is a way of investigating philosophic issues. As opposed to an attempt to resolve questions on the basis of preconceived metaphysical categories, negative Platonism is an open-ended quest to understand the problems of human existence. Patočka's ideal is Socrates, who did not attempt to close off inquiry but instead pursued his "What is?" questions as far as the human mind could take them. Despite, or perhaps because of, his relentless quest to discover the human virtues, Socrates was responsible; his questions emanated from a care for the soul. He wanted to know how to live well. In discovering the answer for himself, he could share it with everyone.

According to Patočka, Plato and Aristotle attempted to answer Socrates' questions, and in doing so, they established metaphysical doctrines. Their students and the generations thereafter were influenced by the two philosophers' metaphysics in such a way as to answer questions before they were asked. While metaphysics might have been intended to be a suit of armor against the abyss, it instead became a straightjacket inhibiting human thought and freedom.

Havel partly agrees with Patočka's analysis. He does not believe that truth can be frozen into metaphysical principle; life is too complicated for that. Yet Havel writes of a unitary "order of Being," which implies a fixed metaphysical principle. Findlay argues that Havel's analysis either "lacks clarity" or is written in a literary form less precise than Patočka's philosophy. But, if Havel actually took Patočka's principles as his own, why was he still attempting—long after Patočka's death—to work out the problems of Heidegger in his prison meditations to Olga? Perhaps Havel disagreed with his mentor.

Havel seems to hold that openness to the question of Being is an insufficient support for morality. He argues instead that morals are grounded phenomenologically, in experience. Wherever there are human beings, there are moral considerations. Being is constructed so that, in every time and culture, human beings have been preoccupied with moral concerns.

Havel's relationship to Patočka is similar to Plato's relationship to Socrates. Plato's dialogues often attempt to discover the nature of a particular virtue (What is justice, love, piety, friendship, courage?). Whenever these virtues are examined, however, certainty about what they really are seems to recede and even disappear under the withering barrage of Socratic questions. But do the virtues vanish in the same way for Plato (and for his readers) as they do for Socrates in the dialogues? After all, if the virtues did not exist, how could we discuss them? We can most clearly see the way Plato attempts to correct Socrates in *Lysis*, a dialogue about friendship. Despite a spirited attempt, Socrates and his young interlocutor cannot seem to discover what "friendship" is. The dialogue ends with both admitting to being more confused than when they started. Socrates' questions serve only to befuddle those engaged in the dialogue. Despite the confusion, however, friendship is evident in *Lysis*. Plato's literary form shows the reader the phenomenon of friendship through the gentle, caring, and thoughtful manner in which the two characters interact.

Havel the artist suggests that Heidegger the philosopher and would-be artist misunderstands the intention of Plato, the artist-philosopher. Heidegger argues that Plato's teaching can be found in the theory of the forms, the otherworldly ideas that exist as metaphysical straightjackets on our freedom and search for the truth. But, Havel's plays imitate Plato's dialogues in their method of pursuing the truth. Plato's teaching is found in real-life relations between the people in the dialogues, not necessarily in their speeches. For instance, we never quite discover a satisfactory definition of justice in *The Republic*, yet it is just that two young men of good character, Plato's brothers, are dissuaded from pursuing the tyrannical life. It is the justice of their education in political moderation that comes to light when the scene of the dialogue is considered, instead of the metaphysical principles of the speeches. Havel's plays often conclude unsatisfactorily, and the characters occasionally offer discourses that their actions contradict. Yet when we reflect on the interpersonal relations of Havel's plays, we see not simply a "representational truth" of common human experience, one created by speech, but a true ground of moral judgment.

Heidegger holds that Socrates is the "purest thinker of the West" because he stood in the "draft" between where we know and yet never know fully, where Being is revealed yet never fully known. Socrates' constant questions made him more aware of the nature of friendship, honor, justice, and the like; yet, he could never give a final definition to any of these qualities, for his wisdom consisted of knowing that he did not know.[86]

Havel responds to Heidegger almost directly. He argues that when we attempt to understand things by questioning them, we often learn that we do not know. But knowing that we do not know results in our having more real wisdom on the subject at hand than if we were to simply accept the common explanation. We do learn a great deal about the beings.[87]

Furthermore, because Socrates could not come to convincing conclusions and occasionally even seemed to confuse himself, he never wrote; he never tried to explain to others what he did not know himself. But Havel writes. He writes because writing shows that the phenomena have a tangible substance. We can give an account of the virtues, even if that account must be presented in the form of a dialogue, as in Plato's work, or in the form of a play, as in Havel's work. In the exchange between real people, we "see" the virtues themselves.

The virtues are visible in human affairs because Being is constructed in such a manner as to make them visible. Being does not dictate that we follow moral guidelines. That would make morals into no more than instincts and thereby eliminate our freedom and dignity. But Being shows us in our everyday experience that morals do exist: Morality is a human possibility. Being presents itself to humans as something good and eternal. "It cannot be an accident," Havel writes in an effort to correct Patočka, "or a mere concord of countless misperceptions if, after thousands of years, people of different epochs and cultures feel that they are somehow parts and partakers of the same integral Being, carrying within themselves a piece of the infinity of that Being." Although the traditions and practices of people and cultures attempt to capture the significance of Being in different ways, all have a similar sense of wholeness that expresses a moral "home" for our existence.[88] Havel explains,

For aren't all religions marked by a belief in a higher authority than the human authority, in the existence of a higher order than the one that we have built on this Earth? Don't they all embrace the notion of a justice higher than earthly justice? Aren't they all based, expressly or by implication, on hope, in that metaphysical meaning of the word on which I have reflected here? Don't they all, in some form or another, take the infinite and the eternal as the ultimate measures of human affairs? Don't they all turn our attention to what is beyond our death? And don't they also derive, from a humility before that which transcends us, moral imperatives, which they offer to us as guidelines to living meaningful lives?[89]

HAVEL AND THE GROUND OF BEING

Perhaps it is appropriate at this point to consider Lawler's objections to Havel's vague spiritual principles. Lawler argues that Havel's efforts to explain transcendent doctrines in a phenomenological way and to heal "the split between the rational and the spiritual" reduce spiritual experience to a kind of everydayness. According to Lawler, Havel attempts to make human beings too comfortable during their time on Earth by assuring them that existence is comprehensible. For Lawler, human beings should never become fully satisfied with life, for to do so entails the vain and ultimately fruitless effort to forget death. Death reminds us of our contingency and vulnerability. Death thereby points to our incompleteness and to our need for God so that we may be whole. Lawler argues that once we comprehend our limits—that death cannot be overcome and that ultimate and certain answers cannot be provided by reason alone—we accept that we are aliens, or strangers, in the universe. All questions about existence seem to lead nowhere. There are no answers other than those provided by faith in a knowing and caring God. Lawler states that a proper account of the human condition

> is based primarily in opposition to systemization and denial of differences. It fundamentally affirms the disorder or plurality that characterizes the liberty of personal identity, showing that human greatness is intertwined with human misery, the awareness of human alienation from Being and the inevitability of death.[90]

Havel does not disagree with the idea that "death, or the awareness of death, is the most extraordinary dimension of man's stay on this Earth, one that inspires dread, fear and awe is at the same time a key to the fulfillment of human life in the best sense of the word."[91] In fact, all transcendent principles—such as "knowledge, love, morality, art"—are efforts to overcome death. Nor does Havel dispute the notion that awareness of death makes us "aliens in the world."[92] While Havel understands the importance of death to human consciousness, he is also aware that people would become debilitated if they dwelled on death at every moment of their lives. Anyone who has been close to death knows that confronting the apprehension of personal oblivion can sap the spirit and undermine the resolve. To accomplish anything, we must forget or ignore that we and everything that we have ever done will disappear. We must have hope that our actions matter. Thus, for Havel, "Death gives us a chance to overcome it not by refusing to recognize its existence, but through our ability to look beyond it, or to defy it by purposeful action."[93]

Lawler is correct that Havel is not religious in the usual sense. Havel does not accept the traditional idea of God, partly because such a God demands things and because Havel does not like to be commanded. Moreover, Havel is "the child of the age of the conceptual, rather than the mystical" and therefore has to work out his idea of what God is rationally and not simply accept God on faith.[94] Havel's attempt to characterize the order of Being is similar to Plato's account of the foundation of being, the Good. The order of Being is not visible itself. It is, like Plato's idea or form of the Good, known only in the reflection of the things it illuminates. According to Havel, the order of Being is "like a blind man touching the woman he loves, whom he has never seen and never will." He nonetheless "sees" her beauty. The ground of Being is "like a light whose source we cannot see, but whose illumination we nevertheless live."[95] In the two dialogues where Plato talks about the ground of being—*Republic* and *Gorgias*—he presents "anthropomorphic" myths about the origins and purpose of the universe, not because Plato is attempting to push human beings into pantheistic "everydayness," but rather to give an account of the Good in which all our actions are grounded.[96] Since the ultimate source of our existence is ineffable, both writers resort to myth to explain the unexplainable. Both writers attempt to present a rational myth, free of superstition and cultural bias. But it is obvious that the myth is not the same as the source of being—the myth is no more than an artistic effort to show that there is both a ground and an order to life. Lawler sees the Gaia principle as the source of Havel's ground for morality; hence, he accuses Havel of paganism. But Havel understands the Gaia principle as a symbol of the human longing for meaning, which is expressed though a myth about the way the order of Being reveals itself in the world. Gaia is not the ground of the order of Being; rather, the spiritual order of Being is the source of Gaia and the human myth about Gaia.

Lawler's characterization of Havel as a pagan mistakes the effort to make the myth rational for an attempt to make existence rational. In fact, Havel claims that there are no simple answers to the mysteries of existence—not even in religious texts. The search for meaning never gives certain, clear answers. We are always "striving for something beyond us." This partly accounts for the diversity of life.[97] "For me," he writes,

> the notion of some complete and finite knowledge that explains everything and raises no further questions is clearly related to the notion of an end—an end to the spirit, to life and to Being. Anything meaningful that has ever been said in this matter (including every religious gospel), is on the contrary remarkable for its dramatic openness, its incompleteness.[98]

Havel disagrees with Heidegger and Lawler that alienation is always the central fact of human existence. Havel suggests that we are capable—as St. Thomas Aquinas's rational theology insists—of comprehending the natural order of life. Why, after all, would God create an irrational universe? Why would God not make a home for us in which our peculiar capacity for reason played some part in making our lives satisfying? Thus, there may be evidence of God's rational plan in the myths that all cultures have about the meaning of existence. Havel alludes to the symbols of an orderly universe in many ways: The anthropic cosmological principle and the Gaia hypothesis are but two examples.

Havel states that he is closer to the Judeo-Christian way of thinking than he is to the tradition developed by classical philosophy, perhaps because his authority, Claude Tresmontant, understates classical philosophy's "concreteness and its respect for the world of the senses." Yet, because Havel attempts to reason his way to responsible moral conduct and rejects, at least formally, dependence on a knowing, caring God to provide the source and authority for morality, he is forced to restate the natural argument for virtue and the way virtue is exercised that the classical philosophers first elucidated.[99]

Havel's rational account of first principles also aims at avoiding "a conflict between different spheres of civilization, culture or religion."[100] In the past, different cultures and religions claimed exclusive possession of the truth. Believers formed communities based on those common beliefs and, of necessity, thereby excluded others, resulting in clashes between those with conflicting principles. Havel understands that these various conceptions of truth might result in a clash of cultures. He worries that global communication makes differences between cultures and religions stand out all the more clearly. Thus, Havel stresses the universal character of all transcendent principles as a way of overcoming a clash of civilizations. He explains,

> I am speaking of something slightly different: the need to grasp and articulate anew humanity's essential, fundamental spiritual experience and to infuse the spirit of this experience into the creation of a new world order, one that would allow us all to live and work together in peace without forcing anyone to give up his cultural autonomy.[101]

CONCLUSION

Havel pays high tribute to Heidegger's ideas by using them as the starting point for, and as a challenge to, his own views. One could almost say that almost everything Havel has written is a response to Heidegger's philosophy. Havel accepts Heidegger's criticism of modern philosophy, its attempts to fully answer all of life's mysteries by mastering the beings, conquering nature, and fully controlling human destiny. Yet this arrogant effort to place the human will at the center of existence disguises the complexity, spontaneity, and heterogeneity of life. Havel rejects the most important element in Heidegger's principles—the proposition that Being is no-thing. Instead, Havel maintains that there is an absolute ground to human experience, a natural world that is the basis for responsible moral behavior. Havel argues that the validity of his position can be established through a phenomenological meditation on our everyday experience.

Where do we turn for proof of this assertion? Havel uses his plays as a testing ground for his ideas and for evidence of his philosophic claims. The dissident Havel employs many of Heidegger's categories when attacking "post-totalitarian" society, and we can most clearly see Havel's agreement with Heidegger in the Czech's valiant opposition to tyranny. Ultimately, however, there is an important difference between the two. Heidegger might argue that the collapse of Communism was caused by a new revelation of Being manifesting itself in history, while Havel argues that Communism fell because its doctrines contravene the natural world and the "order of Being." Havel's complex acceptance and final rejection of Heidegger's philosophy are even more apparent in Havel's plays.

NOTES

1. Edward F. Findlay, "Classical Ethics and Postmodern Critique: Political Philosophy in Václav Havel and Jan Patočka," *Review of Politics* 61 (Summer 1999): 403–426.
2. Václav Havel, *Letters to Olga: June 1979–September 1982*, trans. and intro. Paul Wilson (New York: Knopf, 1988), 147, 190–191, 196.
3. Havel, *Disturbing the Peace*, 152 (see chap. 1, n. 4).
4. Paul Wilson, "Introduction," *Letters to Olga*, 17.
5. Havel, *Disturbing the Peace*, 150.
6. Havel, *Letters to Olga*, 284.
7. Peter Majer, "Time, Identity and Being: The World of Václav Havel," *Twentieth-Century European Drama*, ed. Brian Docherty (New York: St. Martin's Press, 1994), 172–182.
8. Caroline Bayard, "The Intellectual in the Post Modern Age," *Philosophy Today* 34 (Winter 1990): 291–302.
9. Dean C. Hammer, "Václav Havel's Construction of a Democratic Discourse: Politics in a Postmodern Age," *Philosophy Today* 39 (Summer 1995): 119–124.
10. Aviezer Tucker, *The Philosophy and Politics of Czech Dissidence from Patočka to Havel* (Pittsburgh: University of Pittsburgh Press, 2000), 247–248.
11. Compare Richard Rorty's "The End of Leninism, Havel, and Social Hope," *Truth and Progress: Philosophic Papers* (Cambridge: Cambridge University Press, 1998), 3:228–242. Richard Rorty, "The Seer of Prague," *New Republic*, July 1, 1991, 35–40.
12. Edward E. Ericson Jr., "Solzhenitsyn, Havel, and the Twenty-First Century," *Modern Age* 41 (Winter 1999): 3–18.
13. Peter Augustine Lawler, "Havel on Political Responsibility," *Political Science Reviewer* 22 (1993): 20–55.
14. Peter Augustine Lawler, "Havel's Postmodern View of Man in the Cosmos," *Perspectives on Political Science*, 26 (Winter 1997): 27–35.
15. Jean Bethke Elshtain, "Sovereignty, Identity, Sacrifice," *Social Research* 58 (Fall 1991): 545–565; Jean Bethke Elshtain, "Politics without Cliché," *Social Research* 60 (Fall 1993): 431–444; Jean Bethke Elshtain, "Stories and Political Life," *PS: Political Science & Politics* 28 (June 1995): 196–197; Jean Bethke Elshtain, "Václav Havel on Freedom and Responsibility," in *Theory and Practice*, ed. Ian Shapiro and Judith Wagner DeCew (New York: New York University Press, 1995), 464–482.
16. James W. Sire, *Václav Havel, The Intellectual Conscience of International Politics* (Downers Grove, Ill.: Intervarsity Press, 2001), 96; Jean Bethke Elshtain, "A Man for This Season," *Perspectives on Political Science* 21, no. 14 (Fall 1992): 207–211.
17. Havel, *Letters to Olga*, 119, 311–312; "A Word on Words," *Open Letters*, 381 (see chap. 1, n. 13); *Disturbing the Peace*, 158.
18. Martin Heidegger, "Letter on Humanism," *Martin Heidegger: The Basic Writings*, ed. David Farrell Krell (New York: Harper & Row, 1977), 236.

19. Martin Heidegger, "The Word of Nietzsche: 'God Is Dead,'" *The Question Concerning Technology and Other Essays*, trans. and intro. William Lovitt (New York: Harper Colophon Books, 1977), 53–112.

20. Martin Heidegger, *Being and Time*, trans. John MacQuarrie and Edward Robinson (London: SCM Press, 1962), 45–46.

21. Heidegger, "The Question Concerning Technology," in *Basic Writings*, 297.

22. Heidegger, "The Question Concerning Technology," 283–317.

23. Heidegger, *Being and Time*, 398.

24. Heidegger, "Letter on Humanism," in *Basic Writings*, 205.

25. Heidegger, *Being and Time*, 85.

26. Heidegger, "Letter on Humanism," 221.

27. Heidegger, *Being and Time*, 63, 220–222.

28. Rüdiger Safranski, *Martin Heidegger: Between Good and Evil*, trans. Ewald Osers (Cambridge, Mass.: Harvard University Press, 1998), 194–195.

29. Heidegger, *Being and Time*, 269–270 (original emphasis).

30. Martin Heidegger, "The Turning," in *The Question Concerning Technology and Other Essays*, 41.

31. Leslie Paul Thiele, *Timely Meditations: Martin Heidegger and Postmodern Politics*, (Princeton, N.J.: Princeton University Press, 1995), 103.

32. Martin Heidegger, "What Is Metaphysics?" in *Basic Writings*, 111.

33. Havel misquotes somewhat Heidegger's refrain in "The Power of the Powerless," in *Open Letters*, 206. See Martin Heidegger, "'Only a God Can Save Us': The *Spiegel* Interview [1966]," in *Heidegger: The Man and the Thinker*, trans. William J. Richardson, ed. Thomas Sheehan (Chicago: University of Chicago Press, 1981), 57.

34. Jean Paul Sartre, *L'existentialisme est un humanisme* (Paris: Nagel, 1946), 36. Quoted in Heidegger, "Letter on Humanism," 214.

35. Heidegger, "Letter on Humanism," 227.

36. Heidegger, "Letter on Humanism," 239.

37. Jean-François Lyotard, *The Postmodern Condition: A Report on Knowledge* (Minneapolis: University of Minnesota Press, 1984), xxiv.

38. Richard Rorty, *Contingency, Irony, and Solidarity* (Cambridge: Cambridge University Press, 1989), 189.

39. Richard Rorty, *Objectivity, Relativism, and Truth* (Cambridge: Cambridge University Press, 1991), 191. See also Rorty, "The Seer of Prague," where Rorty attempts to distinguish between pragmatic and absolute grounds for resistance. But what is pragmatic about risking one's life, reputation, and sanity for the sake of a principle? From where does the pragmatic principle of resistance arise?

40. Michel Foucault, *Michel Foucault: Beyond Structuralism and Hermeneutics*, ed. Hubert Dreyfus and Paul Rabinow, 2nd ed. (Chicago: University of Chicago Press, 1983), 222, 237.

41. Heidegger, "Being and Time," in *Basic Writings*, 49.

42. Heidegger, "Letter on Humanism," 219.

43. Heidegger, "Letter on Humanism," 210.

44. Thiele, *Timely Meditation*, 69.

45. Martin Heidegger, *Hölderlin's Hymne "Anderke,"* ed. Curd Ochwadt (*Gesamtausgabe*, vol. 52; Frankfurt-Main: Klostermann, 1982), 189–190; quoted in Fred Dallmayr, *The Other Heidegger* (Ithaca, N.Y.: Cornell University Press, 1993), 155, see also 149–199. Heidegger states "Dasein enters with the other into the same fundamental comportment toward the entity asserted about, which is unveiled in the same way" (Martin Heidegger, *Basic Problems of Phenomenology*, trans. A. Hofstadter [Bloomington: Indiana University Press, 1982], 210; quoted in Thiele, *Timely Meditation*, 50).

46. Thiele, *Timely Meditation*, 154. Compare James Madison's argument in favor of institutional stability in *Federalist #49*,

> The reason of man, like man himself, is timid and cautious when left alone, and acquires firmness and confidence in proportion to the number with which it is associated. When the examples which fortify opinion are ANCIENT as well as NUMEROUS, they are known to have a double effect. In a nation of philosophers, this consideration ought to be disregarded. A reverence for the laws would be sufficiently inculcated by the voice of an enlightened reason. But a nation of philosophers is as little to be expected as the philosophical race of kings wished for by Plato. And in every other nation, the most rational government will not find it a superfluous advantage to have the prejudices of the community on its side. (http://libertyonline.hypermall.com/Federalist)

47. See Heidegger's retraction of his earlier assertion that the pre-Socratics expressed Being directly (Martin Heidegger, *On Time and Being*, trans. J. Strambaugh [New York: Harper & Row, 1972], 70).

48. Heidegger, *Being and Time*, 85.

49. Heidegger, *On Time and Being*, 11; quoted in Thiele, *Timely Meditation*, 96.

50. Quoted in Victor Farias, *Heidegger and Nazism* (Philadelphia: Temple University Press, 1989), 284.

51. Martin Heidegger, *Discourse on Thinking*, trans. J. Anderson and E. Freund (New York: Harper & Row, 1966), 68.

52. Michael Allen Gillespie, *Hegel, Heidegger, and the Ground of History* (Chicago: University of Chicago Press, 1984), 173.

53. Havel, *Letters to Olga*, 186–189, 197, 223, 301–302. See also, Havel, "The Power of the Powerless," *Open Letters*, 30–32. Compare Heidegger's remarks on how "they" can preoccupy a person's life (*Being and Time*, 220–222). My thanks to Hedi Hegyi for pointing out the liberating effects of existential philosophy in Communist countries.

54. Havel, "Power of the Powerless," *Open Letters*, 206. See also, *Letters to Olga*, 339.

55. Havel, *Letters to Olga*, 225, 319.

56. Havel, *Letters to Olga*, 264.

57. Václav Havel, "Address at the Opening Ceremony of the Meetings of the International Monetary Fund and the World Bank Group," Prague, September 26, 2000.

58. Havel, *Letters to Olga*, 225–226.

59. Havel, *Letters to Olga*, 311–312, 320.

60. Václav Havel, "The Spiritual Roots of Democracy," *Lapis Magazine*, online, 1991. Thiele argues that Heidegger's theory of "Being-in-the-world," or to "dwell alongside" what already exists, makes ethics "available." Thiele maintains that humans share "representational truth," a universal experience of "standards, procedures, and practices." This common experience of reality is not grounded in traditional metaphysical categories, however. There are no God-given commandments or strict moral codes, such as those proposed in Plato's theory of forms. Yet, it is difficult to see how Thiele's effort to humanize Heidegger's theory makes ethical judgments possible. After all, as Heidegger points out, representational truth is constituted in the culture and society in which people live. Different societies may have had Being revealed in different ways. In fact, Heidegger goes so far as to suggest that truth is different at different times in history and within distinct cultural groupings (Thiele, *Timely Meditation*, 44).

61. Václav Havel, *Summer Meditations*, trans. Paul Wilson (New York: Vintage Books, 1993), 31; "Speech on the National Day of the Czech Republic," Prague, October 28, 1995.

62. Havel, *Letters to Olga*, 187–188, 219.

63. Havel, *Letters to Olga*, 220.

64. Havel, *Letters to Olga*, 324.

65. Havel, *Letters to Olga*, 321–322.

66. Havel, *Letters to Olga*, 321–324.

67. Adam Smith, "Of the Character of Virtue," *The Theory of Moral Sentiments*, part VI (London: A. Millar, 1790; Library of Economics and Liberty, online).

68. Havel, *Letters to Olga*, 266.

69. Havel, *Letters to Olga*, 220, 266, 344–347.

70. Havel, *Letters to Olga*, 147–148, 230.

71. Havel, *Letters to Olga*, 224.

72. Havel, "Politics and Conscience," *Open Letters*, 251.

73. "Europe at the *fin de siecle*," interview with Maximilian Schell, *Society* 32, no. 6 (September–October 1995): 68–72.

74. Havel, *Letters to Olga*, 233.

75. Havel, *Summer Meditations*, 6.

76. Havel, *Letters to Olga*, 140–141.

77. Havel, *Letters to Olga*, 301.

78. Havel, *Letters to Olga*, 242.

79. Havel, *Letters to Olga*, 122–123.

80. Havel, *Letters to Olga*, 206–207.

81. Havel, *Letters to Olga*, 237–238.

82. Havel, *Letters to Olga*, 122.

83. Havel, *Letters to Olga*, 189.

84. Havel, *Letters to Olga*, 339.

85. Findlay, "Classical Ethics and Postmodern Critique," 403–438.

86. Heidegger, *Basic Writings*, 358.
87. Havel, *Letters to Olga*, 329.
88. Václav Havel, "Speech upon Receiving the Jackson H. Ralston Prize," Stanford University, September 29, 1994. See Peter Augustine Lawler, "Havel's Postmodern View of Man in the Cosmos," *Perspectives on Political Science* 26 (Winter 1997): 33.
89. Václav Havel, "The Future of Hope Conference," Hiroshima, December 5, 1995.
90. Lawler, "Havel's Postmodern View of Man in the Cosmos," 27–35.
91. Havel, "The Future of Hope Conference."
92. Havel, *Letters to Olga*, 240, 321.
93. Havel, "The Future of Hope Conference."
94. Havel, *Letters to Olga*, 101.
95. Havel, *Letters to Olga*, 225.
96. Plato, *Republic*, 614b–621d, *Gorgias*, 523a–527e.
97. Havel, *Letters to Olga*, 243.
98. Havel, *Letters to Olga*, 225.
99. Havel, *Letters to Olga*, 196.
100. Havel, "The Future of Hope Conference."
101. Havel, "The Future of Hope Conference."

3

A DISSIDENT IN AN "UNNATURAL" WORLD

Although Václav Havel became famous in the West as a dissident, he was never fully comfortable with the term, since it implies an organized political opposition to Communist rule. The dissident Havel was careful to explain that his disagreement with the Communist regime was an "existential attitude," not a political program. He claimed not to be interested in "politics" as the term is usually understood: He did not seek power and did not belong to a group or party intent on wresting control from the government.[1] But Havel might not have been telling the whole truth.

The term "dissident" took on a special meaning in the Soviet bloc—it could almost have described a particular profession. In fact, Havel argues that people from all walks of life with many professions dissented from the power of the state. Once people were publicly identified as dissidents and became known in the West, they were at least partially shielded from persecution—even Communist governments, it seems, felt the pressure of international public condemnation. This notoriety established a gulf between dissidents and ordinary people, the latter of whom feared that their obscurity made them too vulnerable to publicly resist Communist tyranny.[2] However, dissidents shouldered an increased responsibility to act and speak as the conscience of the nation. On occasion, Havel was tempted to cry out, "I'm not your savior!"[3]

Havel claims that he did not mean to become a dissident: it happened simply as a result of his attempts to capture truth in his art.[4] To cause dissension means to create differences between people, to stir up trouble. But Havel contends that he was not a troublemaker. In fact, he argues that his differences with the Communist government were rooted in his sense of responsibility toward his fellow citizens—and humanity generally—and the obligations placed on everyone by the "order of Being," from which all responsibility derives. It was the Communist government of Czechoslovakia that separated people from the truth and from the natural world of individual discernment, responsibility, and morality. It was the Communists who robbed people of their dignity and personal identity, thereby alienating them from themselves as well as others. Havel's dissent was undertaken not to cause dissension but to maintain his own integrity and perhaps to act as a catalyst for others to achieve a sense of personal autonomy.[5]

Havel's opposition was born when Communism had evolved from its violent and brutal era, described by Aleksandr Solzhenitsyn in *The Gulag Archipelago*. Havel labels his era the post-totalitarian system, a time when show trials, torture, loss of property, deportations, and executions had stopped. Stalin and his henchmen had murdered so many people and destroyed so many lives that even the most ardent Communists had doubts about returning to terror as a method of political control. Communists were not reticent about using power to maintain their position, but under Stalin they had seen so many of their loyal colleagues swept up in the endless purges that they feared a new terror might threaten their own safety, security, and position. By the 1970s and 1980s, the Communist Party had developed less fearsome but more "subtle and selective" methods of maintaining its "leading role in society."[6] Moreover, after Nikita Khrushchev's revelation about Stalin's atrocities, the brutal Communist repression of the Polish and Hungarian uprisings in 1956, and the invasion of Czechoslovakia by Warsaw Pact troops in 1968, hardly anyone actually believed that the high ideals of Communism were practicable.

If so few believed, why did so many obey? If people did not fear violent reprisals, why did they not rise up against the system that oppressed them? How did a social system that originated with the hope of attaining social justice for all end up cynically holding onto power solely for the benefit of its ruling class? What characteristics of the post-totalitarian system enabled it to maintain its hold? Why did Havel oppose it? It was to these questions that Havel turned his attention in essays such as "Dear Dr. Husák," "The Power of the Powerless," and "Politics and Conscience," all written after the high hopes of the Prague Spring had been crushed.[7]

Although Stalinist tactics did not survive into the post-totalitarian era, many people lived with memories of the arbitrary use of terror during the 1950s. The fear that Communists might return to brutality was always in people's minds. People worried that if Communists were provoked and their supremacy threatened, they would return to their former hideous ways in order to retain power. In a sense, the stability of the post-totalitarian era was preserved by a fear of something neither rulers nor the ruled wanted. Moreover, the West accepted the existence of the Soviet bloc as an established fact of international life, according an aura of legitimacy to regimes under Soviet control.[8]

Of course, the authorities had at their disposal a whole range of lesser threats and rewards to control the population. The Communist state was supported by "the ubiquitous, omnipotent" state security police who employed, cajoled, and intimated legions of informers to keep a watchful eye on their fellow citizens. Anyone caught deviating from the party line could be fired and barred forever from work in their chosen career. Those considered the most serious threat were forced to relocate to a part of the country where they could find "suitable work." They were denied passports and could not travel. Their families suffered: spouses could not obtain work, parents were harassed, and—by far the most effective threat—children were not allowed to receive a good education. Fear was so pervasive that the government had no need to suppress free expression. A kind of self-censorship paralyzed artists and intellectuals, who believed that they could not challenge what was conventionally accepted.[9] Paul Wilson writes that Havel describes

> a society governed by fear—not the cold, pit-of-the-stomach terror that Stalin had once spread throughout his empire, but a dull, existential fear that seeped into every crack and crevice of daily life and made one think twice about everything one said and did. This fear was maintained by the Secret Police, "that hideous spider whose invisible web runs right through society," and it reduced human action—and therefore history itself—to false pretense.[10]

Fear was reinforced by a legal system that justified Communist oppression. Laws were written in such a way that anything out of the ordinary, any act of independence or deviation from the norm, was interpreted as the suspect behavior of a "class enemy," or a person in the service of a hostile foreign power. "Everything unusual, risky, self-taught, and unbridled" was illegal.[11] Obedience to the law was based partly on the fear of punishment and partly on the recognition that laws protect people from murder, theft, assault, and other crimes. In the vast array of statutes, it was difficult for average citizens to distinguish which laws served the interests of a civilized society and which were constructed as tools of oppression. For example, the law against disturbing the peace could be equally applied to keep drunks from harassing passersby or to prevent playwrights from staging their plays. Judicial proceedings were the same as in other developed countries; lawyers were employed and witnesses called. Judges deliberated on the evidence, the verdict was decided, and punishment was meted out. Of course, in political cases, the proceedings were a sham, since the verdict had already been decided at the political, not judicial, level. But however artificial, the legal system effectively disguised the arbitrary power of the Communist Party.[12]

Communist rule sprang from one of the most powerful ideologies ever to have taken hold as a social doctrine: the teachings of Karl Marx, which promised equality, liberation, and community.[13] Those who opposed the principles of Communism were, according to the theory, soon to be swept aside by the historical inevitability of the people's demand for social justice. But after 1968, virtually no one in Czechoslovakia believed that the theory could translate into practice. While everyone was expected to pay lip service to the ideals of revolutionary reform, the authorities were hardly focused on abstract ideas of justice. Instead, they promised that the Communist state would provide for the material needs of the people—a pledge the centralized economy could not in the end deliver. Marxism was transformed into a ritual form of communication that legitimized party rule, insulated the leadership from the grim realities of average citizens' daily lives, and supported the status quo. Havel explains:

> The contrast between the revolutionary teachings about the new man and new morality, and the shoddy concept of life as consumer bliss raises the question of why the authorities actually cling so tenaciously to their ideology. Clearly only because their ideology, as a conventionalized system of ritual communication, assures them the appearance of legitimacy, continuity, and consistence, and acts as a screen of the prestige for their pragmatic practice.[14]

Despite the loss of faith in the ideology's revolutionary ideals, its power over the public discourse remained strong in the post-totalitarian era. The ideology became the means by which events were explained, judged, and acted on. Since Marxist doctrine proclaimed that social strife would end after the Communist revolution, the ideology demanded that no discord exist. Havel says, "Society was petrified into the fiction of everlasting harmony."[15]

Ideology mediated reality, masking the explicit meaning of incidents. Havel provides the following example: When a stone window ledge fell from a building on Vodičkova Street in Prague, killing a woman, instead of facing the problem of shoddy maintenance of buildings, the Communist-controlled press explained that local municipal matters were not as important as the more worthy goals of the dignity of mankind and the mission of socialism to humanize the world. Weighed in the scale of human suffering, the news report contended, the plight of one person did not matter. What was important was that Communism triumph over social injustice. According to Havel, the ideology "contextualized" the incident so that its immediate meaning was obscured. What was at stake, Havel explains, was not the fate of mankind but window ledges falling on people's heads. The ideology "separated thought from its immediate contact with reality."[16]

Heidegger is correct that language can mediate our understanding of events. In this case, certainly there were people who accepted the value of socialism over the maintenance of buildings; however, the Czechs demonstrated an even stronger reaction, indicating that Heidegger was wrong and that human value judgments were not determined by the linguistic milieu but were grounded in the natural world accessible through our senses. After all, our regret at a building falling on a passerby's head is just that, no matter how much dialectic reasoning is proffered to explain it away.

Havel's most famous example of the ability of language and symbols to influence or conceal the natural world is presented in his account of why a Communist-era greengrocer would place a sign bearing the slogan WORKERS OF THE WORLD, UNITE! among the carrots and onions. What is he trying to convey or explain? What are his motivations? Who is his audience?

Havel argues that the greengrocer does not really think about what he is doing. He knows, of course, that displaying the sign will show solidarity with those in power. He knows, too, that he can avoid a good deal of trouble if his superiors believe that he accepts Communist doctrines. Yet such thoughts rarely enter his consciousness. He surely does not tell himself the truth: "I am afraid and therefore unquestioningly obedient." In fact, if he were forced to state such an obviously humiliating truth, even to himself, he would be embarrassed. He puts the sign up voluntarily because it is easier to accept what Heidegger calls the "public way"—the ruling opinion of the social milieu in which he lives—which establishes what is accepted as true and worthwhile. The ritual exhibiting of the sign shows shoppers, his boss, political bigwigs, and casual passersby that the greengrocer adheres to the official ideology on which the regime rests, that the authority of those in charge is absolute. If pushed on the question, the shopkeeper might say, "What's wrong with the workers of the world uniting?" But no one challenges him, because the sign is a ritual, reinforcing the authority of the status quo while disguising the greengrocer's complicity in supporting an oppressive regime. Havel explains that "the sign helps the greengrocer to conceal from himself the low foundations of his obedience, at the same time concealing the low foundations of power. It hides them behind the facade of something high. And that something is ideology."[17]

Communism forced people to live a lie. To comply with the ideology, they had to deny what their senses were telling them—that is, they had to suppress the evidence. They had to accept that their lives were satisfying, when in fact their daily existence was stultifying and oppressive. The gulf between the world of observation and the linguistic reality established by propaganda created a kind of moral crisis. People had to ask themselves: Do I play it safe and live the lie, or act on the basis of what I perceive to be true? Should I try to forget the disparity before me, disguise my lack of integrity, and gain at least some modicum of contentment by pursuing material well-being? Havel explains that the difficulty of choice lay not in believing the propaganda and ignoring one's senses but in ignoring both one's senses and the propaganda, thus rooting oneself entirely in "everydayness."

> The profound crisis of human identity brought on by living within a lie, a crisis which in turn makes such a life possible, certainly possesses a moral dimension as well; it appears, among other things, as a deep moral crisis in society. A person who has been seduced by the consumer value system, whose identity is dissolved in an amalgam of the accouterments of mass civilization, and who has no roots in the order of being, no sense of responsibility for anything higher than his own personal survival, is a demoralized person. The system depends on this demoralization, deepens it, is in fact a projection of it into society.[18]

In their early revolutionary stage, Communist regimes were characterized by fanaticism, zeal, and a desire to transform the world. Their goal was "to make an earthly paradise the final end of history, to rid the world of social conflict, of negative human qualities, and even of misery." But, once in power for any length of time, Communist governments became profoundly conservative. They opposed variety, spontaneity, and unpredictability. Post-totalitarian Communist governments fell victim to their own ideology, for they were supposed to have achieved social justice. Even if it did not exist, the pretense had to be maintained. "Society was petrified into the fiction of everlasting harmony," Havel explains.[19] Revolutionary charisma was replaced by "the dictatorship of a political bureaucracy," intent on regularizing all of life.[20]

The centralized planned economy added to the gray, monochromatic way of life. Millions of mammoth, featureless, coffinlike apartment complexes (nicknamed *paneláks*) constructed in the Communist world provide a striking visual representation of how the bureaucracy worked to standardize living conditions. Havel explains:

> Let me exaggerate deliberately. It would be to the greatest advantage of a centrally directed system of production if only one type of a prefabricated panel were produced, from which one type of apartment building would be constructed; these buildings in turn would be fitted with a single kind of door, door handle, window, toilet, washbasin, and so on, and together this would create a single type of housing development constructed according to one standardized urban development plan, with minor adjustments for landscape, given the regrettable irregularity of the earth's surface. In each apartment, of course, there would be the same kind of television set showing the same program.[21]

The post-totalitarian system demanded conformity because it was based on science, the science of social classes and historical development worked out by Marx. While common sense tells us that human beings do not behave with the same consistency as scientific laws, Communist doctrine asserted that they should and did. Any deviation from the results promised by the ideology was suppressed by the ruling elite to prove the ideology correct and thereby retain the legitimacy of the regime.[22] The "truth" of the ideology became a self-fulfilling prophecy.

The ideology claimed to be based on more than mere opinion: It was rooted in a metaphysical certainty. It answered all of life's questions and resolved all of life's mysteries. In an era of "metaphysical and existential uncertainty," Marxist ideology had "a certain hypnotic charm." It offered to "wandering mankind" an escape from doubts and insecurities. It became "a secularized religion" that provided "an immediate home" in which everything became "clear once more." The ideology was seductive because it professed to solve the problem of Being.[23]

Since the ideology already knew the "correct" answers to every problem, social existence was reduced to the administration of details by an anonymous bureaucratic apparatus. "The professional ruler," according to Havel, became the "'innocent' tool of an 'innocent' anonymous power, legitimized by science, cybernetics, ideology, law, abstraction, and objectivity—that is, everything except personal responsibility."[24] Under this bureaucratic tutelage, life became slow, repetitious, boring, and monotonous. Havel explains:

> Between the aims of the post-totalitarian system and the aims of life there is a yawning abyss: while life, in its essence, moves toward plurality, diversity, independent self-constitution, and self-organization, in short, toward the fulfillment of its own freedom, the post-totalitarian system

> demands conformity, uniformity, and discipline. While life ever strives to create new and improbable structures, the post-totalitarian system contrives to force life into its most probable states. The aims of the system reveal its most essential characteristic to be introversion, a movement toward being ever more completely and unreservedly itself, which means that the radius of its influence is continually widening as well. This system serves people only to the extent necessary to ensure that people will serve it. Anything beyond this, that is to say, anything which leads people to overstep their predetermined roles is regarded by the system as an attack upon itself. And in this respect it is correct: every instance of such transgression is a genuine denial of the system.[25]

Of course, those who actually worked in the bureaucracy rarely believed that the authoritative doctrines could transform the world for the better. Instead, public officials paid homage to the ideology while exploiting their positions for either personal gain or their family's advantage. During the era of normalization, Havel argued, "The number of people who sincerely believe everything that official propaganda says and who selflessly support the government's authority is smaller than it has ever been. But the number of hypocrites rises steadily: up to a point, every citizen is, in fact, forced to be one."[26]

Most Czechoslovaks turned away from politics, gave up hope that they could influence the system, and became as cynical as their leaders about looking to their own advantage.

> It is as though after the shocks of recent history, and the kind of system subsequently established in this country, people had lost all faith in the future, in the possibility of setting public affairs right, in the meaning of a struggle for truth and justice. They shrug off anything that goes beyond their every-day, routine concern for their own livelihood; they seek ways of escape; they succumb to apathy, to indifference toward supra-personal values and their fellow men, to spiritual passivity and depression.[27]

Fear, compliance, cynicism, unthinking acceptance of the ideology, and an impoverishment of spiritual inspiration formed the true superstructure of post-totalitarian Communism. The very dullness of the system made it look invincible and thereby supported its existence.

Havel's existential protest against the system was undertaken because "life rebels against all uniformity and leveling; its aim is not sameness but variety, the restlessness of transcendence, the adventure of novelty and rebellion against the status quo."[28] Havel objected to Communism's metaphysical dogmatism, resisted its attenuation of the complexity of Being, and defended the indeterminacy of existence. In his struggles against a dominant but impersonal power, Havel resembles the existentialist followers of Heidegger. There is, however, a crucial difference. Heidegger said one must assert one's own anguished and lonely response to the "public way" because there is no metaphysical approach that can justify an opposition to everydayness other than an assertion of one's will—which itself has no metaphysical ground. There is no such thing as a sense of conscience that supports our decision to stand against the crowd. Conscience is nothing more than the voice of "they." Heidegger maintains that

> a "world Conscience" is a dubious fabrication, and Dasein can come to this only *because* conscience, in its basis and its essence, is *in each case* mine—not only in the sense that in each case the appeal is to one's own most potentiality-for-Being, but because the call comes from that entity which in each case I myself am.[29]

But Havel perceives a natural world, which provides an alternative to the account of reality provided by "the public way." In the natural world, we experience love, hate, friendship, loss, and longing. In the natural world, people feel dismayed when a window ledge falls on a pedestrian's head, distressed when a greengrocer must sell his integrity with his produce, and appalled when row after row of ugly apartments blights the landscape. In the natural world, people use their individual discernment and judgment to make choices about what they think is true, just, and beautiful.

Although the collapse of Communism seems inevitable in hindsight, Havel was never sure whether the natural world would win out over the "pseudo-reality" created by Communist ideology.[30] It was not clear to him, even during his time in jail, that his actions would ever have any tangible consequence. But the natural world not only gave him guidance as to how to act but obliged him to act a certain way.

> Living within the truth, as humanity's revolt against an enforced position, is, on the contrary, an attempt to regain control over one's own sense of responsibility. In other words, it is clearly a moral act, not only because one must pay so dearly for it, but principally because it is not self-serving: the risk may bring rewards in the form of a general amelioration in the situation, or it may not. In this regard, as I stated previously, it is an all-or-nothing gamble, and it is difficult to imagine a reasonable person embarking on such a course merely because he reckons

that sacrifice today will bring rewards tomorrow, be it only in the form of general gratitude. (By the way, the representatives of power invariably come to terms with those who live within the truth by persistently ascribing utilitarian motivations to them—a lust for power or fame or wealth—and thus they try, at least, to implicate them in their own world, the world of general demoralization.)[31]

When Communism collapsed with astonishing speed and with very little violence, Havel interpreted the fall as the victory of practice over theory, individual over group perception, common sense over propaganda, integrity over selfish resignation, and the natural world over ideology. He alluded to his astonishment at the resilience of the natural world by claiming, as president, to have been "pulled forward by Being," as if some mysterious force had defeated all of Communism's lies by placing truth in their place.[32] Although he might be too modest to admit the point, it was also the victory of his understanding of the relationship between nature and Being over Heidegger's.

Ernest Gellner maintains that Havel's analysis of the Velvet Revolution puts its trust "in the eventual victory of simple decency." Although Gellner admires Havel's righteousness, he argues that "Communism was not overthrown by life, by thought" or "by human dignity," but rather by consumerism.[33] Gellner explains:

> What prevailed in 1989 was consumerism and the all-European endorsement of a system which satisfies its imperatives, as against one which conspicuously fails to do so and, in addition, is also oppressive and sleazy. Democracy and decency obtained a free ride on the back of consumerism, and we must be deeply grateful for that. But it is dangerous to delude oneself and suppose that they owed the victory to their inherent political appeal.[34]

It is difficult to agree with Gellner's assertion that a powerful entrenched political system was overthrown so that people could buy better washing machines and spend more time at the mall; human motivations are too complex for a single-factor explanation. If Czechs longed only for a consumer society, why did they choose Havel as president, instead of a business owner or technocrat? People wanted to be free, which meant different things to different people. Some wanted to speak their mind; others hoped to take part in government; a few sought a spiritual revival; and many, of course, wanted to be able to buy the goods available in the West. But even if most people sided with the Velvet Revolution for narrowly economic reasons, that fact does not prove wrong Havel's claim that the natural world prevailed in the overthrow of Communism. Havel's account of the natural world is broader than Gellner's narrow view of morality and decency. For Havel, the natural world includes morality, decency, and responsibility; but it also encompasses the evil inherent in human nature. The natural world rests on the observations of those things we actually experience, for good and bad. Havel might even agree with Gellner's observation that many people sought little more than an improvement in their living conditions when they supported the overthrow of Communism. But Communism demanded that people not say what was on their minds. Communism insisted that the ideology was correct, even when living standards were low. To maintain itself, Communism forced people to lie. Thus, even if a majority supported the Velvet Revolution for the sake of living in a consumer society, they also revolted because their leaders told them that they were already living in a consumer's paradise. They changed their government because the ideology was a lie—they wanted to begin living in truth. The natural world based on human observation won out.

However insightful Havel's analysis is, we can nevertheless ask ourselves why it is still relevant, particularly since it deconstructs a now-defunct political system. The question can be answered only by pointing out once again that—despite the differences—Havel has been profoundly influenced by Heidegger. Like Heidegger, Havel sees the Communist totalitarian system as an offshoot of Western rationalism. Totalitarian systems are "a convex mirror of all modern civilization" and the "avant-garde of a global crisis." Both liberal democracy and Marxist totalitarianism rest on the notion that human rationality can fully comprehend and control Being. According to Heidegger, the philosophy born in the Enlightenment attempts "to nail life and everything living onto a board ... so that everything becomes overseeable, controllable, definable, connectable, and explicable."[35]

Havel too argues that science invades the sphere of the natural world by attempting to replace subjective human judgments with "impersonal and inhuman" knowledge. Science endeavors to fit the phenomena of life into the idiom of its discipline, mathematical formulas, and methodically tested laws. But Havel asks whether human existence is not fundamentally different from the orderly nature that science has so successfully unraveled. He argues that while the rest of nature merely does what it does, humans ask why—that is, humans have Dasein. Havel opposes the modern scientific view of the world, not because it is some sinister force threatening to destroy its maker, but because science is ignorant of the questions that are both most important and closest to us. Even with all of its expertise, science cannot tell us why life without friendship is lonely, why love so moves us, why death so disturbs us, or why a solitary figure who maintains his dignity even while imprisoned so inspires us. Science cannot explain our anxieties and aspirations because none of the beings in nature that science surveys care enough to worry or hope. Value-free science cannot tell us what is valuable. Havel objects to science for the same reason that Aristophanes criticized Socrates in *The Clouds* and for the same reason Socrates, having understood that criticism, took his pursuit of wisdom on a second sailing.

The societies of the West are far less oppressive and far more capable of producing goods and services than the centrally planned Soviet-style economies, but the former are no less guilty of positioning the rationalist understanding of humans in the forefront of public discourse. In fact, the globalization of consumer desires has exacerbated the "anthropomorphic" sense that humans must bend the entire world to their use. It has bolstered a view of life in which the satisfaction of our physical needs acts as an Archimedean first principle motivating all our behavior. While Communism failed to elevate the worker to the central role of human existence, liberal democracies have been successful at turning the consumer into a sovereign lord. Even the "Greens" and environmentalists propose no rival vision of why we will be content when we consume less.

To satisfy the desires of an evermore demanding public, Western societies have created colossal industries to produce goods and services, and equally gigantic bureaucracies to ensure their delivery. Despite the appearance of infinite choice afforded to (and at the command of) consumers, and in spite of the myriad of legally protected freedoms granted to citizens, people in liberal democracies are not able to control important elements of their lives; businesses are too complex; and bureaucracies are too anonymous.

Finally, what will we do even if we are able to create prosperity for all mankind? How will we use our independence and mastery over necessity? Can wealth ever satiate our anxiety and longing? Is not the very achievement of Western consumer societies proof that making the world our standing reserve—only to be put to work for our own good—does little to explain what our good is?

Perhaps more than any other public figure, Havel faced these post-Communist problems even before Communism imploded. His reflections on such problems are manifest in two ways: In his art he tries to give an account of the natural world and virtue's place in it, whereas in his politics he attempts to provide an arena for the exercise of that most human of traits, moral choice.

NOTES

1. Havel, "Politics and Conscience," *Open Letters*, 269 (see chap. 1, n. 13).
2. Havel, "The Power of the Powerless," *Open Letters*, 168–171.
3. Havel, *Disturbing the Peace*, 72 (see chap. 1, n. 4).
4. "I Take the Side of Truth," interview with Antoine Spire, in *Open Letters*, 247.
5. *Disturbing the Peace*, Havel's book-length interview with Karel Hvížala, is misnamed. Its Czech title is "A Long-Distance Interrogation." The change was made because the publisher feared that Western readers would not get the joke.
6. Havel, "The Power of the Powerless," *Open Letters*, 131; "Dear Dr. Husák," *Open Letters*, 53.
7. See Jonathan Van Loo, "Ideological Coercion in Czechoslovakia: Understanding Freedom of Expression and Crisis of Identity in Václav Havel," *Proteus* 14, no. 2 (Fall 1997): 28–32.
8. Havel, "The Power of the Powerless," *Open Letters*, 128.
9. Havel, "Dear Dr. Husák," *Open Letters*, 65.
10. Paul Wilson, introduction, *Disturbing the Peace*, xi.
11. Havel, "The Trial," *Open Letters*, 103.
12. Havel, "Article 202," "Article 203," *Open Letters*, 109–124.
13. Havel, "Stories and Totalitarianism," *Open Letters*, 334.
14. Havel, "Dear Dr. Husák," *Open Letters*, 61.
15. Havel, "Stories of Totalitarianism," *Open Letters*, 336.
16. Havel, "On Evasive Thinking," *Open Letters*, 11.
17. Havel, "The Power of the Powerless," *Open Letters*, 133.
18. Havel, "The Power of the Powerless," *Open Letters*, 153.
19. Havel, "Stories of Totalitarianism," *Open Letters*, 334–336.
20. Havel, "The Power of the Powerless," *Open Letters*, 127.
21. Havel, "Stories of Totalitarianism," *Open Letters*, 343.
22. Havel, "Stories of Totalitarianism," *Open Letters*, 334–337.
23. Havel, "The Power of the Powerless," *Open Letters*, 129.
24. Havel, "Politics and Conscience," *Open Letters*, 257.
25. Havel, "The Power of the Powerless," *Open Letters*, 134–135.
26. Havel, "Dear Dr. Husák," *Open Letters*, 56.
27. Havel, "Dear Dr. Husák," *Open Letters*, 57.
28. Havel, "Dear Dr. Husák," *Open Letters*, 71.
29. Heidegger, *Being and Time*, 333 (see chap. 2, n. 20).
30. Havel, "The Power of the Powerless," *Open Letters*, 139; *Letters to Olga*, 150 (see chap. 1, n. 19).
31. Havel, "The Power of the Powerless," *Open Letters*, 153.
32. Havel, *Summer Meditations*, xvi (see chap. 2, n. 61); "New Year's Address to the Nation," Prague, January 1, 1990, "Speech to Joint Session of U.S. Congress," February 21, 1990, Washington, D.C.

33. *Summer Meditations*, 5.

34. Ernest Gellner, "The Price of Velvet: Thomas Masaryk and Václav Havel," *Telos* 94 (1992/1993): 191–192. Tucker takes the same line of criticism in *The Philosophy and Politics of Czech Dissidents*, 167–169 (see chap. 2, n. 10).

35. Martin Heidegger, "Heidegger's Letter to the Boss's Daughter," *Telos* 77 (Fall 1988): 126; quoted in Thiele, *Timely Meditation*, 193 (see chap. 2, n. 31).

4

AN IRONIC PLAYWRIGHT

THE ABSURDITY OF THE ABSURD

Havel's plays are ambitious, complex, and difficult to interpret. There is even a debate over what genre Havel uses. Many of his most important works employ erratic dialogue, repetitious speeches, chronological shifts, and exaggerated social and interpersonal relations. They have been labeled "absurd, depressing, upsetting, shocking," and a "dead end."[1] Even his "protest" plays—those dealing with his experiences as a dissident—display a sense of the absurd and surreal.[2]

There are a number of reasons why Havel might have chosen a perplexing style. First, and most obvious, Havel's absurd plays are funny. Characters do silly things, repeat affectionate lines to different lovers, walk off stage and reappear in different clothes from the opposite end of the stage, attempt to hold conversations with finicky machines, and get thoroughly drunk while making fools of themselves. At the end of one play, Havel has the stage smoking so heavily that a fireman, instead of the cast, appears for the final bow. Why the levity? Perhaps because Communists take themselves so seriously. As is the case with many social reformers, Communists believe (or at least act as if they believe) that their "cause"—the brotherhood of the human race and social justice for all—is so important that no one should (or could) make fun of it. Social reformers are the sternest of optimists, for although they maintain that it is possible to make the world better, they consider it bad taste to have any fun while changing it. Havel's funny plays remind us that life is full of comedy and that reformers are so caught up in their goal of making everyone happy in the future that they make people miserable in the here and now.

Second, Havel lived under what has been termed a "post-totalitarian" government. The period of post-totalitarianism was rarely fearsome; it attempted to maintain order and normalcy by subtly involving people in the workings of the regime through promises of professional advancement or through threats of professional demotion. The punishment for nonconformity was less severe under post-totalitarianism than during Stalin's reign, but overt opposition to the system was considered treason to the homeland and disloyalty to the socialist cause. Open resistance could result in "interrogations, investigations, detentions, provocations, searches, house arrests, buggings, prosecutor's charges, trials, jail sentences, labor camps, prison hospitals," and social ostracism and isolation.[3] In such a climate, absurd or surreal theater provided Havel with a mechanism for presenting, yet concealing, his intentions: he could plausibly claim that his work had nothing to do with politics, Czechoslovakia, or criticism of the regime. Havel was able to stage *The Garden Party* and *Memorandum* during the 1960s. "In fact," Milan Kundera says, "if these two plays are my favorites among all his work, it is because I was still able to see them in Prague, in superb productions that were entirely faithful to the author's spirit."[4]

Third, the very fact that absurd or surreal theater provided a cover indicates, of course, that Havel was attempting to criticize the politics of those in control of his homeland. As Stanislaw Baranczak points out,

> The despotic oppression of language, custom, stereotype, institution, any automatism with which man replaces the irregularity, spontaneity, and uniqueness of his self is a theme that runs through the Theater of the Absurd. Havel did not invent it, he merely transplanted the theme and its corresponding dramatic techniques onto the ground of the specific experience of the inhabitant of a Central European police state.[5]

Havel's using the theater of the absurd challenges the monochromatic conformity of life under post-totalitarianism. The very complexity of Havel's plays contradicts the one-track economic explanation of existence promulgated by Communist ideology. In his groundbreaking work on the theater of the absurd, Martin Esslin explains that

> instead of a linear development, [absurd plays] present their author's intuition of the human condition by a method essentially polyphonic; they confront the audience with an organized structure of statements and images that interpenetrate each other and that must be apprehended in their totality, rather like different themes in a symphony, which gain meaning by their simultaneous interaction.[6]

Peter Steiner argues that an appreciation of absurdity grew out of the very fabric of life in Czechoslovakia.[7] The government declared the nation to be a laborers' paradise, but the workers were ruthlessly exploited by bureaucrats who ruled in their name. The leaders incessantly proclaimed dedication to the brotherhood of man but sought to maintain their position by capitalizing on the weaknesses and self-interest of their citizens, cajoling people to spy on one another. The state-run media detailed the progress achieved under socialism, yet it was apparent everywhere that society was gray, uniform, and stagnant. Artists and intellectuals were said to have complete freedom, but Czechoslovakia was actually, in Kundera's accurate image, "a literary Biafra."[8] As we shall see, Havel's semiautobiographical "protest plays" *Audience*, *The Unveiling*, and *Protest*—which are among the least surreal of his works—depict the absurd life of a dissident during the stifling era of normalization, the period following the Soviet invasion that crushed the Prague Spring of 1968.

A fourth and more far-reaching explanation of the playwright's artistic choices emerges from Havel's account of the crisis of modernity. He explains that the theater of the absurd is

> the most significant theatrical phenomenon of the twentieth century, because it demonstrates modern humanity in a "state of crisis," as it were. That is, it shows man having lost his fundamental metaphysical certainty, the experience of the absolute, his relationship to eternity, the sensation of meaning—in other words, having lost the ground under his feet. This is a man for whom everything is coming apart, whose world is collapsing, who senses that he has irrevocably lost something but is unable to admit this to himself and therefore hides from it.[9]

But what is the source of the crisis? What are its effects? What, if anything, can be done about it?

According to Havel, Niccolò Machiavelli was the first to proclaim that human beings could fully control nature, could bend all of nature's resources to human use by making politics into a "technology of power."[10] The modern world, Havel writes,

> has been dominated by the culminating belief, expressed in different forms, that the world and Being as such is a wholly knowable system governed by a finite number of universal laws that man can grasp and rationally direct for his own benefit. This era—beginning in the Renaissance and developing from the Enlightenment to socialism, from positivism to scientism, from the Industrial Revolution to the information

revolution—was characterized by rapid advances in rational, cognitive thinking. This, in turn, gave rise to the proud belief that man, as the pinnacle of everything that exists, was capable of objectively describing, explaining and controlling everything that exists, and of possessing the one and only truth about the world. It was an era in which there was a cult of depersonalized objectivity, an era in which objective knowledge was accumulated and technologically exploited, an era of belief in automatic progress brokered by the scientific method. It was an era of ideologies, doctrines, interpretations of reality, an era when the goal was to find a universal theory of the world, and thus a universal key to unlock its prosperity.[11]

What happens when human beings have all of nature at their command? . . . when everything becomes an object for human use? . . . when nothing stands above or beyond human beings to give them guidance about how to live? Havel explains that "this condition is characterized by a loss of metaphysical certainties, of the experience of the transcendental, of any superpersonal moral authority, and any kind of higher horizon." We live in the "first atheistic civilization," he reasons; "we are going through a great departure from God which has no parallel in history."[12] Without belief in a transcendent realm, humans seem to be caught in a never-ending flux of events and historical occurrences, all leading nowhere and signifying nothing.

One of the most important consequences of the absence of ordering principles is the loss of identity. How can we understand what we are when nothing above or beyond ourselves provides any meaning? Of course, we could attempt to define ourselves, giving free rein to our freedom and will. Yet such an activity is often frustratingly unsuccessful. To put the problem in practical terms: When we look in the mirror, we want to see someone who is attractive, witty, smart, and self-assured. Havel explains that the "need for self-affirmation is not essentially reprehensible. It is intrinsically human, and I can hardly imagine a human being who does not long for recognition, affirmation, and a visible manifestation of his own being."[13] We want to have admirable traits, but we are never sure that we possess them. Our true nature always remains something of a mystery to us, and even when we explain ourselves—or especially when we give a written account of ourselves—the act of explanation and writing, the self-awareness changes us.[14] We grasp what we are only by our relation to others. Those around us define us by indicating how attractive, witty, smart, and self-assured we really are.

It is all well and good to say that others define us, but what standards are they using to judge us? How do they know how to value a self? When human beings believe in God, such judgments are relatively simple. People gauge themselves by how well they live up to the word of God. In the modern age, when human beings, not God, are the measure of all things, the definition of self becomes at once an urgent yet illusory goal. The name given to this state of uncertainty is nihilism, and the philosopher who Havel seems to believe most fully faced nihilism is Martin Heidegger, whose writings became the central theme of Havel's prison memoir.[15]

Why has existence become absurd? Havel says the answer is that Western civilization has adopted the egotistical principle that humans can control all of life through science and technology and that scientific rationality can explain life itself. As Heidegger has aptly pointed out, such a project was bound to fail since science cannot provide an account of Being and does not explain human consciousness—Dasein—or resolve our anxiety over death. The Enlightenment raised hopes that human beings could be happy with their time on Earth, but such hopes were inevitably dashed, and the result was disillusionment and nihilism.

Western culture, at least, adopted the scientific project but in return abandoned transcendent principles that direct human actions. Those guided by Enlightenment doctrines have no higher principles by which to define themselves. Havel attempts to counter the loss of identity, which might be defined as the absence of a relationship beyond one's mundane existence. He does so by showing the absurdity of humanity's current condition while pointing beyond that absurdity to the more "natural" view of life, which always has within it transcendent principles, such as love, hate, honor, justice, friendship, and the like—that is, the human virtues and vices that seem to be with us always and everywhere.

We might compare Havel's plays to Plato's dialogues. Plato's characters are certain they understand the virtues. When Socrates questions them, however, their certainty vanishes. Socrates' various companions think that they know what the virtues are, but they cannot clearly give an account of their form. In the modern world, partly as a result of the assault of Heidegger's philosophy on metaphysics, people no longer believe that transcendent virtues exist: only individual values are considered valid. Havel's absurd plays begin where Socratic wisdom ends, with the knowledge that we know that we do not know. Havel's task, then, is much like Plato's, only in reverse. Havel attempts to construct a world in which we can see the virtues. In Plato's work, we can never get a full account of the form of the virtues, but we see people talking about virtues and behaving in virtuous ways. After all, virtues do have a reality if we can discuss them in common. In Havel's plays we see the virtues more by their absence. We are forced to believe that they exist because we notice them by their absence or when they are in contrast to characters who, like Vanek, exhibit attributes such as courage.

In a sense, then, Havel agrees with Heidegger that we understand the world in a mediated way. One of the things that has mediated our world is Heidegger's philosophy. Absurdity is necessary because we look at life through the mediated lens of the exhaustion of modern metaphysics. Havel's "philosophic" reflections may not lead to philosophy as such, but they do lead to philosophic poetry. Havel's poetry attempts to restate the argument for the natural world, a world in which human beings confront moral choices at almost every turn. We act as if there were virtues that help us resolve those moral dilemmas.[16]

Havel uses the theater of the absurd quite differently from the earlier existential playwrights who created the genre. Esslin explains that "Theatre of the Absurd strives to express its sense of the senselessness of the human condition and the inadequacy of the rational approach by the open abandonment of rational devices and discursive thought."[17] According to Eugène Ionesco, "Absurd is that which is devoid of purpose. . . . Cut off from his religious, metaphysical, and transcendental roots, man is lost; all his actions become senseless, absurd, useless."[18] Havel's absurd theater makes us face doubt so that we can see meaning in a new way. He explains that

> the sensation of absurdity is never—at least not as I understand it—the expression of a loss of faith in the meaning of life. Quite the opposite: only someone whose very being thirsts for meaning, for whom "meaning" is an integral dimension of his own existence, can experience the absence of meaning as something painful, or more precisely, can perceive it at all. In its tormented absence, meaning may have a more urgent presence than when it is simply taken for granted, no questions asked—somewhat in the way one who is sick may better understand what it means to be well than one who is healthy. I believe that genuine absence of meaning and genuine unbelief manifest themselves differently; as indifference, apathy, resignation and decline of existence to the vegetative level. In other words, the experience of absurdity is inseparable from the experience of meaning; it is merely, in a manner of speaking, its "obverse," just as meaningfulness is the "reverse" of absurdity. Absurdity, therefore, cannot be thought of as something a priori negative or even reprehensible.[19]

For Havel, "Absurdity is the experience that something has, should, or could have aspired to meaning . . . in the awareness of meaning's absence, the longing for meaning announces its presence again." He argues, "Without this assumption of meaning or a longing for it, the experience of nonsense—absence of meaning—would be unthinkable. . . . That is the case with so-called absurd art which, more than anything else—because it is a desperate cry against the loss of meaning—contains faith." Since the experience of meaning is a kind of faith, we also experience its "natural antithesis" as "nothingness." Thus life is a constant tension between the poles of meaning and nothing. To surrender our judgment entirely to faith makes us too self-righteous and blind to life's complexities (like Plato's characters), but to "surrender" to nothingness leads to "apathy." Being discloses itself partially to us. We get a hint of what is proper and fitting, but we do not receive a roadmap. If we were given too much, there would be no choice and therefore no freedom or dignity. We would lose our consciousness and become animals who act on instinct.[20]

Havel argues that his plays—indeed, any good theater—must have a meaning, even beyond what the author intends. There should be something indeterminate about the plays, and the audience ought to share some of the work in uncovering each play's meaning. When the audience must work to provide meaning, in whatever form, the interpretation is truly theirs and has been understood because they formulated it. Havel identifies a ground for human meaning, which negates Heidegger's claims. But because we cannot know the ground in a scientific or precise way, Marx is incorrect as well. Havel constructs his absurd plays so that the audience or the reader must work to comprehend their meaning. In the plays, as in life, moral choices are rarely simple or easy. The effort to understand the plays involves the viewer's being more fully embedded in their meaning. Viewers are forced to sort out the meaning of the plays and to make judgments about the characters for themselves. Understanding Havel's plays is a little like learning a language. It is much easier to read and listen to a foreign language than to speak it. But we can be considered fully fluent in a language only when we can converse easily in it. In the same way, viewers can learn more fully about Havel's plays by pondering them, and they can learn more about life by fully engaging in its complexity and mystery.

Havel's plays compress reality to bring forth meaning. They "amplify" reality to "display" Being. Good theater attempts to re-create the complexity of existence; it is open to many interpretations. If the author attempts to give too clear a "message," the play becomes mere ideology and takes on the character of "socialist realism."[21]

Often Havel's plays are set in bureaucratic structures, ones that lack spontaneity and humanity. The artificial order of the setting is meant to mirror the lack of order in the very organizations that attempt to organize life. The plays show that such organizations actually conceal life's deeper order. The plays confront us with an empty world, a world that has in fact been made into standing reserve. Yet, at the moment we might be tempted to despair that we have no guidance or meaning in our lives, the plays show us that "where everything is permitted, nothing can surprise," that conventions can "only be challenged or broken down when they already exist." "In short," Havel asks, "mystery would be unthinkable without some kind of order because how else do mysteries declare themselves except by deviating from a given order, thus providing a disturbing insight into the unknown territories of the 'higher structures'?"[22]

The plays are, for Havel, "merely a warning. In a very shocking way, they throw us into the question of meaning by manifesting its absence."[23] He writes of his method that "this demystification should be so shrewdly handled that almost no one notices how it happened and, at the same time, almost everyone realizes, with astonishment, that it has happened."[24] For Havel, Being is constructed in such a way as to give humans an awareness of authoritative moral order. His absurd plays are not "an expression of a loss of faith. . . . Quite the opposite, only someone whose being thirsts after meaning . . . can experience the absence of meaning as something painful . . . the experience of absurdity is inseparable from the experience of meaning; it is merely, in a manner of speaking, its obverse."[25] To better understand Havel's philosophic teaching, we turn to a closer examination of the plays.

WHO IS FERDINAND VANEK?

Václav Havel's semiautobiographical *Audience* (1975), *The Unveiling* (1975), and *Protest* (1979) are perhaps the most accessible of his plays.[26] The success of *Audience* gave rise to a unique theatrical occurrence in which four playwrights—Havel, Pavel Kohout, Pavel Landovsky, and Jiri Dienstbier—used "Ferdinand Vanek" as the central character in a total of eight plays.[27] Although Havel's Vanek plays have generally been well received, they have been given wildly different interpretations.

M. C. Bradbrook maintains that Vanek has "that quality defined by medieval schoolmen as *synteresis*—the divine spark, the implanted seed of God which endows man with integrity and acts as his compass for movement."[28] Marketa Goetz-Stankiewicz perceives "a common idea of human value" running through the Vanek plays. "Vanek posits his own scale of values, which can be defined by what it is *not*; it is not materialistic; not opportunistic; it is not intolerant and not arrogant."[29] According to Phyllis Carey, "Vanek . . . is a threat" to those in power "by virtue of being an authentic human being."[30] For Lesley Chamberlain, Havel's plays are about what it is to live a lie, and the protesters who occur in them, like Ferdinand Vanek, give the lie definition. This is why Vanek . . . has been called more of a dramatic principle than a character. He says and does little, but somehow his mere presence causes those around him to wrap themselves in ideological contortions.[31]

Tamara Trojanowska offers perhaps the most positive view of Havel's intention. She sees Havel as "an optimist because he holds that human nature is perfectible." Although Vanek is "marginalized" by the oppressive system under which he lives, *Audience* shows him in "the central position," in which he is contrasted with "the unappealing image of people who allow others, false standards, or forced expectations to define them. Havel diagnoses the abnormal duality of the oppressed and the oppressive society and its ethical consequences."[32]

Stanislaw Baranczak's appraisal of Vanek is less sympathetic. Rather than view Vanek as a moral paragon, Baranczak sees Vanek's dissident stance as a matter of personal taste. For Baranczak, Vanek

> has no choice; he must stick to his own basic right to follow the voice of his conscience. That is not because of moral haughtiness, but for the simple reason that he is unable to force himself to do things or utter words that he considers wrong or false. In a sense, he lives among his compatriots like a foreigner in Paris: he is aware that all the French eat escargots, and he is even able to grasp abstractly their reasons for doing so, but he is physically incapable of forcing the slimy invertebrates down his throat.[33]

In a review of a New York production of *A Private View* (*Audience* and *The Unveiling* staged together), Robert Brustein complains that Vanek is too gentle and mild-mannered toward those who have cooperated with a despotic government. Although he is

> modest and charming in the face of the most irritating provocations . . . it is these provocations, and Vanek's gentle response to them that ultimately undermine one's faith in the veracity of the proceedings, and leave one wishing Havel had found a more direct way to express his outrage and contrast his own behavior with that of his craven friends.[34]

The most negative assessment of the Vanek character is offered by Alfred Thomas, who argues that the plays of the "Vanek cycle . . . are more complex, darker studies of the human spirit than the Czech tradition of 'humanist' criticism would suppose." Thomas disagrees with Goetz-Stankiewicz's interpretation of Vanek as a "positive hero." For him, "there simply is no hero." All the characters, including Vanek, are contaminated "by corruption, greed and the lust for power." To call Vanek a hero mistakenly gives the plays a "happy ending" and misses their "tragic-comic absurdity." Thomas maintains that "Havel's drama is of a distinctly darker hue" than many commentators have suggested, for he is "a direct spiritual descendant of Franz Kafka and Jaroslav Hašek."[35]

Perhaps explanations of the trilogy are so varied and contradictory because the Vanek character is a bit of a mystery, even to Havel himself. He claims to have written *Audience* for a few "friends," stating, "It never occurred to me that the play might be saying something (more or less significant) to other people, people who do not know me or my situation and who are ignorant of my having worked in a brewery." What surprises and pleases Havel most "is that something apparently happened which, I think, does or should occur with all art, namely that the work of art somehow exceeds its author, or is, so to speak, 'cleverer than he is,' and that through the mediation of the writer—no matter what purpose he was consciously pursuing—some deeper truth about his time reveals itself and works its way to the surface."[36] Havel's demurral may be no more, as Pavel Kohout suggests, than his "characteristic modesty," for his plays do seem to have a message relevant to more than a few of his "friends."[37]

Although both positive and negative readings of Havel's Vanek plays are persuasive, no critic has yet been able to fully explain why the message of the plays is so mixed and why, for some, it is so confusing. Havel uses Vanek as a "dramatic principle," to highlight the absence of moral behavior on the part of the plays' other characters. Thomas is correct that the plays show us a sort of moral void, for although Vanek is the "hero," he does not carry the dialogue, he hardly acts, he rarely if ever denounces the government or chastises his fellow citizens, and he seems uncertain that his dissident position has merit. Yet it is the lack of clearly stated moral principles that makes us aware of the presence of morality, and the source of the plays' dramatic tension is the fact that questions of morality are the only things in dispute.

Despite his seeming shortcomings, Vanek is not a badly drawn character—in fact, he is quite compelling. Havel attempts to show through him the complexity of effecting moral conduct. Vanek's relationships with his less-than-noble interlocutors show disinterested observers that it is possible to distinguish moral from immoral behavior. Those not directly engaged in the moral dispute—that is, the audience (as the title of the most celebrated of the plays implies)—come to recognize the existence of moral principles. Thus justified are the more positive critical assessments of Havel's intention in the *Vanek* plays. Vanek is obviously more courageous and moral than his "craven friends," yet Vanek is never self-righteous, perhaps because he is more confident about what is wrong with his society than he is about how to make it right. Vanek seems to be guided by some unspoken drive to resist evil and defend human dignity. He does not disparage those whose moral voice is less powerful. He is aware that other people are enveloped in a web of social connections, professional ambitions, and family responsibilities that makes it difficult for them to dissent. It would be undignified and evil of Vanek to condemn people for what are, after all, common human failings.

Havel's plays are also difficult to decipher because they are both polyphonic and multilayered. Clearly, they intend to expose some of the social neuroses prevalent under Communism, especially its post-totalitarian variant. They also are more general meditations on what Havel perceives as "the crisis of human identity." People may come to believe that their lives have no purpose beyond the satisfaction of their biological functions. We eat, sleep, laugh, cry, and die, but to what purpose? Are we no more than material constructs capable of wondering about our final return to matter? Havel explains his effort to locate human identity through his art as follows:

> The problem of human identity remains at the center of my thinking about human affairs. If I use the word "identity," it is not because I believe it explains anything about the secret of human existence; I began using it when I was developing my plays, or thinking about them later, because it helped me clarify the ramifications of the theme that most attracted me: "the crisis of human identity." All my plays in fact are variations on this theme, the disintegration of man's oneness with himself and the loss of everything that gives human existence a meaningful order, continuity and its unique outline.[38]

To comprehend the plays, we must view them not only as attacks on the system of post-totalitarianism under which Havel lived but also as more comprehensive expressions of the search for human identity in the postmodern era, when all transcendent principles have been called into question. They aim to show us a foundation for moral behavior.

AUDIENCE

Audience is a conversation between Vanek, a dissident playwright, and his Foreman, a brewmaster in a regional brewery.[39] The action takes place in the Foreman's office, where Vanek has been invited for a talk. It is not immediately clear what the Foreman has in mind; the discussion rambles because the Foreman is embarrassed and uneasy about what he will ask Vanek to do. Perhaps to overcome his reticence, the Foreman imbibes twelve bottles of beer during the course of the exchange—eleven before he falls asleep and one after he awakes—and is subsequently moved to take four restroom breaks.[40] The Foreman asks Vanek many times how things are going, encourages him not to be depressed, offers him beer, and inquires whether he has taken his tea break. Vanek politely assures the Foreman that things are going fine, that he is not depressed, that he does not like beer, and that he has not had his tea break yet. Vanek's gentle, compliant, and courteous manner eventually drives the Foremen to blurt out, "With you a man never knows what's what . . . you don't say anything . . . Gawd knows what you're thinking . . . you just keep saying 'yes,' 'of course' . . . and 'thank you'. . . ." Later, he sarcastically disparages Vanek's polite habit of speech: "'I'm delighted we've been drawn closer together,' 'I appreciate your frankness'—why do you keep talking like that?"[41]

The Foreman attempts to become pals with Vanek, offers him an easier job in the warehouse, and reminds him that he, the Foreman, took some personal risk to give Vanek a job. Finally, the Foreman gets around to the real reason for the meeting. "They"—the secret police—have been making inquiries about Vanek. In particular, the person who has been asking for reports on Vanek is Tonda Masek, one of the Foreman's school chums, a "decent sort" who had been helpful to the Foreman when he got into a bit of trouble. The problem is that Vanek is so polite and well mannered that the Foreman has no idea what to report, other than that Vanek occasionally hides in the lab when he needs a rest from work, has been seen "in town with Marge from the bottling plant," and had the "boys in Maintenance" fix the central heating in his house. The Foreman then tries to cajole Vanek into writing reports on himself. After all, the Foreman claims, he is only a working man, whereas Vanek is a writer. What would it hurt if Vanek wrote a few reports to the secret police to help out the boss who gave him a job? At first Vanek refuses to inform on himself, but later he has second thoughts.[42]

Audience exposes the way post-totalitarian governments attempted to entangle people in the workings of the regime. Masek probably was a boyhood friend of the Foreman. Is it really spying when friends exchange gossip? Masek helped the Foreman out of a legal mess. Doesn't the Foreman owe him a bit of information in return? Moreover, the Foreman himself is under surveillance; "Mlynarik," who works on "the separator," turned him in for pilfering beer from the factory and selling it to the manager of a pub.[43]

No one in the Vanek trilogy makes overt threats, although all the characters are aware of the consequences of disobedience—they inquire about Vanek's previous stays in jail. Since all are mindful that they are being watched, they censor themselves. The secret police are never actually mentioned in any of the Vanek plays; instead, they are evoked through roundabout illusions. "They come here and ask about you," the Foreman informs Vanek in a lowered voice. And since everyone knows that everyone is being watched, there is every reason to be sensible and stay out of trouble. Thus, the Foreman advises (nigh threatens) Vanek to avoid his friend and fellow dissident Pavel Kohout. After all, the Foreman explains to Vanek, "Kohout won't give you a job."[44]

Audience shows how an odd sort of solidarity existed in post-totalitarian Communist societies. Since the authorities were intrusive and all-powerful, and since they owned everything, average people constantly attempted to avoid detection. They formed a kind of silent conspiracy against the state. To preserve some modicum of autonomy, people had to "all stick together," as the Foreman says, to thwart the domination of the Communist Party nomenclature. It is ironic that post-totalitarian social cohesion was based on opposition to a state apparatus whose principal reason for existence was to represent the communal aspiration of mankind.

To further complicate matters, informers were everywhere. A person could never be sure if opposition to the state, no matter how trivial, was being reported. The solidarity one felt with others who opposed the state had to be weighed against the fear that the trusted person might actually be an informer. The Foreman reveals this dilemma in his advice to Vanek. His expressions of solidarity—"People ought to help one another" and "We all have to stick together"—have to be weighed against his skeptical pronouncements—"People are proper bastards" and "Don't trust nobody nowadays."[45]

Audience must also be understood as a critique of Marxist theory. According to Marx, the basis of class division is economic. Once class divisions are abolished, not only will social inequity disappear, but estrangement and conflict between individuals will be resolved. Vanek's relationship with the Foreman shows that Marx was wrong. The antagonism between Vanek and the Foreman has nothing to do with money and has everything to do with education. Real class differences arise not simply from economic inequalities, as Marx indicated, but from disparities in the level of education. The Foreman does not really understand what drives Vanek; he is surprised that Vanek receives so little compensation for his plays. He assumes that high intellectual standing, the life of a playwright, must provide big monetary rewards. He cannot grasp why Vanek would write plays and not be well paid for the work. But Vanek does not have more money than the Foreman. He does not seek money for his art, being more interested in maintaining his creativity and intellectual freedom than in pursuing wealth.[46]

Despite making more money than Vanek, the Foreman feels inferior to his employee. The Foreman claims to be "just an ordinary common or garden brewery foreman" and "an uneducated brewery yokel." He worries that Vanek doesn't "think much" of him. He believes that Vanek is an "intellectual" and a "fine gentleman" who is "always on top even when you're down."[47]

The Foreman uses his inferiority as a source of power against Vanek. He attempts to make Vanek feel guilty for having led the privileged life of an intellectual. According to the Foreman, Vanek spends his time "sitting at home . . . nice and cozy and warm . . . sleeping late in the morning." The Foreman tries to overcome Vanek's reluctance to bring a famous actress friend of his to the brewery by complaining, "Of course, if you don't think we're good enough for her down here . . . don't invite her."[48] In the end, the Foreman uses his inferiority as a tool to get Vanek to spy on himself. The Foreman claims that Vanek is a "gentleman" who has "principles" but won't "soil his hands." Vanek puts "principles before people" because he is from a "clever lot." The authorities are "scared" of him since people "write" about him. However, "Never mind me," the Foreman whimpers to Vanek, "*I* can be allowed to wallow in my own slime. . . . Nobody gives *me* a hand, nobody is scared of me. . . . I'm just good enough to shovel muck out of which your principles can grow." The Foreman breaks into sobs on Vanek's shoulder.

Few critics notice that Vanek succumbs to the Foreman's passionate outburst. James W. Sire, who does see Vanek's shift, explains it away as part of Havel's irony.[49] In *Protest*, Havel himself alludes to Vanek's change of heart, having Stanek mention the "muddy ending" of *Audience*. When Vanek returns to the Foreman's office at the conclusion, he behaves less like the well-mannered intellectual that he is and more like one of the boys. He drinks a proffered beer "straight away" instead of affably refusing it. He changes his polite tone. "It's all a bloody mess," he complains when the Foreman asks him how things are going. Although he does not agree to spy on himself or write out reports about his activities for the Foreman, perhaps Vanek may give the Foreman some tidbits to report to his friend in the secret police.[50]

As odd as it might seem, the Foreman is right. He really is caught. If he were to ignore the requests of the secret police, he might lose his job, become a social outcast, or even end up in jail for his earlier misdeeds. Unlike

Vanek, who is an internationally known playwright, the Foreman would have little support from outside the country. A display of courage on his part would be known only to himself and his immediate family and friends. It is doubtful that his disobedience would have any effect on the Communist authorities. Vanek seems aware of the merciless entanglements of post-totalitarian governments, and he compromises his morals just enough to keep the Foreman out of trouble.

If we consider *Audience* outside its historical context, we can see that Havel uses it as a vehicle for investigating the postmodern condition. In postmodern theory, there are no grounds for morals; yet, as we know, every society enforces a moral code. Richard Rorty and other postmodern thinkers maintain that our morals are shaped by our communities. Rorty argues that human beings are "centerless networks of beliefs." Moral principles are nothing but "discourses," none conclusive. No belief, no practice, no way of life, is superior to any other. What seem like individual subjective choices are really acts determined by our cultural milieu. Gary Kochhar-Lindgren explains that

> postmodernist reflection . . . suggests that contemporary subjectivity occurs as the subjected nexus of linguistic, familial, political, cultural, economic, and electronic grids of power that crisscross the individual at every instant. This world-system, which creates the conditions for a certain institutionalization of objectivity and subjectivity, exists in turn only because through a complex historical process the world has come to be viewed as a representation, a picture. If the world is a picture, then the subject is fixed in that picture as a wide-eyed spectator of the framed scene—apparently looking on from the outside, but actually absolutely dependent upon the determinations of the system.[51]

Rorty argues that Havel's dissident stance was little more than a subjective refusal to tolerate personal oppression, not an ethical position based on an objective standard of morality.[52] Rorty does contend that objective principles such as relativism, multiculturalism, and eclecticism are most compatible with liberty and tolerance. However, he and other postmodern thinkers reject foundationalism and therefore offer nothing other than personal preference to explain why liberty is better than servitude. Rorty's position makes us wonder why we should favor liberty or tolerance in the first place. In the end, Rorty falls back on convention to defend his preferences. When "historical circumstance allows," it is possible to have an "agreement about political topics." In other words, for people who by chance are born and raised "on our side of the English Channel" in a democratic culture, liberal democracy is a beneficial and worthy choice because other people in our culture have similar prejudices. As for those with "unusual views" who disagree with his democratic sentiments, Rorty indicates that "extensive attempts at an exchange of political views have made us realize we are not going to get anywhere."[53]

The values that framed the dominant community in Communist Czechoslovakia were hardly those that Rorty embraces. In a population of fifteen million, two million were members of the Communist Party. Because the secret police recruited an army of informers to spy on their fellow citizens, most people avoided political discussions entirely, preferring to concentrate on private matters. In Czechoslovakia one could get ahead, not by ability or hard work, but by obsequious obedience to the party line and by fawning over those in power. Not surprisingly, a culture of corruption flourished. Kickbacks and payoffs were required to enter the university, to earn a promotion at work, or to receive adequate medical care. Since the state owned almost everything, and since there were often shortages of even basic necessities, many people pilfered what they needed. "He who does not steal from the state deprives his family" was a common refrain among people whose political situation led them to justify theft.

Vanek is the outsider in this society. He does not accept the "enframement" of his community. All of Vanek's fellow characters attempt to pressure Vanek into acquiescing as the Foreman does:

> FOREMAN: Important thing is that we should all stick together. . . .
> VANEK: Yes, I agree. . . .
> FOREMAN: I don't know what *you* think, but I always say there's nothing like a good crowd. . . .[54]

As Baranczak explains:

> It is not Vanek who, from the heights of his moral purity as a fighter for human rights, accuses the corrupt society of indifference; it is his society that accuses Vanek of the same—yes, of indifference. In the eyes of a citizen whose main concerns are promotion at his workplace, getting his daughter into a university, and building himself a dacha in the country, Vanek looks like a dangerous instigator and rabble-rouser.[55]

Vanek's stoic and indomitable opposition is evidence that there is such a thing as courage and that human beings are not merely products of their culture—nor should they be if that culture is evil. There must be some other basis for morality. As Havel puts it, "Consciousness precedes Being, and not the other way around."[56]

THE UNVEILING

In *The Unveiling* Vanek goes to visit his friends Vera and Michael for the unveiling of their newly redecorated apartment. Although we never discover what Vera and Michael do for a living, they are likely part of the technocratic or managerial class that enjoyed a fairly decent life under Communism. They seem to be reasonably well paid, since they can afford to ostentatiously redecorate their apartment. They also enjoy more freedom than most Czechoslovaks; Michael has recently returned from Switzerland at a time when travel abroad was restricted to the privileged few. Both look down on manual labor, expressing horror that Vanek has been reduced to working in a brewery.

Thomas argues that "Michael and Vera have sold out to the regime."[57] However, it is more likely that they are apolitical or perhaps even hostile to politics. They insist that Vanek get his "situation resolved" (his legal troubles arising from being a dissident), and they are aghast that he is "mixed up with those Communists . . . Kohout and his crowd."[58] Rather than sell out, they merely want to lead a normal life, have nice possessions, raise well-behaved children, take pleasure in their personal intimacy, and be left alone by the state. As with many Czechoslovaks during the depressing era of normalization that followed the crackdown of the Prague Spring, Michael and Vera have retreated from any thought of public activity to concentrate entirely on improving their private lives. They are intelligent people who have assessed the situation in their country and abandoned hope of reform. They have turned their attention "inward"; they "fill their homes with all kinds of appliances and pretty things" and "are preoccupied far more with themselves, their families and their homes . . . in short, the material aspects of their private lives."[59] It should not escape our attention that Havel's ironic characterization indicates how Communism made post-totalitarian people almost exclusively interested in private material gain.

Michael and Vera cannot be considered selfish. Quite the contrary, their overriding concern is to improve Vanek's personal life: they want him to become more like them. Their advice could fill a self-help book. Not only should he have his "situation . . . resolved," but he should also stop chasing waitresses and spending too much time at the pub with his unsavory friends. He should change his life, redecorate his apartment, get in shape, take cooking lessons, settle the differences with his wife, improve his sexual technique, have children, and begin writing again, especially if the plays have a chance of being published or produced.

Overwhelmed by this torrent of unsolicited advice and unwilling to give up his opposition to the state—with all the consequences that resistance entails—Vanek gets up to leave. But Vera breaks into hysterical sobs, accuses him of selfishness, and calls him a "disgusting, unfeeling, inhuman, egotist!"[60] As in *Audience*, Vanek relents and decides to stay at the unveiling. After all, if Vera and Michael have made an accommodation with the regime, it is because they want to lead normal lives. Is it not natural for people to long for a comfortable life, a collection of fine possessions, a loving relationship, and a good family? Wouldn't it be unjust for Vanek to condemn Michael and Vera for seeking what most people want most of the time? Does not the quest to live a satisfying life justify making an accommodation to an oppressive government? Perhaps even more so than Michael and Vera, Vanek knows what he has sacrificed to maintain his moral principles: he has no children, few prospects for a career, a troubled marriage, and an unhealthy lifestyle.

Like *Audience*, *The Unveiling* can be read as a meditation on "the crisis of human identity." Michael and Vera are the perfect postmodern couple who would surely subscribe to Rorty's position that there should be "no high altars, and instead just . . . lots of picture galleries, book displays, movies, concerts, ethnographic museums, museums of science and technology, and so on—lots of cultural options but no privileged central discipline." [61] Their eclectic taste in furnishings is evident in the living room, where sits an

> antique table, surrounded by soft, modern seats. A mass of sundry antiques and curious objects decorates the room—for example, there is an art-nouveau marquee, a Chinese vase, a limestone baroque angel, an inlaid chest, a folkloristic painting on a glass pane, a Russian icon, old hand-mortars and grinders, and so on; a niche in the wall houses a wooden Gothic Madonna; a rococo musical clock adorns the fireplace, and a Turkish scimitar hangs above it. The dining area is furnished in a "rustic style," with a wooden farm-cart wheel on the wall; the floor is covered with a thick, shaggy carpet, on it lie several Persian mats and, near the fireplace, a bear skin with a stuffed head: down stage left stands a filigreed wooden confessional.[62]

The confessional has lost its relationship to the sacred and is now a "fantastic object." Michael and Vera serve Vanek "sautéed groombles" from Switzerland and oysters with just "a few drops of woodpeak." They are particularly proud of the "electric almond peeler" that they have brought back from the West.[63] They are fully immersed in what Martin Heidegger calls "everydayness." The ordinary things of life, the beings, engage all of their concerns. Only when they consider—briefly—the fate of their young child do they ponder the "mystery" of Being and how human beings are, again to paraphrase Martin Heidegger, thrown into existence.[64]

Vanek's friends are nice, exactly the kind of pleasant but not overly committed human beings who Rorty believes are essential for establishing a peaceful, wholesome world. They are sophisticated, urban, and tolerant members of a society built by global communication and multinational corporations. Havel explains that this global society has created a "state of mind or of the human world [that is] called post-modernism. For me, a symbol of that state is a Bedouin mounted on a camel and clad in traditional robes under which he is wearing jeans, with a transistor radio in his hands and an ad for Coca-Cola on the camel's back."[65] However, the global community "is but a thin and recent veneer," and the people who are part of it feel neither loyalty to it nor sense of community within it.[66]

Vera and Michael are nice for exactly the same reason that they have eclectic tastes. They do not believe in anything—or perhaps they believe in many things but have no basis for any of those preferences. They would not consciously hurt anyone, because they do not feel strongly enough to undertake such spirited actions. They are caring people: if they lived under a liberal democracy where protest is safe, they would likely join organizations dedicated to social justice. However, in a totalitarian setting, they would never expose themselves to danger in defense of principles—say, freedom or dignity—because those values are no more valid than any others. They certainly would not participate in human rights organizations such as Charter 77; speak out against unjust arrests and imprisonment; or withstand the harassment, surveillance, interrogations, and possible prison sentences that dissident activities frequently provoke. Although they might wish to live in a just society, their lack of conviction makes them feel no civic responsibility to work for political change. They are primarily dedicated to private concerns. Their lack of metaphysically grounded principles combined with their participation in the global society has made them little more than self-interested consumers.

The Unveiling shows that it is possible to construct an identity on personal preference; yet, people who live this way are fickle, inconstant, shallow, self-interested, timid, and socially irresponsible. We are drawn from Vera and Michael's lack of civic courage to Vanek's steadfast commitment to something beyond himself. Just as in *Audience*, the audience is led to discover that moral behavior is recognizable in everyday life.

PROTEST

In *Protest*, Vanek is asked to visit Stanek, a writer and evidently a former colleague during the Prague Spring. Vanek has not seen Stanek for many years, most likely because Stanek has avoided a meeting. Stanek has sold out to the regime in order to write and produce for state-run television. At first it is unclear why Stanek renews the relationship. Stanek asks Vanek about his life and is particularly curious about whether Vanek had been beaten during his stays in jail. When Vanek assures him that he was not, Stanek berates the society in which he lives for its "cringing" acceptance of tyranny.[67]

After the niceties are over, Stanek gets to the point. He wants Vanek to write in protest against the incarceration of Javurek, a pop singer who is hated by the authorities "because he sings the way he does." In his spare time, it seems that Javurek has been having an affair with Stanek's daughter, Annie, and has made her pregnant. Stanek hopes that a protest published by Vanek's contacts abroad will secure Javurek's release.[68]

When Vanek reaches into his briefcase and produces the very kind of document that Stanek had hoped for, the real tension in the play begins. Stanek is faced with a clear moral choice. Should he sign the protest himself? Or should he leave it to Vanek and the others who have become "professional" dissidents to press Javurek's case? In a long dialogue, Stanek presents the argument for each course of action. Subjectively, he would feel much better if he signed the protest. By his moral actions he would reclaim his self-respect, free himself from the self-censorship that has been necessary to promote his career, regain a measure of respect from his former writer friends who have become dissidents, and register his opposition to a government that maintains its position by intimidation and lies.

On the objective side, Stanek reasons that if he signs the letter, he will lose his job, and his son will be denied entrance to the university. Moreover, it is unlikely that Stanek's joining a protest would help Javurek. Dissidents have become a class apart, isolated by the authorities, distrusted by the people, and resented by intellectuals; their ability to influence events is limited to making symbolic appeals to the West, which the West mostly ignores. If Stanek were to go over to the opposition, the authorities might even dig in their heels and prosecute Javurek more forcefully to show that they cannot be intimidated. Stanek convinces himself that disobedience to the state might also be detrimental to society as a whole. Dissident activities make it possible for those in power to justify harsh restrictions; the very existence of dissidents indicates that enemies threaten the state. Far better, Stanek concludes, to work from the inside, to change things slowly, and to stay in a position where it is possible to make beneficial, if marginal, changes to the system.

Stanek finally decides not to sign the protest, but not before insulting Vanek. Stanek accuses him of talking "more than he should have" in prison. At this reproach Vanek "jumps up" and stares "wildly" at Stanek. *Protest* is the only play where Vanek gets angry. Perhaps Vanek is distraught because there is some truth to the barb and, even more, because he realizes that there is a great deal of submerged animosity in Stanek's disparaging remark.[69] Writing before the collapse of Communism, Kohout explains the intellectuals' attitude toward dissidents, with reference to Vanek's creator:

> To once critical intellectuals, the overwhelming majority of whom have by now come to an arrangement with authority, he poses no less of a problem. To them he is an inconvenience greater than authority itself since he proves them guilty of a life-sized lie: in front of the world, their families, and even themselves. Whereas authority knows his momentary powerlessness, to this group of despondents Václav Havel is a very real danger—because the future threatens to prove him right, and that will necessarily mean a condemnation of them. They hate him, but at the same time, just to be sure, they obsequiously curry favor with him, only to slander and denounce him the next moment.[70]

Stanek proves to be correct. Javurek is released either because the authorities lose interest in him or because of Stanek's influence. Once again, Vanek concedes the point to his antagonist and is even relieved that he did not send the protest off to the West a few days earlier: "They would've got their backs up and kept [Javurek] inside."[71]

In spite of the "objective" success of Stanek's behavior, we are clearly led to believe that his stance is inspired by little more than the desire to save his own skin. In contrast, Vanek has nothing to gain by protesting the injustice committed against Javurek. The comparison between Stanek's pragmatic cowardice and Vanek's courageous resistance to evil indicates that moral behavior also has an "objective" existence, one readily appreciated by the most "objective" participant and the "positive hero" of Havel's play— the audience.[72]

If postmodernists are correct, there can be no standards for moral behavior, and our actions must therefore be based on pragmatism. What works we will keep; what fails we will throw out. Such a principle may seem practicable where the rule of law is established, a civil society exists, and citizens control the political process and thus their own destinies. But Vanek can never be sure that his disobedience will have concrete results. He surely never could have foreseen the collapse of Communism. There was nothing pragmatic about risking his life, reputation, and sanity for the sake of his principles. His resistance is rooted in something beyond the pragmatic calculations that led Stanek to a cowardly decision.[73]

VANEK AS MORAL EXAMPLE

Havel's Vanek plays show us the response of three groups—workers, the middle class, and intellectuals—to post-totalitarianism. Members of each group have their own excuse for not opposing the oppression under which they live. The plays are sympathetic to their plight, for each play demonstrates the complex web of pressures and fears that lead people to comply with tyranny. It is this considerate treatment that caused confusion among interpreters of the Vanek trilogy, many of whom seem to want moral choices to be cut and dried. Yet, it is clear that sympathy toward those caught in a bad situation is not the same as justification of their lack of moral responsibility.

In contrast to the complicity of these groups, Havel presents Ferdinand Vanek. Although Vanek is the main character, he does very little talking. Vanek's associates carry on the conversation, and he reacts. He is the straight man who exposes the foibles of others. He resembles Jaroslav Hašek's *Good Soldier Švejk*, the symbol of Czech resistance to domination and oppression. Švejk complies with the letter of the commands of his Austro-Hungarian rulers but always in a way that undercuts the spirit of those orders.[74] Vanek, too, is outwardly compliant but inwardly firm. He is sure that his country's government is pernicious, but he is unsure that his resistance will ever achieve concrete changes; hence, he is never sanctimonious or scolding. He is aware that political opposition can cost one's career, family, and friends—too high a price for most people to pay.

Vanek is so reticent and self-effacing that we never fully understand what makes him courageously defy evil. He makes no grand speeches or gestures. He gives no account whatsoever of his actions. We are aware of his defiance only through what others say about him. Yet we are absolutely certain that Vanek is more moral and courageous than the other characters; it cannot be denied that he, and he alone, resists evil. While others are "enframed" by the contingencies of their social conditions, Vanek demonstrates his freedom by expressing his responsibility to the truth of the natural world. As Trojanowska states, "Havel's emphasis on the moral dimension of freedom offers an alternative to the dull pragmatism of the world which deprives itself of the possibility of [transcendence]."[75]

Through Vanek, Havel establishes a phenomenological and experiential ground for virtue and morality. We see the absence of virtues in Vanek's interlocutors, but we become aware that our sense of the absence implies that the virtues exist. Havel's plays contradict those who insist that morals are nothing but illusions based on culturally determined values. He forces his audience and readers to ask: Do I really believe that Stanek is as moral as Vanek? If not, how can my moral judgments be explained? Must not some moral ground exist for me to see the moral superiority of Vanek? Havel directly challenges the relativist position. If relativists are correct that values are mere illusions, should not they explain why they would choose Stanek's cowardice over Vanek's courage? Should not they be responsible for explaining why the universal human understanding of courage and cowardice that they themselves experience is merely a mirage?

Havel's prephilosophic challenge to relativism is not meant to be irrational, nor is it merely based on feelings or emotions. What might be mistaken for a lack of philosophic sophistication is rooted in the phenomena of everyday life, as is the most complex philosophy. After all, Socrates constantly used practical experiences gained from farmers, musicians, shoemakers, and horse trainers to prove his philosophic points. Aristotle's *Politics* begins with the words "we see," as if to show that philosophic speculation must begin with what we experience, and that experience inevitably includes judgments about morality.

Havel attempts to overcome the metaphysical principle laid down by Friedrich Nietzsche, who claimed that "judgments, value judgments . . . can in the last resort never be true . . . the value of life cannot be estimated. Not by a living man, because he is party to the dispute, indeed its object, and not the judge of it; not by a dead one, for another reason."[76] Havel's absurd theater places a distance between the audience and the action of the plays, making it possible for the spectator to be not a party to the dispute but rather a disinterested judge. Thus Havel displays Vanek's courage as well as the absence of virtues in Vanek's interlocutors. We become aware that our sense of the absence implies that the virtues exist. "Categories like justice, honor, treason, friendship, infidelity, courage, or empathy," Havel explains,

> have a wholly tangible content, relating to actual persons and important for actual life. At the basis of this world are values which are simply there, perennially, before we ever speak of them, before we reflect upon them and inquire about them.[77]

The plays thus present a foundation for morality. Unless there was a foundation, antifoundationalists would hardly notice its absence; unless there was a ground to make sense of the world, "there could be no wounding by nonsense."[78] The mistake relativists make is to want morality to be simple, universal, with the same apodictic certainty as science. But if morality were as certain as science—that is, if we behaved according to scientific laws the way the rest of nature does—we would lose our freedom and dignity: We would act instinctively, according to a predetermined pattern. We would have no Dasein. The essence of the relativist claim against morality is that no single universal rule can be applied everywhere. But is this not an admission that relativists accept a form of morality as a standard by which to judge its absence? From where did this form arise? Havel, however, maintains that general rules of conduct construct the human condition; that is, there is a natural world. The uncertainty arises because people are free to ignore the rules and because, of course, human beings have varying degrees of good judgment. Hence, the application of general codes to particular circumstance is inevitably perplexing, intricate, and difficult; and "the way of a truly moral politics is neither simple nor easy."[79]

The Vanek character pursues the highest form of responsible behavior while revealing the enormous complexity and risk that moral actions entail. He avoids the twin dangers of self-righteous dogmatism and nihilistic relativism. He is steadfast in his belief that evil must be resisted, but he does not arrogantly condemn those caught in the web of an evil situation.

THE GARDEN PARTY

The most well-known and often-performed of Havel's plays is *The Garden Party*. As is the case with many of Havel's works, the piece has no real plot, nor is it set in any specific country.[80] Unlike the great Russian dissident writer Aleksandr Solzhenitsyn, who admitted that his *Candle in the Wind* was a failure because it was not set in Russia, Havel seems comfortable writing plays that have no cultural home. *The Garden Party* deals with the workings of a bureaucracy, one that might exist in any country but probably is most likely to be found in a post-totalitarian nation. Havel's bureaucratic organizations never really do or produce anything; they seem to exist only to manage the bureaucracy. The language of the characters in the organizations is nonspecific, rarely refers to an actual object or event, and could be applied to any bureaucratic situation. Havel's characters are a strange mixture of linguistic repetition, jargon, and cant. Yet they seem to know something. None of them is completely ridiculous, for that would reduce the works to farce.[81]

The main character of *The Garden Party* is Hugo Pludek, a young man who enjoys playing chess with himself since he has the capacity to become—rather than pretending to be—his own opponent. Hugo's parents are concerned about his future and arrange an interview with Francis Kalabis (a "childhood chum" of Hugo's father) in hopes of establishing their son's career. We never meet Kalabis, who sends a telegram excusing himself from the meeting because he must attend "the Garden Party of the Liquidation Office." Hugo's mother suggests that Hugo go to the Garden Party to find a job and secure his future.

When Hugo arrives at the Garden Party, he finds that a decision has been made to liquidate the Inauguration Service. When he questions the director about this decision, Hugo discovers that the Liquidation Office too is slated for liquidation, an impossible feat since only the Liquidation Office can liquidate bureaus. If it is liquidated, there will be no means of completing its liquidation. Hugo, who is particularly adept at mouthing platitudes and spouting nonsensical bureaucratic jargon, is the only one who can plot a way out of this logical morass. Thus, he is "assigned the extremely honourable and important task of constructing on the ruins of the former Liquidation Office and the Former Inauguration Service a great new institution, a Central Commission for Inauguration and Liquidation."[82]

Hugo is the perfect "organization man." He seems to have no inner life, and he can perform any function and deliver any form of speech the bureaucracy demands. When he returns from the Garden Party, even his own family fails to recognize him. He speaks of himself in the third person. He seems to have entirely lost his identity to the organization. Hugo has become his own clichés. Of course, Hugo may only be pretending to be a soulless bureaucrat—as the sophistication of some of his speeches might suggest—in order to advance his career in the organization. But is this more likely a tragic interpretation of Hugo's fate? If Hugo is only acting as if he has no inner life, then the pretense demonstrates how oppressive and alienating bureaucracies can become, and it highlights even more starkly the intrusiveness of "social mechanisms and the situation of man crushed by these mechanisms."[83] Whether Hugo is an authentic organization man or is just feigning to be one, his banality and emptiness are a warning about the stultifying effects of the modern world's bureaucratic structure, which, Havel writes,

> draws everyone into its sphere of power, not so they may realize themselves as human beings, but so they may surrender their human identity in favor of the identity of the system, that is, so they may become agents of the system's general automatism and servants of its self-determined goals.[84]

The audience learns from Hugo's vacuousness that an essential element of what it means to be human is lost in the life of an organization man; and the essentially human becomes, although never defined, of utmost importance as the result of its absence from the play.

THE MEMORANDUM

The Memorandum is the longest of Havel's plays, and doing justice to this complex, multilayered comedy would entail many pages of analysis. It is a satire on the inevitable policy shifts that occur in every centralized state. Written in the 1960s, it pokes fun at the "nomenclature" who, in order to keep their jobs during one of those shifts, publicly admit the "mistakes" they made during the Stalinist era. It mocks the raw personal ambition of people who claim to rule in the name of "the masses." It exhibits the hollowness of human beings who ascribe to an ideology. It highlights the "dictatorship of the ritual," where "power becomes . . . anonymous" and where "individuals are . . . pushed aside by faceless puppets, those uniformed flunkeys of the rituals and routines of power."[85] The play is also about the relationship between language and Being, and for brevity's sake, we will limit the discussion to that topic.

Joseph Gross, director of a bureaucratic organization that does God-knows-what, arrives at work one day and finds on his desk the Memorandum, written in what seems to be gibberish. He discovers that Jan Ballas, his subordinate, has surreptitiously instituted a new campaign to replace the "natural" language with "Ptydepe," a synthetic language meant to clarify communication among the staff by placing their work "on a truly scientific basis."[86] When Gross opposes the change, Ballas blackmails him into accepting the initiative because the director once took an official rubber stamp home, against regulations, and purchased an in-box with his own funds and without the requisite purchase form.

Gross attempts to have the Memorandum translated but discovers that only those with an authorization are permitted to have documents translated and, furthermore, that only those who understand Ptydepe are authorized to receive authorization. In an effort to escape this conundrum, Gross attends Special Ptydepe Classes at the Translation Center. Lear, the Ptydepe instructor, explains that, in Ptydepe, the more often a word is used, the shorter it is, whereas less-often-used words are longer; hence, "whatever" becomes "gh," and "a wombat" has 319 letters. The principle behind Ptydepe is that words in the natural language are too closely related, and their meanings overlap. In

Ptydepe, each word must be fully distinct from every other to avoid any confusion and make communication perfectly clear to all parties. An example of how easily a synthetic language is learned is presented:

> LEAR: Generally speaking, the interjection "boo" is used in the daily routine of an office, a company, a large organization when one employee wants to sham-ambush another. In those cases where the endangerment of an employee who is in full view and quite unprepared for the impending peril is being shammed by an employee who is himself hidden, "boo" is rendered by "gedynrelom." The word "osonfterte" is used in substantially the same situation when, however, the imperiled employee is aware of the danger. "Eg gynd y trojadus" is used when an employee who has not taken the precaution, or the time, or the trouble to hide wants to sham-ambush another employee who is also in full view, in case it is meant as a joke. "Eg jeht kuz" is used in substantially the same situation when, however, it is meant in earnest. "Ysiste etordyf" is used by a superior wishing to test out the vigilance of a subordinate. "Yxap tseror najx" is used, on the contrary, by the subordinate towards a superior, but only on the days specially appointed for this purpose.[87]

Gross regains control of the organization when a sympathetic secretary translates the Memorandum. It turns out that unnamed higher authorities are suggesting that Gross "liquidate with the greatest possible resolution and speed any attempt to introduce Ptydepe into your organization."[88] Armed with this directive, Gross puts an end to the false path of Ptydepe. But his victory is short-lived, for Ballas undertakes a new initiative to introduce into the organization "Chorukor," a synthetic language that attempts to make words with similar meanings sound as similar as possible.

The Memorandum is one of Havel's Heideggerean thought experiments. If language is the house of Being, then why shouldn't humans be able to construct a perfectly accurate and scientific language in which the meaning of words is absolutely clear? Gross tells us we cannot displace natural languages, for they were "created by the centuries-old tradition of national culture" and "therefore [have] become part of our consciousness and our means of understanding the world."[89]

Further, interspersed between language lessons and bureaucratic infighting are remarks about everyday interests and events (in fact, these take up most of the play's dialogue). The main characters ask the secretaries to make coffee or to go shopping for limes when usually scarce fruit unexpectedly shows up at the greengrocers. There is a great deal of discussion about what is being served for lunch and whether the goose is crispy. The men make salacious remarks about how attractive the secretaries are and how available they might be. Ballas uses the Ptydepe campaign to displace Gross and become director.[90] Fearful that he might again get into trouble, Gross refuses to help the secretary who is dismissed for translating the Memorandum without authorization.

Havel does not doubt that language plays an important part in what we think, as his essay on the power of speech, "A Word about Words," attests.[91] But *The Memorandum* shows that certain human desires, needs, passions, ambitions, longings, and shortcomings are not under the dominion of words. Those human traits have a phenomenological and experiential basis, which language cannot entirely master or change. Since human beings are neither perfect nor (in the post-Communist jargon of the day) transparent, no language can be perfect either. Language is not the only house of our Being; inherent characteristics apparently make up part of the self and therefore our existence.

THE INCREASED DIFFICULTY OF CONCENTRATION

In *The Increased Difficulty of Concentration,* Havel experiments with several of Heidegger's themes. The play does not have much of a plot or even a chronology. The action jumps forward and backward in time. Characters exit one part of the stage in the present only to promptly reappear at another part of the stage at a past or future time. The play is nominally about Dr. Eduard Huml, a social scientist who is being interviewed at his apartment by a group of social scientists using their new invention, Puzuk, a machine capable of scientifically understanding the human psyche. To analyze all the variables that constitute a human personality, Puzuk must collect data, as any "real" social scientist would; therefore, the team schedules an interview with Huml for just that purpose. However, Puzuk is temperamental and is also sensitive to variations in temperature. "He" (as they refer to the machine) refuses to ask any questions until conditions are just right. The team of social scientists hovers around "him," hoping to undertake the study.

Huml is himself interested in the human psyche; he is dictating a book on the topic to his young secretary, Blanka. Huml presents an interesting argument concerning the relationship between individual personality and wider social and cultural norms.

> HUML: Ah! Yes—(*Begins to pace thoughtfully to and fro, while dictating to* BLANKA, *who takes it down in shorthand.*)—and thus attach to various

things various values—full stop. Therefore, it would be mistaken to set up a fixed scale of values, valid for all people in all circumstances and at all times—full stop. This does not mean, however, that in all of history there exist no values common to the whole of mankind—full stop. If those values did not exist, mankind would not form a unified whole—full stop. Yet, as a rule, each man—each period—each social group—has its own scale of values, by which the basic, universal values are in a certain way made more concrete—full stop. At the same time, an individual scale of values is always somehow related to other—more general—scales of values—for instance, to those belonging to a given period—which form a sort of framework, or background, to the individual scales—full stop. Would you mind reading me the last sentence?
BLANKA: (Reads) "At the same time, an individual scale of values is always somehow related to other, more general, scales of values, for instance, to those belonging to a given period, which form a sort of framework, or background, to the individual scales."
HUML: That's pretty good. Let's go on. Among the most basic values of present-day man one can include, for example, work—in other words—the opportunity to do that which would enable man to fulfill himself completely, to develop his own specific potentialities, his relationships with other people, his moral principles—certain convictions regarding his concept of the world, his faith in something to which he can commit his life—full stop. Got it?
BLANKA: Yes.
HUML: Good. And now a new paragraph, please. The state in which man finds himself after he has satisfied one of his particular needs—i.e., when he has achieved a particular value—is called happiness—full stop.[92]

Huml lives by his words, for his most pressing concern is neither his book nor his interview with Puzuk, but rather his active love life. He has promised his wife that he will break off his affair with Renata, his mistress; likewise, using almost identical language, he has promised Renata that he will end his marriage. While dictating the manuscript to Blanka, he makes an impulsive attempt to seduce her, an effort she resists. Finally, when Puzuk's interview fails, Huml consoles his fellow social scientist Miss Balcar by initiating what seems to be a new affair.[93]

What are we to make of these sexual antics? What meaning do they give to the play? Indeed, why does Havel portray romantic dalliances and marital infidelity in so many of his works? We could ascribe Havel's fascination with the topic to his own shortcomings as a husband.[94] But such an explanation would mean that his artistry is little more than a public airing of his dirty laundry. Such an interpretation would not go very far in helping us understand "the crisis of human identity." Rather, Havel seems to be suggesting that in an age when people's self-image is not shaped by reference to a higher, spiritual notion of existence, they must look to others ("the other") to provide them with cues about their self-worth. Are they attractive, witty, intelligent, and so on? When the objective moral and spiritual universe recedes, the inner subjective quest to discover meaning ascends. Havel ascribes promiscuity not simply to the fact that "morals have broken down" or that people no longer fear divine punishment but to the subjective need to discover oneself in the encounter with others. There are, of course, few more intimate or ego-enhancing ways to "know thyself" than to be seen as sexually attractive to another.

In the end, the quest to define ourselves through sexual fulfillment is bound to fail. First, once the initial excitement of the chase wears off and the relationship becomes routine, the ego-boosting satisfaction of a sexual liaison is diminished. Second, as stated earlier, self-identity cannot be fully constructed by an "other," since others are themselves unsure of their identity. Finally, the recognition one receives from another is not rooted in anything permanent, but there is a desire in our souls to understand our lives with reference to something eternal. Even those who deny existence of a spiritual realm insist that this "non-spiritual truth" is true for all times and places. Perhaps this is why Havel is fond of quoting Heidegger's statement "Only a God can save us now."

One way of discovering something lasting about the psyche is through science. We could even argue that an important aspect of the philosophic project since the Enlightenment has been to understand ourselves by identifying the laws that dictate our behavior. Biology, medicine, social science, and the effort to map the human genome are all endeavors to grasp and perhaps control the human psyche. But, as the wandering eyes of Havel's characters seem to indicate, it is impossible to fully understand what motivates human beings. Our likes and dislikes, attractions and aversions, romances and heartbreaks are mysteries even to ourselves. Havel has Huml make the point that science cannot fully comprehend human beings:

> HUML: Nothing easier, if you really care to know. For example, it should be enough to point out the rather obvious fact that things which from one angle appear as predictable may from another angle appear as coincidental, and vice versa; because predictability and coincidence are no absolute categories, nor are they any objectively existing and differentiated spheres of reality—their extent depends merely on the chosen viewpoint, or angle. It can't be helped, from the scientific point of view

everything is always to some extent predictable, while science itself is but a gradual disclosing of this predictability; what we call coincidental is either that which lies beyond the radius of predictability, or simply that which so far we've been unable to establish as predictable. In other words, your endeavour to isolate the element of coincidence and use it as a means of shaping human individuality bears no relationship to science whatsoever. Moreover, it is bound to miss its goal completely. Why? Because it replaces reality—i.e., an objective totality—with a chimera of one of its specific relative and wholly subjective aspects. Science is able merely to keep reaching up towards the totality of a unique personality. It can do this within the limits of that which—at a given moment—it is capable of illuminating and describing as predictable. It can never reach beyond these limits, because man, as an objective totality, fundamentally contains the dimensions of infinity. And I'm afraid the key to a real knowledge of the human individual does not lie in some greater or lesser understanding of the complexity of man as an object of scientific knowledge. The only key lies in man's complexity as a subject of human togetherness, because the limitlessness of our own human nature is so far the only thing capable of approaching however—imperfectly—the limitlessness of others. In other words, the personal, human, unique relationship which arises between two individuals is so far the only thing that can—at least to some extent—mutually unveil the secret of those two individuals. Such values as love, friendship, compassion, sympathy and the unique and irreplaceable mutual understanding—or even mutual conflict—are the only tools that this human approach has at its disposal. By any other means we may perhaps be able more or less to explain man, but we shall never understand him—not even a little—and therefore we shall never arrive at a basic knowledge of him. Hence, the fundamental key to man does not lie in his brain, but in his heart. (MISS BALCAR *begins to cry softly.*)

(*Surprised*) Why are you crying? (MISS BALCAR *goes on crying.* HUML *is baffled. Pause.*)

I didn't mean to hurt you.... (*Kisses her*)[95]

Puzuk has been invented to predict the unpredictable. Miss Balcar claims that he is capable of explaining "human individuality." If Puzuk operated as advertised, it would be possible to understand and foretell the behavior of every human being. Although the technicians who manage Puzuk never mention the idea, once individuality is grasped, the logical next step is to harness and control it. A workable Puzuk would make human beings into standing reserve, for if they could be manipulated and used for purposes other than their own, they would lose their freedom and dignity. If human beings were reduced to standing reserve, to what end should they be put? What is the goal of human life? If it is possible to make human beings into standing reserve, does this not imply that at the core of their being is no-thing?[96]

Is it Havel's view—put in Huml's recitation—that we have no sense of our identity? Are we a complete mystery to ourselves? If we had no sense of self whatever, we would lose a sense of time, as happens when we are ill or unconscious. As Heidegger makes clear in *Being and Time*, it is our confrontation with Being that gives us a sense of time. We want our lives to have meaning beyond the passing of seasons, so we take pictures while on vacation, remember stories to tell our grandchildren, and record important events and call it history. We even mark out time by reference to some extraordinary event, for example, the birth of Christ.

The Increased Difficulty of Concentration dramatically makes the point that if we had no self-identity, events would occur randomly—past and future would become the present. "All my plays," Havel wrote to his wife, Olga,

> as I have said several times already, deal in one way or another with the theme of human identity and the state of crisis in which it finds itself. . . . The disintegration of human identity also means (psychologically) the disintegration of existential continuity and therefore (philosophically) the disintegration of time (as an intensely experienced dimension of Being). I first tried to indicate this specifically in *The Increased Difficulty of Concentration* and it is presented consistently (nonthematically, or rather not as a "subject").[97]

But, except when we are incapacitated, we do have a very definite sense of time, which means, of course, that we do have at least some awareness of our own identity. We live in the odd gray area of knowing, yet not knowing, about ourselves, and this makes life complicated, mysterious, and somehow comprehensible. While the characters in Havel's plays never seem to grasp their own longings, the audience is made to see the ancient verity of Socratic wisdom: self-awareness begins in knowing that we do not know.

Part of individual identity is a perception of Dasein. Of course, most people have no idea what the term means, but they are aware, even if in fleeting glimpses, of the ineffable mystery of life and death. They recognize in the vulnerability of others the contingency of their own condition. Thus Dasein is somehow more than mere consciousness or the ability to speak. Puzuk can speak, but he does not seem to possess Dasein. Language may be the house of Being, as Heidegger suggests, but it is not the house of Dasein. Dasein is constituted by a confrontation with death, an experience that can be learned only from the passing away of others. At its most basic level, Dasein rests on the mutual throwness of other people. Thus, although Dasein seems to be a subjective individual experience, it is actually a social phenomenon. Most important for Havel, Dasein is the origin of responsibility toward others, for we can all become aware of our mutual plight. Even the most soulless of Havel's characters, Hugo (*The Garden Party*), is able to paraphrase Shakespeare, "What a rich thing is man, how complicated, changeable, and multiform."[98] A machine such as Puzuk could not gain Dasein without being aware that he was destined to reenact the tragic end of those who were no more. Could a machine ever achieve such empathy? Could a machine identify with the death of humans? Havel's Puzuk does not pass the test, for although it can speak, it is interested only in its own comfort.

The Increased Difficulty of Concentration suggests that our identity is mysterious yet not altogether devoid of content. We have an awareness of time as well as an awareness of the sequence of events that roots us in the phenomenal world. We also experience Dasein, even if rarely; and this experience shows us that our own lives are inextricably intertwined with others of our species with whom we can feel sympathy and experience community. For Havel, at the very core of our identity there is Dasein, which is open to a sense of responsibility toward others. We see that Puzuk has no Dasein because it has no relationship with others and therefore no responsibility toward others. Huml, however, certainly understands the concerns of others, but he is irresponsible because he has little regard for the longing and needs of those around him. Therefore, while Dasein establishes the possibility of grounding one's identity in responsible behavior toward others, it does not force or require such behavior. Dasein merely opens the possibility for moral action.

TEMPTATION

There are two places where Havel specifically takes up the theme of evil, the play *Temptation* and the essay "Thriller," the latter of which is named after Michael Jackson's music video. Most commentary on Havel's ideas, including, of course, this book, makes much of his efforts to delineate a defense of moral responsibility. But Havel's ubiquitous reminders that we should behave responsibly would be unnecessary if human beings did not act irresponsibly. In fact, many of the leading characters in Havel's plays are incapable of moral actions. Henry Foustka (*Temptation*) fails to protect his young admirer, Marketa, when she attempts to publicly defend him. Josef Gross (*The Memorandum*) allows his secretary, Maria, to be fired even though her benevolent act of translating a document from Ptydepe restored his position as director. Eduard Huml makes lovely speeches about the human moral sense, but he attempts to seduce every woman he meets.

Temptation forces us to ask, What is evil? At first glance, *Temptation* seems to cover the same ground as *The Increased Difficulty of Concentration*, but the former is much darker.[99] Its subject matter is the modern fixation with science as the only explanation of existence. In *The Increased Difficulty of Concentration*, it becomes obvious that science is utterly incapable of accounting for human passions. *Temptation*'s characters find each other tempting in all kinds of ways that scientific models could not begin to decipher.

Temptation's main character, Dr. Henry Foustka, works at an institute whose task is to combat irrationality, that is, any belief not based on science; but Foustka, just like Goethe's Faust, dabbles in the occult. Foustka's Mephistopheles is an unkempt cripple named Fistula who barges into Foustka's apartment, promising to teach him the secrets of irrational mysticism. When Foustka rejects the idea, Fistula makes a show of his powers by promising that Marketa, the beautiful young secretary who works at the institute, will fall in love with Foustka at the next evening's office party. In a way the seduction does occur, for Marketa falls hopelessly in love with Foustka when he describes a morally ordered universe.

> FOUSTKA: I'll begin, if you don't mind, by taking a new tack. Has it ever occurred to you that we wouldn't be able to understand even the simplest moral action that doesn't serve some practical purpose? In fact, it would have to seem quite absurd to us if we didn't recognize that hidden somewhere in its deepest depths is the presumption of something higher, some sort of absolute, omniscient, and infinitely fair judge or moral authority through which and within which all our activities are somehow mysteriously appraised and validated and by means of which each one of us is constantly in touch with eternity?
> MARKETA: Yes, yes, that's exactly how I've felt about it all my life! I just wasn't able to see it, let alone say it so beautifully.
> FOUSTKA: So there you are! What's even more tragic is that modern man has repressed everything that might allow him somehow to transcend himself, and he ridicules the very idea that something above him might even exist and that his life and the world might have a higher meaning of some sort! He has crowned himself as the highest authority, so he can then observe with horror how the world is going to the dogs under that authority!
> MARKETA: How clear and simple it is! I admire the way you're able to think about everything so . . . so, well, in your own way somehow, dif-

ferently from the way most people usually talk about it, and how deeply you feel all those things! I don't think I'll ever forget this evening! I have a feeling that I'm becoming a new person every minute I'm with you. Please forgive me for saying it so openly, but it's as if something were radiating from inside of you that—I don't understand how I could have walked by you so indifferently before—it's simply that I've never felt anything like this before.[100]

But the romance never materializes because Foustka's flirtation with mysticism is revealed; Fistula turns out to be an informer. To save his career, Foustka denies his commitment to occult studies, claims that he is investigating mysticism only to oppose it, volunteers to inform on those who truly accept the preternatural, and stands by while Marketa loses her job and ruins her reputation attempting to defend him. For all his talk of a higher meaning, Foustka fails to act morally.[101] Foustka sells his soul but not for the same reason as Faust. Faust wants what science promises, human mastery over the natural world. Beginning with the Enlightenment, the human race made that deal with its destiny, choosing to focus on material well-being rather than spiritual improvement. Foustka's temptation is less grand; he merely wants to save his skin.

Obviously, *Temptation* is meant to comment on the post-1968 period of "normalization" in Czechoslovakia, where, by some estimates, 20 percent of the population informed on their fellow citizens to the secret police. Many others protected their jobs and safety by pretending to be loyal subjects of the Communist regime. Yet Havel's intent seems to go deeper than exposing the faults of his fellow citizens. Foustka is lying to himself as well as to others. As his conversation with Marketa indicates, he knows what morality is, but he hides his unethical behavior even from himself. Havel explains:

> I enjoy writing rhetorical speeches in which nonsense is defended with crystal-clear logic. I enjoy writing monologues in which pure truths are expressed with veracity and subtlety, truths which are pure lies from beginning to end. Even more, I enjoy writing speeches that balance on a knife's edge: the audience members identify with the truths expressed in them, yet they sense a scarcely perceptible tinge of mendacity, given the situation and context, and they become uneasy, wondering how it was all meant. In *Temptation*, for example, Foustka expounds his opinions on the basic questions of being to Marketa, and in doing so he tells her things that are almost identical to what I believe myself and what, in similar words and in all seriousness, I have said elsewhere, such as in my letters from prison, or in this conversation. At the same time, there is something

subtly false in what Foustka says. He says it—and this is something we should not miss—partly because he is trying to get Marketa to fall in love with him, and he succeeds. So he is, be it ever so subtly, abusing his own truth, one that he has, by honorable means, arrived at himself.

But is it still truth, then? Isn't just such a subtle abuse of the truth, and of language, the real beginning of Foustka's misery, and of the misery of the world we live in? The audience should not be entirely clear about these things; the ambivalence should disquiet them, all the more so because from their own experience—that is, if they are men—they would know that we are often at our most eloquent in formulating important truths when we set out to charm women with them.[102]

Foustka's obfuscations, lies, and self-deceptions are a sign of the difficulty of understanding human identity even for oneself. There is a part of us that always escapes even our most vigorous attempts at self-examination. We lie to ourselves, and we discover the fabrications only later, on reflection. This inability to define our identity indicates that we are not fully capable of constituting our own being through an act of will. We cannot become what we say we are, for if we could, then Foustka's claim would be true—he would have been working to both promote the occult as well as undermine it. Making a statement and earnestly believing it in the moment do not make the statement true. There is an existential reality to truth beyond us. Heidegger and the postmodernists are not entirely correct when they argue that "language is the house of Being." There is a difference between what people say and what they do. The audience of *Temptation* is fully capable of seeing Foustka's groveling deceit and debasement. When we come "face to face with the distillation of evil," might we not "recognize what is good"?[103]

In the ancient world, myths served to portray the nature of good and evil. But since the Enlightenment, little credence has been given to myths. Perhaps because science has no way to explain evil, modern society has had great difficulty comprehending and combating it. According to Havel, science "has succumbed to a large and dangerous illusion." It believes that "everything can be rationally explained" once "a ray of scientific light" is cast on it. But the wars, brutal ideologies, and death camps of the twentieth century—the most rationalistic of all ages—indicate that science cannot protect us from evil. Havel argues that there is an irrational element in the human soul, one that can never be fully controlled or understood by science. Perhaps there is even some ungovernable impulse to do evil. Evil, like morality, has a phenomenological basis. The source of that evil, Havel suggests with his mythical explanation, lies buried deep in the human heart.[104]

THE BEGGAR'S OPERA

Havel commented that he has "fewer reservations" about *The Beggar's Opera* "than any other play." In a letter to his wife, he lamented that it was not performed more often and suggested that it needed to be "discovered" and properly "understood by someone."[105] *The Beggar's Opera* is based on a 1728 play of the same name by John Gay, which also became the inspiration for Bertolt Brecht and Kurt Weill's *Die Dreigroschenoper,* or *The Three Penny Opera* (1928), from which the popular song "Mack the Knife" was taken. Because of Brecht's Marxist sympathies, Communist governments in Central and Eastern Europe allowed and perhaps even encouraged productions of *The Three Penny Opera* during the 1950s and 1960s. The three plays have significantly different aims, and a comparison of the works will help make Havel's intent clear.

A good starting point is to ask why Havel "rewrote" this well-known play. One suggestion holds that Havel used the title "as a convenient façade behind which the 'untouchable' playwright could hide from the censor's prying eyes."[106] But if a leading dissident such as Havel were discovered tampering with such a favored production as Brecht's play, it would have been perceived by the Communist government as an act of civil disobedience. A more satisfying explanation for Havel's potentially dangerous rewrite is that the Czech playwright wanted to highlight the difference between his construction of absurd plays as a device for uncovering and disclosing the truth, and Brecht's use of "epic" theater as an ideological tool.

Gay's Beggar's Opera

Gay's *Beggar's Opera* tells the story of a conflict between rival criminal bands. The daughter of one of the gang leaders, Polly Peachum, falls in love with her father's archrival, Macheath. Macheath is an amoral ladies' man who is married to Polly, Lucy Lockit, the police captain's daughter, and perhaps four other women.[107] He also surrounds himself with a coterie of prostitutes who are associated with his underworld enterprises. Macheath is a charming and handsome scoundrel who plays on the romantic longings of young women to fulfill his own lascivious and nefarious desires. The dramatic tension of the play centers on the conflict between Polly and Lucy, who discover that they are married to the same rogue. Social convention, their own pride, and their parents' disfavor all militate against their relationship with Macheath; yet, the two young women seem hopelessly in love.[108] Because of their commitment to a villain, the women are disgraced in the eyes of both society in general and their parents in particular. When their fathers, Mr. Peachum (the criminal) and Lockit (the police captain), conspire to protect their daughters by having Macheath arrested and hanged, the women plead for his release. Polly even helps Macheath escape, although he is recaptured.

Just as it seems Macheath will really go to the gallows, the Player and the Beggar intervene and encourage the rabble, including the audience, to demand that Macheath be set free since "an Opera must end happily."[109] This seeming act of compassion, however, reveals the true state of morals in eighteenth-century England, where

> through the whole Piece you may observe such a Similitude of Manners in high and low Life, that it is difficult to determine whether (in the fashionable Vices) the fine Gentlemen imitate the Gentlemen of the Road, or the Gentlemen of the Road, the fine Gentlemen—Had the Play remain'd, as I at first intended, it would have carried a most excellent Moral. 'Twould have shown that the lower sort of People have their Vices in a degree as well as the Rich: And that they are punish'd for them.[110]

In its time, Gay's play was shocking because it showed how love could flaut all social conventions. By making the unprincipled Macheath the play's "hero"—who knows how to manipulate love's intensity for his own pleasure—and by allowing him to escape punishment, Gay satirizes the hypocrisy and decadence of British society. "The key point," John Richardson explains of Macheath, "is not that he stands for something, but that he stands against expectation and illusion."[111] Gay presents a social criticism of British mores, especially the perceived corruption of the administration of Prime Minister Robert Walpole, by uncovering how that society's practices fail to measure up to its principles.

Brecht's Three Penny Opera

Brecht's *Three Penny Opera* uses many of the same characters and situations as Gay's *Beggar's Opera*. Macheath is present as Mackie ("Mack the Knife"); Mr. Peachum is the head of the beggars' ring; the corrupt police captain is renamed Brown; and Lucy Brown (daughter of the policeman) and Polly Peachum are manipulated and mistreated by Mackie.[112] Brecht's treatment of the play does not endeavor to point out the hypocrisy of upper-class morals; rather, it is meant to strip "bare the middleclass corpus of ideas." Brecht hopes that his audience will learn to "criticize human behaviour from a social point of view" and thereby come to comprehend "the social laws under which they are acting."[113] Brecht is well aware that the musical elements of the play will entertain, but his goal is to give the audience "instruction" and "enjoyment in learning" in their "class situation."[114] Brecht's play is overtly Marxist, "a representation of the . . . social science method tool known as dialectic materialism" that seeks to emancipate humans from nature and transform society by awakening a "sense of confidence" in the "possibility of change in all things."[115]

G. W. Pabst's film adaptation of *The Three Penny Opera* is even more explicit than Brecht's play in presenting a Marxist critique of capitalist society. When Mackie must flee for fear of arrest, leaving his wife Polly in charge of his gang, she effortlessly transforms the criminal enterprise into a bank—there being no difference between banking and theft in Marxist ideology. Mr. Peachum stages a march of beggars to promote his own interests, but the demonstration of the "masses" takes on a life of its own conveying the wretched conditions of the poor, the selfishness of the rich, the injustice of bourgeois society, and the power of the masses. The movie's final scene unmasks the designs of those who aspire to control and manipulate the masses.

> MR. PEACHUM: Today I've seen the power of the poor. . . . Your money and my experience, a mighty business.
> MACKIE: Why do they need us, if they're so powerful?
> MR. PEACHUM: They don't know it, but it's we who need them![116]

Havel's Beggar's Opera *in Its Social Milieu*

Peter Steiner places Havel's *Beggar's Opera* in its historical milieu, arguing that the adaptation satirized Czechoslovak society just as Gay's original lampooned England's. Steiner points out that Havel wrote *Beggar's Opera* in 1972 just as the stark realization had set in that the Prague Spring was dead and that its brief flowering of freedom and creativity would have no lasting effect. Even worse was the dawning recognition that the repressive, unimaginative, and dreary era of normalization would become the governing doctrine of the nation. Steiner reads *Beggar's Opera* as Havel's commentary on how people coped with this grim reality.[117]

Havel's play is more sinister than Gay's. Havel's Macheath does not stand out because of his lack of morality. He is neither a contrast to the other characters in the play nor an indictment of the morals of his society. In fact, all of the characters steal, cheat, and especially lie. Havel's Macheath is actually more gullible than his fellow characters; the prostitute Jenny fools and betrays him three times. In Havel's *Beggar's Opera*, everyone is amoral — with the possible exception of the pickpocket, Filch, who goes to the gallows. Mr. Peachum enlists his daughter to use sexual favors to spy on Macheath. Mrs. Peachum encourages her husband to have a mistress. The police are bigger crooks than the criminals are; in fact, Police Captain Lockit controls the underworld syndicate. Lies and deception are the rule, not the exception. Most of the characters use others for their own ends. All of the major players are driven exclusively by calculations of self-interest. They think nothing of morals because morals do not exist.[118] John Keane explains, "Selfishness is 'reality,' and . . . the system encourages and depends upon chronic lying, double-crossing, back-stabbing, trickery, the greedy pursuit of self-interest as it is defined at that particular moment. To act in contrary ways, for instance to embrace precepts like honesty or care for others, would amount to pure foolishness."[119] Perhaps the one character whom Havel portrays without irony is a drunk who incongruously appears and yells out, "Long live freedom of the press."[120]

During the era of normalization, many people came to an accommodation with the Communist regime. Some spouted the Communist Party's lies, claiming that the regime supported individual freedom, economic equality, and civic responsibility, when in reality the government was supported by Warsaw Pact troops. Other, subtler people joined the Communist Party in hopes of reforming it from the inside. These reform-minded Communists convinced themselves that "they were rescuing something, or, at least . . . preventing still worse men from stepping into their shoes" and that the greater opportunity, special perks, and higher social status they enjoyed were not the real reason for "their dirty work."[121]

In Havel's *Beggar's Opera* Peachum plays the role of those willing to come to an agreement with a "world that has changed." He counsels Filch to give up his "fidelity to the pure code of honor among thieves," which is no more than "thralldom to abstract principles." Peachum insists that those who work in the "no-man's land between the underworld and the police" are the "real heroes" since they "contribute to the objective interests" of the under class.[122]

In real-life Communist Europe, a significant group of people became state security police (StB) informers. Some StB informants rationalized their betrayal of friends and associates with the thought that they were helping those on whom they spied. They reasoned that their reports to the StB were less damning than those that a "real" informer might submit. They played a double game of deceit, or at least they believed that they were both deceiving their friends and lying to the authorities. Havel represents this form of self-deception, particularly in a speech that Mr. Peachum makes to Lockit:

> Have you any idea at all what it's like spending years fighting against the underworld while you're living in it and trying to maintain its confidence? Years of turning evidence against robbers and cutthroats while having to play the role of their benefactor, without a slipup, I might add? Years of fighting crime while appearing to commit it? Do you have the slightest inkling of what that means? Wearing two faces for so long?[123]

Of course, even if it were true that the information uncovered by these operatives, who pretended to be dedicated to the state, was not particularly damaging to the people under surveillance, it did not necessarily mean that the scrutiny was harmless. The population developed an "existential fear," the sense that they were always being watched. People could never be sure whether informers were pretending to be committed to the state or were pretending to pretend and were thus actually dedicated and loyal to the government. The "ubiquitous, omnipotent state police," Havel declares, was "the hideous spider whose invisible web" ran through the "whole of society." Under such conditions people were always fearful and always felt compelled to lie, pretending to be stalwart supporters of the government and its policies. All "naturalness and authenticity turned into a kind of endless dissimulation."[124]

Havel's Beggar's Opera *and the Reconstruction of the Natural World*

Although Steiner's interpretation of *The Beggar's Opera* has merit, its focus on the historical milieu overlooks Havel's more comprehensive and philosophic intent, present in almost all of his plays. *The Beggar's Opera* creates a world in which everyday moral and ethical behavior is absent. It is, in a sense, the sort of existential reality that Friedrich Nietzsche imagined and that postmodern theorists claim is true. "Judgments, value judgments concerning life ... can in the last resort never be true," Nietzsche explains, since a "living man ... is party to the dispute, indeed its object."[125] Havel tests whether such an amoral society can actually exist.

In Gay's *Beggar's Opera*, Peachum attempts to protect his daughter from the unscrupulous charms of Macheath.

> PEACHUM: And what then? You would not be so mad as to have the Wench marry him! Gamesters and Highwaymen are generally very good to their Whores, but they are very Devils to their Wives.[126]

In Havel's version, Peachum pursues his career goals by encouraging his young daughter to be sexually permissive.

> PEACHUM: Is it true that you're sleeping with the Captain?
> POLLY: Wasn't that what you wanted, Father?
> PEACHUM: So it's true then! Wonderful, Polly! Keep it up.[127]

Havel's Peachum wants Polly to feign a strong attachment to Macheath, but he is worried that the married couple might actually be in love.

> POLLY: I want to be happily married. I want children. I want to be able to bring them up, to keep house. . . .
> MRS. PEACHUM: Tell me the truth now; you have fallen in love with him?
> *Polly . . . bursts into tears. . . .*
> PEACHUM *looks at her in shock, then roars*: Leave my table—you slut![128]

In Gay's play, Mrs. Peachum expresses a belief in traditional restriction on sexual license. She is worried that her daughter is rebelliously engaged in an intimate romance with Macheath.

> MRS. PEACHUM: How the Mother is to be pitied who has handsome Daughters! Locks, Bolts, Bars, and Lectures of Morality are nothing to them: They break through them all. They have as much Pleasure in cheating a Father and Mother, as in cheating at Cards.

Gay's Mrs. Peachum faints when she discovers that Polly has run off and married Macheath.[129]

In Havel's *Beggar's Opera*, Mrs. Peachum is not worried about Polly's moral conduct but is only concerned that her daughter may not be using her intimate relationship to deceive Macheath and may actually care for him. In fact, traditional sexual taboos are so convoluted in Havel's society that men who are not promiscuously cheating on their wives are mocked. Even more astonishingly, wives insist that their husbands discharge this responsibility. The madam Diana attempts to shame Peachum into complying with this social convention.

> DIANA: Still, there's more than one good joke going the rounds in London about your upright Puritanism.
> MRS. PEACHUM: Diana's right, Willy. We've overlooked that, and perhaps we were wrong. Shouldn't we put a stop to wagging tongues once and for all? . . .
> PEACHUM: Don't be ridiculous. As a womanizer I'd be a joke.

> DIANA: A successful womanizer is never a joke.
> PEACHUM: And what makes you think I could pull it off?
> DIANA: Why don't you let me take care of that?
> MRS. PEACHUM: Diana knows what she's doing, Willy.[130]

In Havel's upside-down world, characters exhibit what might be considered odd behavior. First, prostitutes consider any act of kindness or affection on the part of their customers abnormal.

> BETTY: Get out of here, you disgusting pervert! Pig! ...
> DIANA: What's wrong, Betty?
> BETTY: He kissed me on the forehead and then had the gall to stroke my hair!
> DIANA: What's wrong with that?
> BETTY: Madam! I sell my body here as an honest woman, but no cheap bum is going to think he owns my soul as well. What does he think I am? ... This wasn't an honest-to-goodness perversion, it was just pure filth.
> VIVKI: Betty's right.... Soon they'd be making declarations of love right to our faces—.[131]

Second, mothers willingly make their daughters into prostitutes, as Madam Diana states when she scolds Macheath for hiding from the police in her establishment.

> DIANA: You must be out of your mind! ... I'm directly responsible for these girls to their mothers.[132]

Third, the prostitute Jenny, who reads Descartes and is perhaps the most unscrupulous character in the play, betrays Macheath three times because she claims to love him.[133]

In Gay's *Beggar's Opera*, when Polly and Lucy discover that they are both married to Macheath, they pretend to get along, but Lucy is jealous and would "sooner bear to see thee hang'd than in the Arms of another."[134] Later, she tries to poison Polly. Havel's wives actually accept Macheath's polygamy; they are not rivals, and they do not deceive one another. Despite Macheath's lies and betrayal, their only concern is that he might be executed for his reprehensible deeds.

> *Polly and Lucy begin to wail; they both fling themselves on Macheath, kissing him passionately and weeping hysterically.*[135]

Now what are we to make of this strange world that Havel has created? While Gay presents Macheath as a foil, to unmask the disjunction between

London's moral principles and its real practices, his play does assume that there are moral standards. Havel mixes traditional virtues such as honesty, honor, integrity, fidelity, and compassion with their sudden reversal or abandonment. We never know when a character is displaying authentic traits or is just pretending to be decent to get his or her way. It is this odd juxtaposition of morality and amorality that makes us aware of the ubiquitous nature of moral norms and individual virtue. For instance, Havel's presentation of the two women when they discover they are married to the same man highlights the more common, or more natural, human reactions to betrayal and dishonesty. In the ordinary world, would not Polly and Lucy react to duplicity with shock and dismay, as Gay's characters do, instead of willing acceptance, as do Havel's?

It is unclear that families could exist if they were based on the mutual exploitation of family members as presented in Havel's play. What would women be like if they were sexually exploited at a young age by their parents? How would a man react to a wife who insisted that he be unfaithful? How would children behave if affection did not exist among family members? Why would parents undertake the difficult task of raising children if the parents themselves were wholly self-interested? Families are the places where morals and manners, the rules by which civilization exists, are passed from one generation to the next. If parents did not nurture their children, if there were no love and affection in families, then children would become undisciplined, erratic, and barbarous. No society could survive if a large segment of its population were made up of such people.[136]

In Gay's play, Macheath is the only inveterate liar; in Havel's, almost everyone lies. If people lied to one another at every turn in order to gain their own advantage, no one would believe anything anyone else said, and the simplest communication would be impossible since language is an agreement of words that have meaning. How could society exist without an ability to communicate?

If no one ever kept one's word, there could be no law and few viable social conventions. If people behaved on the whim of the moment, as do Havel's characters, they would lose that ability peculiar to the human race of projecting their will into the future—that is, of deciding not just what will happen in the present but how they will behave in a time that has not yet occurred. Human beings would not have foresight and would thus lose the capacity to control their own destiny.

Of course, amoral people do exist: many deceive others and use them for their own ends. Every society has thieves, liars, and cheats. How can moral conduct be "natural" if such people exist? The characters in Havel's *Beggar's*

Opera never seem to experience genuine friendship, love, or shame. They are always motivated by narrow self-interest and merely pretend to care for others. If love, friendship, and community did not exist, if they had no true content, then it is not clear that we would talk about them. If people did not believe that others shared these common human experiences, they would never allow themselves to be deceived. They would realize that all the talk was meaningless and that they would no longer trust anyone's good intentions.

Havel's absurd play makes us imagine what human behavior would be like if the virtues did not exist, almost as if Socrates were present, relentlessly questioning his friends until the virtues somehow disappeared. Havel then re-creates something like Plato's theory of the forms. We know the virtues exist, because if they did not, life would be like an absurd play, empty of meaning. However difficult they are to fully grasp, the virtues must exist, or "love or human communication becomes an empty sequence of habitual functions, gestures and phrases, phrases about love and community."[137] If reality were established by language, as Paul DeMan and other postmodernists argue, then it would be impossible to lie. Reality would be what people say it is at the moment. But Havel shows that there are lies. Although language mediates our understanding of the phenomena, language can never fully establish or create our experience of the world. Therefore, our experience of the virtues—as well as that of love, friendship, and community—must have some permanence or form. They must exist, as Havel points out, "beyond the horizon of the visible world, in that realm wherein dwells the Word that was in the beginning and is not the word of man."[138]

Havel's *Beggar's Opera* suggests that if criminal behavior became the rule, not the exception, society would break down. In fact, criminal conduct is not viable, because every society has rules of conduct that decent people accept as the norm. Amoral people are successful because they take advantage of the honesty of others, playing on their decency, and tricking them into believing that at work is the usual, or normal, trust people put in one another. Liars and cheats pretend to be as honest as everyone else in order to get their way. But does this not mean that there are normal patterns of behavior, that there are morals, and that trust is the usual way in which people interact in every society?

No doubt some individuals are antisocial and amoral. For them, both force and threat of force might be the only means to subdue their aggressive behavior. But most people do not abuse their parents, beat their children, steal from the grocery store, wantonly destroy public property, or kick their pets. All people calculate their own interests, but we also observe that many people feel sympathy for others, have a sense of social responsibility, and exhibit a capacity to judge when their self-interest becomes destructive of social norms.

If Heidegger is correct that Being is no-thing, then there cannot be a higher or transcendent set of principles that guide our actions. Havel's *Beggar's Opera* might be the world in which we actually live. But Havel makes us wonder how moral codes arose in the first place. Why are people not self-interested always and everywhere? Havel's play is a thought experiment intended to show the unreality of an amoral world. No human society has ever existed, or could ever exist, under the conditions Havel creates in *The Beggar's Opera*. Since we have no example of an amoral society, can we therefore assume that moral, or responsible, actions between people are somehow natural—what Havel labels that natural world? Can we not say that Being is constructed in such a way as to give humans an awareness of morality?

Havel versus Brecht

It could be argued, as Brecht does, that morality is a human construct passed down from one generation to the next. Morals are no more than conventions—invented to meet the needs of social interaction—whose origins have been lost in the mists of time. According to Brecht's Marxist interpretation, morals are the ideological supports justifying the power relationships of society. In his plays, "human behaviour is shown as alterable; man himself as dependent on certain political and economic factors and at the same time as capable of altering them."[139]

But Brecht's argument merely pushes Havel's question back further. Why did all societies establish moral rules? Why have narrow self-interest, dishonesty, theft, and cruelty—especially to the innocent—been proscribed in every culture known to us? Why does every society celebrate honesty, courage, integrity, and other virtues? Could it be that Being dictated these restrictions and that humans discovered, rather than invented, morality? Havel explains:

> In this world, categories like justice, honor, treason, friendship, infidelity, courage, or empathy have a wholly tangible content, relating to actual persons and important for actual life. At the basis of this world are values that are simply there, perennially, before we ever speak of them, before we reflect upon them and inquire about them.[140]

The difference between Gay's satire, Brecht's epic musical, and Havel's absurd play can now be made clear. Gay pokes fun at his society not because it lacks moral principles but because its citizens regularly breach those precepts. Brecht rejects the very concept of morality since there is no fixed human nature or eternal principles of any kind. He uses theater as an ideological weapon to criticize existing economic and power relationships and to foster a revolutionary spirit against them. To highlight the dialectic development of consciousness, Brecht maintains that plays should not have a fixed, or final, form; that their productions should change with the times; and that their plots ought to be experiments. Brecht uses various devices (such as musical interludes and narrators) to remind the audience that they are not witnessing the "truth" but merely viewing a production designed to raise consciousness. Properly constructed theater "must amaze its public, and this can be achieved by a technique of alienating the familiar."[141]

Havel claims to "respect Brecht, but . . . only in his non-Brechtian moments . . . when the thing, as it were, becomes bigger than he is," that is, when his plays do not become an "ideologist's study."[142] Havel must have found it amusing that, in spite of his ideological commitment to staging plays according to the prevailing ideology (instead of to the written text), Brecht sued Pabst for changing his plot.[143] As Havel says, even relativists have a fixed point of belief; or, at the very least they accept relativism as true. Brecht's fixed point of belief is Marxist ideology, and although Brecht claims to be open and tolerant, he is more interested in preaching a particular, narrow concept of human motivation (that everything can be reduced to greed and money) rather than displaying human life in all its complexity. Absurd theater does not attempt to preach or convert people to a particular political doctrine. "It does not have that kind of arrogance," Havel explains. "It leaves the instructing to Brecht."[144]

While Brecht attempts to alienate people from their situation, making them unhappy and therefore a vehicle for social change, Havel's absurd theater begins with an awareness that in the modern world the familiar is already alien. Havel does not satirize moral principles, because in the contemporary world many serious people believe that no moral or metaphysical order exists. Havel's play manifests a "state of crisis" in which people have "lost the ground under [their] feet" and where the "world is collapsing" and "everything is coming apart."[145] Yet, Havel's play is not nihilistic. It highlights the absurdity of the modern world, in which people believe in nothing, but it also imagines an even more absurd situation in which people act as if they believe in nothing. Gay criticizes the practices of his society from the vantage of its principles. Havel reconstructs a ground for moral principles by showing that the ordinary social practices of everyday life exhibit moral principles. The phenomena themselves provide a metaphysical ground for morals.

Havel does not argue that people must follow moral codes. He is quite aware that people often behave badly. He would oppose any effort to make people follow hard and fast rules, which, after all, is what the Communists tried to do. Life is too complex and various for a simple and universal code to apply always and everywhere. Rather, Havel attempts to lay the groundwork for the possibility of responsible behavior. He does so by first showing the impossibility of living a life without morals and then by providing phenomenological examples of moral dictates.

NOTES

1. Havel, *Letters to Olga*, 298 (see chap. 1, n. 19).
2. The clearest exception to the absurd and surreal genres is Havel's play *Tomorrow*, which details the final political steps leading to the overthrow of Austro-Hungarian rule and the creation of the First Republic in Czechoslovakia. Havel wrote the play in 1988; the title is suspicious given the events of the next year (Václav Havel, *Tomorrow*, in *Czech Plays*, ed. and trans. Barbara Day [London: Nick Hern Books, 1994], 1–26).
3. Stanislaw Baranczak, "All the President's Plays: Irony Comes to Power in Prague," *New Republic*, July 23, 1990, 27–33. Baranczak explains that "the Central European writer's taste for the absurd, for dark humor, produces in him the saving art of 'maintaining constant distance' from the world while never completely disengaging from it. Paradoxically, it is exactly the art of distance that allows you to see your subject from up close." For Havel's harassment at the hands of the secret police, see Václav Havel, "Reports of My House Arrest," in *Open Letters*, 215–229 (see chap. 1, n. 13).
4. Kundera, "A Life like a Work of Art," 16 (see chap.1, n.1).
5. Stanislaw Baranczak, "All the President's Plays: Irony Comes to Power in Prague," *New Republic*, July 23, 1990, 27–33.
6. Martin Esslin, *The Theatre of the Absurd* (London: Eyre & Spottiswoode, 1962), 33.
7. Peter Steiner, *The Deserts of Bohemia: Czech Fiction and Its Social Context* (Ithaca, N.Y.: Cornell University Press, 2000).
8. Quoted in Mark Brandenburg, "Under the Ice: Czechoslovakia's Stirrings under the Ice," *New Republic*, April 23, 1984, 13–16. See also, Václav Havel, "Six Asides about Culture," trans. E. Kahout, in *Václav Havel: Living in Truth*, ed. Jan Vladislav, intro. George Steiner (London: Faber and Faber, 1986), 124–125. Biafra had endured a deadly famine.
9. Havel, *Disturbing the Peace*, 53 (see chap. 1, n. 4).
10. Havel, "Politics and Conscience," in *Open Letters*, 256, 259.
11. Václav Havel, "Speech at World Economic Forum," Davos, Switzerland, February 4, 1992.
12. Havel, *Disturbing the Peace*, 10–11; see also, "It Always Makes Sense to Tell the Truth," in *Open Letters*, 94–95.

13. Václav Havel, "Speech upon receiving the Sonning Prize," Copenhagen, May 28, 1991.

14. Havel, *Letters to Olga*, 160.

15. Havel calls the letters to Olga his "Heideggerean meditations" (*Disturbing the Peace*, 158). See also, Richard Rorty, "The Seer of Prague," *New Republic*, July 1, 1991, 35–40.

16. Havel, *Letters to Olga*, 154.

17. Esslin, *The Theatre of the Absurd*, 17.

18. Eugène Ionesco, "Dans les Armes de la Ville," *Cahiers de la Compagnie Madeleine Renaud Jean-Louis Barrault* (Paris), no. 20 (October 1957); quoted in Esslin, *The Theatre of the Absurd*, 17.

19. Havel, *Letters to Olga*, 177.

20. Havel, *Letters to Olga*, 152, 342–343.

21. Havel, *Letters to Olga*, 285.

22. Havel, *Letters to Olga*, 198.

23. Havel, *Disturbing the Peace*, 54.

24. Havel, *Letters to Olga*, 289.

25. Havel, *Letters to Olga*, 177.

26. Havel, *Audience*, trans. George Theiner; *The Unveiling*, trans. Jan Novak; *Protest*, trans. Vera Blackwell, in *The Garden Party and Other Plays* (New York: Grove Press, 1993).

27. Marketa Goetz-Stankiewicz, ed., *The Vanek Plays: Four Authors, One Character* (Vancouver: University of British Columbia Press, 1987).

28. M. C. Bradbrook, "Václav Havel's Second Wind," *Modern Drama* 27 (March 1984): 124–132.

29. Goetz-Stankiewicz's introduction to *The Vanek Plays*, xxii, xxvii.

30. Phyllis Carey, "Living Lies: Václav Havel's Drama," *Cross Currents* 42 (Summer 1992): 200–211.

31. Lesley Chamberlain, "Play It Again, Václav—The Wisdom in Havel's Plays," *World and I* 16 (August 2001): 76.

32. Tamara Trojanowska, "Living in Margins and Mazes or Freedom Worth Reconsidering: Mrozek's *The Emigrants* and Havel's *The Audience*," *Canadian Slavonic Papers/Revue canadienne des slavistes* 36 (September–December 1994): 397–411.

33. Stanislaw Baranczak, "All the President's Plays: Irony Comes to Power in Prague," *New Republic*, July 23, 1990, 27–33.

34. Robert Brustein, "Review of *A Private View*," *New Republic*, March 12, 1984, 27. Brustein might have said that Vanek should be more self-assured, more assertive, and more take-charge—that is, more American and less Czech. Havel explains, however, that "Czechs and Slovaks are not passionate people." Václav Havel, "Farce, Responsibility, and the Future of the World," in *Open Letters*, 356.

35. Alfred Thomas, "Review of *The Vanek Plays* and *Living in Truth*," *Slavic Review* 51 (Summer 1992): 348–351. See also Michael L. Quinn, "Ferdinand Vanek, or Compliant Protest," *Text and Presentation,* ed. Karelisa Hurtigan (Lanham, Md.: University Press of America, 1990), 73–81.

36. Václav Havel, "Light on a Landscape by Václav Havel," in Goetz-Stankiewicz, *The Vanek Plays*, 237–238.

37. Pavel Kohout, "The Chaste Centaur," in Goetz-Stankiewicz, *The Vanek Plays*, 241.

38. Havel, *Letters to Olga*, 145.

39. For Havel's own, less-sympathetic treatment of his Foreman in the brewery, see Havel, "It Always Makes Sense to Tell the Truth," *Open Letters*, 89–93.

40. Of course, we do not know how large the bottles of beer were. In any case, Czechs are renowned for their prodigious beer drinking. I once sat at a common table in a pub with two men who had drunk forty pints of beer. It was five thirty in the afternoon.

41. Havel, *Audience*, 201, 205.

42. Havel, *Audience*, 206, 207, 208.

43. Havel, *Audience*, 196.

44. Havel, *Audience*, 195, 199. Foreman did not really go out on a limb to get Vanek work at the factory since there was "a shortage of labour" in that region (194). On the pervasive presence of the secret police in post-totalitarian societies, see Václav Havel, "Dear Dr. Husák," *Open Letters*, 54–55.

45. Havel, *Audience*, 187, 191, 192, 196.

46. Havel, *Audience*, 190. Havel's views on the flaws of Marx's theory are influenced by Aleksandr Solzhenitsyn. See "Power of the Powerless," "Politics and Conscience," "A Word about Words," in *Open Letters*, 150, 171, 208, 266, 270, 380. For a full account of the defects of Marx's misunderstanding of human nature, see James F. Pontuso, *Assault on Ideology: Solzhenitsyn's Political Thought* (Lanham, Md.: Lexington Books, 2004), chap. 4.

47. Havel, *Audience*, 193, 198, 201, 207–209.

48. Havel, *Audience*, 197.

49. James W. Sire, *Václav Havel: The Intellectual Conscience of International Politics* (Downers Grove, Ill.: Intervarsity Press, 2001), 39.

50. Havel, *Audience*, 208–209. Jan Novak's translation has Vanek imitating the brewmaster by buttoning his fly as he enters the room. When asked how things are going, he responds with a more forceful expletive than that in the Theiner translation (Goetz-Stankiewicz, *The Vanek Plays*, 25–26).

51. Gary Kochhar-Lindgren, "The Vertiginous Frame: Václav Havel, Martin Heidegger, and Everyday Life in a Disjointed Germany," *Picturing Cultural Values in Postmodern America*, ed. William G. Doty (Tuscaloosa: University of Alabama Press, 1995), 37.

52. Richard Rorty, "The Seer of Prague," *New Republic*, July 1, 1991, 35–40. Rorty cannot account for his own civic courage. At some personal risk of arrest from the Communist authorities, he lectured for the Jan Hus Educational Foundation in Czechoslovakia—that is, in what has come to be called "the black university." See Barbara Day, *The Velvet Philosophers* (London: Claridge Press, 1999), 101, 177, 286, 288.

53. Rorty, *Objectivity, Relativism, and Truth*, 191 (chap. 2, n. 39).
54. Havel, *Audience*, 191.
55. Baranczak, "All the President's Plays," 27–33.
56. Václav Havel, "Speech before a Joint Session of the U.S. Congress," Washington, D.C., February 21, 1990.
57. Thomas, "Review of *The Vanek Plays*," 349.
58. Havel, *Unveiling*, 233–234. Vanek's (Havel's) friend Pavel Kohout had been a Communist in his youth.
59. Havel, "Dear Dr. Husák," *Open Letters*, 58.
60. Havel, *Unveiling*, 237.
61. Richard Rorty, *Essays on Heidegger and Others* (Cambridge: Cambridge University Press, 1991), 132.
62. Havel, *Unveiling*, 215.
63. Havel, *Unveiling*, 219, 220–221, 232.
64. Havel, *Unveiling*, 224.
65. Václav Havel, "Address to the Senate and the House of Commons of the Parliament of Canada," Parliament Hill, Ottawa, April 29, 1999.
66. Václav Havel, "Speech to the Latin American parliament," Sao Paulo, Brazil, September 19, 1996.
67. Havel, *Protest*, 244–245.
68. Havel, *Protest*, 251.
69. Havel, *Protest*, 265.
70. Kohout, "The Chaste Centaur," 243–244.
71. Havel, *Protest*, 265.
72. Havel, *Disturbing the Peace*, 201.
73. For a discussion of Havel's and Rorty's pragmatism, see Patrick J. Deneen, "The Politics of Hope and Optimism: Rorty, Havel, and the Democratic Faith of John Dewey," *Social Research* 66 (Summer 1999): 577–597.
74. Jaroslav Hašek, *The Good Soldier Švejk and His Fortunes in the World War*, trans. Cecil Parrott, with the original illustrations by Josef Lada (New York: Crowell, 1974).
75. Trojanowska, "Living in Margins," 411.
76. Friedrich Nietzsche, *Twilight of the Idols; or, How to Philosophize with a Hammer*, trans. R. J. Hollingdale (New York: Penguin, 1968), 30.
77. Havel, "Politics and Conscience," 251.
78. Havel, *Disturbing the Peace*, 201.
79. Václav Havel, "Speech at New York University," New York, October 27, 1991.
80. According to Veronika Ambros,

> Václav Havel's *Zahradní slavnost* (*The Garden Party*) will be used to illustrate the authentication of the dramatic fictional world. In Martin Esslin's view, the play belongs within the Theater of the Absurd. *The Garden Party*, however, is a special, Czech variety of this

category. In the 1960s, critics often labeled contemporary Czech drama "model-drama," a tag based on certain features that these plays have in common: presenting a possible world and modeling rather than depicting or representing the actual world. In contrast to the existential core of such plays as Beckett's *Waiting for Godot*, the Czech authors construed a model of a hypothetical world, one where political and moral issues of power distribution are raised. (Ambros, "Fictional World and Dramatic Text: Václav Havel's Descent and Ascent," *Style* 25, no. 2 [Summer 1991]: 310–319.)

But according to Eugène Ionesco, everyday language "is nothing but clichés, empty formulas and slogans" that must be "split apart in order to find the living sap beneath" (Ionesco, "The Playwright's Role," *Observer*, June 29, 1958; quoted in Esslin, *The Theatre of the Absurd*, 95).

81. For a treatment of the odd language used, see Ambros, "Fictional World and Dramatic Text," 310–319.

82. Václav Havel, *The Garden Party*, trans. Vera Blackwell, in *The Garden Party and Other Plays* (New York: Grove Press, 1993), 7, 48–49.

83. Havel, *Disturbing the Peace*, 65, 193. My thanks to Shirley Kagan and Matthew Dubroff, the intrepid "theatrical consultants" of this chapter, for pointing out the sophistication of Hugo's speeches and thus the "theatrical" quality of his soullessness.

84. Havel, "Power of the Powerless," *Open Letters*, 143.

85. Havel, "Power of the Powerless," *Open Letters*, 139.

86. Havel, *The Memorandum*, trans. Vera Blackwell, in *The Garden Party and Other Plays*, 63.

87. Havel, *The Memorandum*, in *The Garden Party and Other Plays*, 86.

88. Havel, *The Memorandum*, in *The Garden Party and Other Plays*, 113.

89. Havel, *The Memorandum*, in *The Garden Party and Other Plays*, 64.

90. "Like the specialized jargon of most professionals, Ptydepe represents an elitist code that paradoxically limits human communication both to a small group of *cognoscenti* and to those issues that can be analyzed and labeled" (Phyllis Carey, "Living Lies: Václav Havel's Drama," *Cross Currents* 42, no. 2 [Summer 1992]: 200–211).

91. Havel, "A Word about Words," *Open Letters*, 377–389.

92. Havel, *The Increased Difficulty of Concentration*, trans. Vera Blackwell, in *The Garden Party and Other Plays*, 139–140.

93. For an analysis of Havel's depiction of women, see Jude R. Meche, "Female Victims and the Male Protagonist in Václav Havel's Drama," *Modern Drama* 40, no. 4 (Winter 1997): 468–476.

94. See John Keane, *Václav Havel: A Political Tragedy in Six Acts* (New York: Basic Books, 2000), for an account of Havel's private life.

95. Havel, *The Increased Difficulty of Concentration*, in *The Garden Party and Other Plays*, 179–180. See also Walter Schamschula, "Vaclav Havel: Between the Theater of the Absurd and Engaged Theater," *Fiction and Drama in Eastern and Southeastern Europe: Evolution and Experiment in the Postwar Period*, ed. Henrik Birnbaum and Thomas Eekman (Columbus, Ohio: Slavica, 1980), 337–348.

96. Havel, *The Increased Difficulty of Concentration*, in *The Garden Party and Other Plays*, 170–171.

97. Havel, *Letters to Olga*, 92.

98. Havel, *The Garden Party*, 50.

99. After watching a performance of the play, Havel's biographer felt "a little afraid. Not even I can see to the bottom of its depths. . . . The final vortex warns against a horrible and unmanageable end. Vašek [Havel] is skillful at representing this vortex" (Edá Kriseová, *Václav Havel: The Authorized Biography*, trans. Caleb Crain [New York: St. Martin's Press, 1993], 218).

100. Václav Havel, *Temptation*, trans. Marie Winn (New York: Grove Press, 1989), 33–34.

101. "An inseparable aspect of the crisis of identity is a conflict between words and deeds. . . . I've often addressed that problem in my plays" (Havel, *Letters to Olga*, 305).

102. Havel, *Disturbing the Peace*, 193–194.

103. Havel, *Disturbing the Peace*, 199. See also, Paul I. Trensky, "Václav Havel's 'Temptation Cycle,'" *Czechoslovak and Central European Journal* 10, no. 2 (1991): 84–95.

104. Havel, "Thriller," *Open Letters*, 285–290.

105. Havel, *Letters to Olga*, 62, 63, 86, 304.

106. Peter Steiner, introduction to Václav Havel's *The Beggar's Opera*, trans. Paul Wilson (Ithaca: Cornell University Press, 2001), xvi.

107. John Gay, *The Beggar's Opera* (Charlottesville, Va.: Electronic Text Center, University of Virginia Library, [1728] 1765), 3:15.

108. Gay, *The Beggar's Opera*, 3:10.

109. Gay, *The Beggar's Opera*, 3:16.

110. Gay, *The Beggar's Opera*, 3:16.

111. John Richardson, "John Gay, *The Beggar's Opera*, and Forms of Resistance," *Eighteenth Century Life* 24, no. 3 (2000): 20.

112. Bertold Brecht, *The Three Penny Opera*, ed. and trans. John Willett and Ralph Manheim (New York: Arcade Publishing, 1994).

113. Bertolt Brecht, "On the Use of Music in the Epic Theatre," in *Brecht on Theatre*, trans. John Willett (New York: Hill and Wang, 1986), 86.

114. Bertolt Brecht, "On Experimental Theatre," in *Brecht on Theatre*, 132.

115. Bertolt Brecht, "A Short Organum for the Theatre," in *Brecht on Theatre*, 193, 202.

116. G. W. Pabst, *The Three Penny Opera*, adapted from the musical by Bertolt Brecht and Kurt Weill (London: Lorrimer Publishing, 1984).

117. Steiner, introduction to Havel's *The Beggar's Opera*, ix–xxxi.

118. Havel, *The Beggar's Opera*, 84.

119. Keane, *Václav Havel*, 235–236.

120. Havel, *The Beggar's Opera*, 26, 67.

121. Havel, "Dear Dr. Husák," *Open Letters*, 55.

122. Havel, *The Beggar's Opera*, 42.
123. Havel, *The Beggar's Opera*, 66.
124. Havel, "Dear Dr. Husák," *Open Letters*, 53–55.
125. Nietzsche, *Twilight of the Idols*, 30.
126. Gay, *The Beggar's Opera*, 1:4.
127. Havel, *The Beggar's Opera*, 9.
128. Havel, *The Beggar's Opera*, 20.
129. Gay, *The Beggar's Opera*, 1:8.
130. Havel, *The Beggar's Opera*, 11.
131. Havel, *The Beggar's Opera*, 52, 56.
132. Havel, *The Beggar's Opera*, 49.
133. Havel, *The Beggar's Opera*, 71–74.
134. Gay, *The Beggar's Opera*, 2:15.
135. Havel, *The Beggar's Opera*, 61.
136. See James Q. Wilson, *The Moral Sense* (New York: Free Press, 1993), 141–164, in support of Havel's point on families as well as on the "naturalness" of the virtues.
137. Havel, *Letters to Olga*, 242.
138. Havel, "A Word about Words," *Open Letters*, 389.
139. Brecht, "On the Use of Music in the Epic Theatre," in *Brecht on Theatre*, 86.
140. Havel, "Politics and Conscience," *Open Letters*, 250–251.
141. Brecht, "A Short Organum for the Theatre," in *Brecht on Theatre*, 192.
142. Havel, *Letters to Olga*, 285.
143. Brecht, "The Film, the Novel and Epic Theatre" (from *The Three Penny Lawsuit*) in *Brecht on Theatre*, 47–49.
144. Havel, *Disturbing the Peace*, 54.
145. Havel, *Disturbing the Peace*, 53.

5

FREE MARKETS AND CIVIL SOCIETY: CITIZEN IN THE GLOBAL ECONOMY

In 1994 then prime minister Václav Klaus and playwright-president Václav Havel engaged in a spirited debate over proposed changes to the Czech constitution that would have decentralized power and strengthened the authority of local governments. Although few commentators at the time grasped the significance of the exchange, the dispute became the basis of a long-standing feud between the Czech leaders. The controversy was fought over "regionalism," as it was characterized in the press, and it went to the heart of the difficult transition that post-Communist countries faced as they began establishing free-market economic systems and building the social structures necessary to support democracy. Even beyond the immediate political and economic issues involved in the Czech Republic, the discussion raised questions concerning the nature of human beings and the most fitting way to organize social life in the post–Cold War era.[1]

KLAUS: IT'S THE ECONOMY

When Václav Klaus became prime minister in 1992, his first concern was to transform the cumbersome, centrally planned Czech economy. He argued that a free-market economic system would be more efficient, competitive, and just. He rested his hopes on coupon privatization, a scheme that he hoped would transfer ownership of state-run industries into private hands. For a nominal fee, every Czech could become a kind of stockholder in a number of Czech industries. Klaus reasoned that private owners would insist that companies show a profit, forcing businesses to adopt efficient management techniques. The government would no longer be required to subsidize unwieldy Communist-inspired industries, making it possible to reduce taxes or to spend tax revenues on more worthy projects. Although he was careful to protect a number of key domestic industries, Klaus also promoted the principle of opening Czech markets to foreign firms. He calculated that once Czech companies were faced with foreign competition, they would have to produce more marketable goods than had been the case under central planning.

In his widely distributed *The Ten Commandments of Systemic Reform*, Klaus argues that strictly political issues are both secondary and instrumental to economic reforms.[2] For Klaus, political matters were important in only four areas. First, a post-Communist leader had to introduce a competitive political party system. Second, a leader had to use the party system as a vehicle for building popular support during the euphoric, or initial, stage of the transition, in order to create a ruling coalition capable of carrying out economic reforms. Third, once the painful transition to the free market began, the leader had to oppose demands by "vested interest groups" to continue subsidies to large state-run programs and enterprises; furthermore, the leader had to resist "populist pressure to inflate the economy" as a means of alleviating some of the economic hardships. Finally, the leader had to present a clear and optimistic vision of the long-term benefits of a market-oriented system and use that vision as a "permanent campaign" to keep the reform spirit alive.[3]

Klaus said very little about the difficulties of establishing a democracy. He did not seem to think that a democracy would be particularly difficult to create. He believed that once a competitive party system was put in place, democracy would be fully established. If pushed on the matter, he maintained that good citizenship is founded on, and the result of, a rational calculation of self-interest. *Homo politicus* is a corollary of *Homo oeconomicus*. Since the combination of free-market economics and parliamentary democracy is, in the long run, most likely to satisfy people's interests, he believed there to be no need to worry about founding institutions to nurture a democratic character. Whatever the social arrangement, Klaus argued (quoting Adam Smith with approval) that "the strongest motive is 'the uniform, constant, and uninterrupted effort of every individual man to better his condition.'" If human nature is constant, then a calculation of "incomes and prices" plays a role in "any economic (and noneconomic)" decisions.[4] The key to creating and maintaining democratic government is none other than establishing an economic system that offers the highest wages relative to the price of goods—the free market. For Klaus, what works according to Smith's "invisible hand" is not only the economic system but also the political arrangement.

One final component must be added to complete Klaus's view of post-Communist reforms. He maintains that, regardless of how painful it is to particular groups or individuals, the transition to capitalism is moral because it maximizes human freedom. Freedom, for Klaus, is not merely the absence of government control, although this is certainly important; rather, freedom is an integral part of living a satisfying human life. "I believe," he asserted, that

> capitalism, of course, democratic, is the only system that makes possible material prosperity and political, economic, and human freedom. Capitalism encompasses the economic, political, and moral and cultural (or to put it differently, spiritual) worlds. It is sometimes suggested that the three worlds . . . are divisible into compartments. I prefer . . . to speak about three dimensions of one system. The logic of human behavior in all of them is identical, and it would be a disaster to accept the accusations of the enemies of democratic capitalism who say that economic behavior is egotistical whereas political behavior is or should be altruistic, that economic transactions and morality are incompatible, that culture is noble and superior whereas financial markets are nasty and inferior.[5]

For Klaus, the freedom associated with capitalism is also moral because it "helps the poor escape from poverty better than any other system." Freedom unlocks the potential for "human creativity" and "gives a chance to the human mind, to wit, invention, discovery, and enterprise, a system based on the ethic of hard work and not envy."[6]

HAVEL: CIVIL SOCIETY AND DEMOCRACY

Although Havel's politics are admittedly "slightly left of center," he did not oppose a rapid transition to a free-market economy.[7] In fact, he praised Klaus for his "uncompromising stance" in favor of free-market reforms and stated that, as then finance minister, Klaus "had the most positive influence" on the final form of the sweeping changes made toward economic freedom. Like Klaus, Havel argues that the most natural way to organize economic life is not to organize it too much. According to Havel, the free exchange of goods and services is "the only natural economy, the only one that makes sense, the only one that can lead to prosperity, because it is the only one that reflects the nature of life itself," which is "infinitely and mysteriously multiform."[8] Havel goes so far as to suggest that the only "economic system that works" is a market economy. The free market works because "everything belongs to someone—which means that someone is responsible for everything."[9]

However, Havel argues that the free market depends on certain prerequisites that its strongest advocates seem to ignore:

- the free market depends on fair and voluntary exchanges;
- fair and voluntary exchanges depend on the enforcement of contracts;
- the enforcement of contracts depends on a stable legal system;
- a stable legal system depends on public officials and citizens willing to obey the law; and
- the willingness to obey the law depends on a sense of civic responsibility.

Havel explains:

By the way, it is a great mistake to think that the marketplace and morality are mutually exclusive. Precisely the opposite is true: the marketplace can work only if it has its own morality—a morality generally enshrined in laws, regulations traditions, experiences, customs—in the rules of the game, to put it simply. No game can be played without rules. (It is no coincidence that many ancient religious books come with both a moral codex and something like a set of regulations for commerce.)[10]

Havel criticized Klaus for making free-market economics into a new kind of ideology, one that had to be followed even if the facts did not support the theory. Havel argues that life is too complicated to fit into any single model, even one that allows the variety bred by economic freedom. While Marxism expects people to always think about others—man as a species being—Klaus believes that people think only of themselves and always calculate their narrow economic self-interest. Havel maintains that neither extreme is valid. People often think of their own interests, but they also have a sympathy for others, a sense of responsibility to the broader community, and a capacity to judge when their self-interest is becoming destructive to social norms. Havel is also aware that being cognizant of one's responsibilities is not the same as behaving morally. Havel agreed with Klaus that an economic transition was necessary, but Havel maintained that the more difficult task—the transition to civic responsibility—was also needed. Havel insists that economic liberty does not necessarily create good citizens or responsible human beings; civic virtue has to be nurtured.

While Klaus seems to believe that liberty is a good in itself, Havel is more interested in how freedom is put to use. For example, there is the obvious fact that some people who strive exclusively for economic gain are selfish and care little about their fellow citizens. Evidence of that selfishness was visible in the many scandals associated with the coupon privatization in the Czech Republic. But rampant corruption is merely an indication of a deeper problem, one caused both by the legacy of Communism and by the nature of the modern technological world.[11]

Havel implies that no matter how well constructed the governmental structure or how efficient the economy, the fate of a nation ultimately rests on the character of its people. Generally, human beings do not act for the good of the community or obey the law unless they feel some dedication and loyalty to the system under which they live. He writes:

> I am convinced that we will never build a democratic state based on rule of law if we do not at the same time build a state that is—regardless of how unscientific this may sound to the ears of a political scientist—humane, moral, intellectual and spiritual, and cultural. The best laws and the best-conceived democratic mechanisms will not in themselves guarantee legality or freedom or human rights—anything, in short, for which they were intended—if they are not underpinned by certain human and social values. What good, for instance, would a law be if no one respected it, no one defended it, and no one tried responsibly to follow it? It would be nothing but a scrap of paper. What use would elections be in which the voter's only choice was between a greater and a lesser scoundrel? What use would a wide variety of political parties be if not one of them had the general interest of society at heart?[12]

"Civil society" is often defined as the interconnecting activity through which citizens participate in and learn to feel loyalty toward the laws of their nation. Although the term "civil society" was first coined in 1767 by Adam Ferguson,[13] it was Alexis de Tocqueville who brought the concept to life. Tocqueville visited the United States in the 1820s to learn how a backward, half-civilized, unsophisticated, and semiliterate people (Americans), without so much as a single opera house, could make democracy work, whereas the most intellectually and culturally advanced nation on Earth (France) had failed completely at the endeavor.[14] To oversimplify, what Tocqueville discovered was that Americans had a civil society and the French did not.

Havel uses the term "civil society" the way Tocqueville did. He explains:

> What, in fact, is a civil society? In the most general terms, we could perhaps describe it as a society in which citizens participate—in many parallel, mutually complementary ways—in public life, in the administration of public goods, and in public decisions. The extent, the manner, and the

institutional form of this participation depend predominantly on the participants, on their initiative and imagination, even though these are naturally exercised within a certain legal framework. Thus, it is a society that not only gives wide latitude for both individual and group creativity as an important component of public activity, but is directly founded on such creativity. The functions of the state and of its structures in such a society are limited only to that which cannot be performed by anyone else, such as legislation, national defense and security, the enforcement of justice.[15]

It was exactly the kind of activity associated with a civil society that "was the target of the most brutal attack on the part of communist regimes."[16] Communism was more than "the dictatorship of one group of people over another. It was a genuinely totalitarian system; that is, it penetrated every aspect of life and deformed everything it touched, including all the natural ways people had developed of living together. It profoundly affected all forms of human behavior."[17] Communism "systematically mobilized the worst human qualities, like selfishness, envy, and hatred."[18] Under Communism Czech society lost the art of politics. The party maintained power by keeping a watchful eye on almost everyone. The fear of being observed and the anxiety of not knowing who was engaged in spying created distrust and interfered with ordinary social interactions. People "learned not to believe in anything, to ignore one another, to care only about [themselves]. Concepts such as love, friendship, compassion, humility, or forgiveness lost their depth and dimension." A sense of apathy developed, a feeling that ordinary people could not control events or even their own destinies. This was especially true in Czechoslovakia when hopes raised by the Prague Spring dissolved into the rigid era of normalization.[19]

Communism undermined people's moral sense for many reasons: It asked too much of people, expecting them to care for strangers as much as for their families, friends, neighbors, townsfolk, and fellow citizens. It made all responsibility communal rather than individual. It was materialist and asked people to believe that material rewards mattered, not a higher moral sense. It was ideological. It was anthropocentric; it attempted to supply a total answer to all of life's problems through scientific certainty. In an attempt to fulfill the ideology of a universal classless society, the Communist system stressed uniformity and worked to "make everything the same." "From Berlin to Vladivostok," Havel explains, "the streets and buildings were decorated with the same red stars. Everywhere the same kind of celebratory parades were staged. Analogical state administrations were set up, along with a whole system of central direction of social and economic life." Party control destroyed the web of social interactions that make up nonideologically based societies. It covered nations with a "shroud of uniformity, suffocating all national, intellectual, spiritual, social, cultural or religious variety."[20] Communists attempted to control every social group—or more accurately, to establish and guide any organization or activity that occurred "right down to every bee-keepers' association."[21] People did "volunteer" to take part in civic organizations, but since these civic bodies were tools of state control, participation became a despised duty, or worse, a kind of collaboration with an evil system.

The consequence of Communist control, according to Havel, was to dissolve the social and cultural mechanisms through which pre-Communist people had learned to live together in harmony. In essence, civil society was all but destroyed, and with it, "politics itself as a field of practical human activity" was "annihilated."[22] Traditional institutions and practices were replaced by the artificial conformity of "socialist fraternity." The problem for post-Communist countries has been that civil society is not simple to recreate. "It is easy," Havel says,

> to make everything the same by force, to destroy the complex and fragile social, cultural, and economic relationships and institutions built up over centuries, and to enforce a single, primitive model of central control in the spirit of a proud utopianism. It is as easy to do that as it is to smash a piece of antique, inlaid furniture with a single blow from a hammer. But it is infinitely more difficult to restore it, or to create it directly.[23]

Havel declares that local governments are the breeding grounds of democracy. At the local level, politics exist on a human scale; people can see and understand the issues facing them and the solutions available to them. Decentralized administration encourages participation on a wider scale. Many citizens—not just politicians involved with the national government in the capital—can learn to recognize societal problems and formulate policies to solve them. Havel reasons that the anomie and apathy bred by the Communist system can be overcome if citizens are made to accept responsibilities and work together for a common goal. Moreover, if citizens had a hand in making the laws, they would come to trust their elected officials, feel greater satisfaction in their own actions, and be more likely to obey the laws. The only way to relearn the art of self-government, Havel contends, is by doing it.

Havel argues that local government can take on many tasks "more quickly and efficiently" than a central administration can because local people know more about the issues.[24] Localities can adjust more readily to new issues, adapt more quickly to changing situations, and "encourage a more sensitive response to the multifarious needs of life, which can scarcely be centrally monitored." In fact, although Havel has often been described as impractical, he observes quite sensibly that one of the surest ways to reduce both the size of the bureaucracy and the cost of government—the latter, one of Klaus's key goals—is to shift state-run programs into local or private hands.[25]

Havel's position is similar to those of James S. Coleman, Pierre Bourdieu, Glenn Loury, Michael Woolcock, and Robert D. Putnam.[26] According to this diverse group of scholars there are three types of "capital": physical, human, and social. Physical capital consists of the land, buildings, machines, and money used to produce things. Human capital is the education, skills, experience, and abilities that an individual acquires over a lifetime. Social capital is the capacity of a group of citizens to accomplish tasks and to promote its members and their goals. Coleman explains:

> Social capital . . . comes through changes in the relations among persons that facilitate action. If physical capital is wholly tangible, being embodied in observable material form, and human capital is less tangible, being embodied in the skills and knowledge acquired by an individual, social capital is less tangible yet, for it exists in the *relations* among persons. Just as physical capital and human capital facilitate productive action, social capital does as well. For example, a group within which there is extensive trustworthiness and extensive trust is able to accomplish more than a comparable group without that trustworthiness and trust.[27]

Klaus seems to believe in the rational actor model of human behavior, which includes only physical and human capital. Havel, however, maintains that social capital is an important mechanism for accomplishing tasks. Social capital is more difficult to create, since it depends on the long-term interactions of mutual confidence and responsibility. Communism did much to destroy those fragile connections, and Havel's hope is that the face-to-face contacts gained only through participation are what build the new, mutual interactions of trust and obligation. Moreover, as we shall see, Havel goes beyond the proponents of social capital by arguing that active participation is itself a human good and is not merely an instrument for achieving goals, be they individual or group.

Havel claims that localities also provide a kind of laboratory for innovation and experimentation. In the end, such localities materialize more creatively because they require less standardization. "The central rationality of the state—be it ever so enlightened—cannot continue to take the place of the pluralistic richness of ideas, the knowledge, the experience, and the inventiveness of individuals and the great variety of associations they naturally create."[28]

People are more community oriented in small towns. Citizens know one another not abstractly but personally. In small towns, people are friends, not mere acquaintances. Moreover, smallness means that reputation and shame are important elements in enforcing social norms. "People in small towns" writes James Q. Wilson, citing a number of sociological studies, "are in fact and not just in legend more helpful than those in big cities."[29]

There is a risk that local authorities will not "behave as purposefully as the state" or enact regulations as enlightened or as technically competent as would the national government. "But," Havel reminds his constituents, "democracy is a system based on trust in the human sense of responsibility, which it ought to awaken and cultivate." The risk that the localities will behave provincially "is far outweighed," Havel advises, by the "sense of civic solidarity and an interest in public affairs" that is nourished when people take an active role in shaping their own future. In small societies, obedience to the law is based on friendship with one's fellow citizens and the reputation one has within the community, not on the enforcement power of the state. The "experience of participating" imbues citizens with "a feeling of responsibility for the whole, and thus, indirectly, good relations with their own country." In essence, when people share the act of governing, they not only become more committed to their region, but they also transfer that patriotic loyalty to the nation as a whole.[30] Havel states:

> It is not true that decent decentralization estranges citizens to their state; on the contrary, in a decentralized environment they feel much greater shared responsibility for its working, because they are drawn in it, if only on a local level. In other words: general responsibility for our fatherland and our pride is anchored by a tangible responsibility for a microcosm in which we live. And only through what we can see and feel for ourselves we discover the best, what we cannot see that easily and what we do not feel directly.[31]

Voluntary organizations are the second prop of civil society. They provide even more entry points into public service. Havel explains that these groups include

> free association of people in different types of organizations, ranging from clubs, community groups, civic initiatives, foundations and publicly beneficial organizations up to churches and political parties. People associate in these organizations in order to accomplish things that a group can do better than an individual. This kind of association which leads to an authentic self-structuring of the society emanates from interests other

than those linked directly with business or material profit; and . . . these not-for-profit activities do not serve only those who take part in them, but bring a wider benefit that can be, in one way or another, enjoyed by everyone.[32]

A vigorous civil society protects against popular tides of passion and demagogic appeals by potential leaders. "It constitutes a true guarantee of political stability," Havel states. "The more a community develops all organisms, institutions, and instruments of a civil society, the more resistant it is to various political windstorms or upheavals."[33] In Havel's view, civil society is a more valuable safeguard of human liberty than the free market.

In an age when mass communication dominates almost every aspect of human life, people often become alienated from their politicians and political system. Events seem to occur beyond the control of most citizens, and policies are adopted with little or no real consultation with the populace. It is little wonder then that the contemporary era, although the most democratic in history, is also one in which many people are deeply distrustful and cynical about politics. What worries Havel is

> the depersonalization and dehumanization of politics that has come about with the progress of civilization. An ordinary human being . . . seems to be receding farther and farther from the realm of politics. Politicians seem to turn into puppets that only look human and move in a giant, rather inhuman theater; they appear to become merely cogs in a huge machine, objects of a major civilizational automatism which has gotten out of control and for which nobody is responsible. . . . Under these circumstances, many people hardly ever see a politician as a person anymore. Instead, a politician is a shadow they watch on television, not knowing whether he is speaking impromptu or reading a text written for him by anonymous advisers or experts from a screen hidden behind the cameras. Citizens no longer perceive their politician as a living human being, for they never have and will never see him that way. They see only his image, created for them by TV, radio and newspaper commentators. If they want to ask a politician a question they can usually do so only in writing, and receive a reply from a nameless member of his staff.[34]

To combat this skepticism and mistrust, citizens must feel that their voice matters. Havel makes the point in almost metaphysical terms: human beings are constructed to seek recognition of the self. The only way to gain this recognition is through community action. To live fully decent lives, people must participate with one another in the mutual shaping of destiny.

> The most important aspect of civil society is yet another thing—it is the fact that it enables people to realize themselves truly and entirely as the beings that they potentially are, that is, as the species called *zoon politicon*, or social animal. Human beings are not only manufacturers, profit-makers or consumers. They are also—and this may be their innermost quality—creatures who want to be with others, who yearn for various forms of coexistence and cooperation, who want to participate in the life of a group or of a community and who want to influence that which happens around them. . . . People desire to be appreciated for that which they give to the environment around them. Humanity constitutes a subject of conscience, of moral order, of love for our fellow humans. Civil society is one of the ways in which our human nature can be exercised in its entirety, including its more subtle elements, which are more difficult to grasp, but are perhaps the most important of all.[35]

Havel's argument recalls Aristotle's: Man is a political animal. Social life is necessary for human survival, since individuals cannot survive in the wilderness. However, social life requires that humans deal with other people whose interests may conflict with their own. Living as part of a community presents both a challenge and an opportunity for human beings. People are forced into situations where potential conflicts with others are possible, but social life encourages people to resolve those conflicts. Only through political activity can humans maintain peace and order. Politics require that citizens help their community decide what policies it should adopt to resolve conflicts. Therefore, politics depend on the use of speech and reason. Only in political life can individual character be developed to the fullest, for only in a social setting can citizens exercise their particularly human traits—speech and reason—to the fullest. Political life affords people the opportunity to be recognized by others for their humanness. Havel explains, "I believe in face-to-face contact, the kind of communication that prevailed at the agora. The great challenge of the present era is to seek out forms of democracy that suit the present times while reviving the very face-to-face contact that marked the birth of democracy."[36]

KLAUS'S RESPONSE TO THE CIVIL SOCIETY: IT'S STILL THE ECONOMY

In a strongly worded address before the Czech parliament in December 1997—dubbed by the press as the "Ten Commandments Speech"—Havel rekindled the debate over how to build a civil society. Havel accused the recently resigned Klaus government of "an apathetic, or almost hostile, attitude toward everything that bears even a distant resemblance to a civil society." Klaus responded by calling the speech "confrontational" and interpreted it as a "challenge." Klaus considered Havel too left of center or perhaps even a closet socialist—a suspicion reinforced by admissions Havel made on the subject.[37]

Klaus declared that "the last eight years have been a battle between two world visions." Havel's views "pointed to a vision of the world that is diametrically opposed to right-wing thinking, and showed how deep is his ignorance of the workings of the market economy and a free society."[38]

Klaus opposed decentralization. He feared that strong local governments would thwart his ambitious economic reforms. His reasoning was that provincial elections were likely to return former Communists to power because, in some regions, they were the only people with administrative experience. Furthermore, the Czech Communist Party was the second largest mass-based group in the nation, ranking only behind labor unions. Communists had little enthusiasm for Klaus's free-market programs. If they were to gain local office, they could create islands of resistance to modernization, in much the same way that the local councils had opposed the reforms promoted in Britain by Klaus's hero, Margaret Thatcher.

Even where Communists were not elected, Klaus believed that workers in localities with antiquated industrial plants might use their political leverage to protect their jobs. It was subsidies of inefficient industries that helped to cause the collapse of Eastern Europe's managed economies. The model Klaus seemed to have in mind was that of Asia. There was little democracy in Taiwan or Hong Kong, but there was a great deal of individual freedom and economic growth. A free-market system had to allow inefficient enterprises to fail, creating personal suffering and social upheaval. If the people hurt by the transition became too powerful, they might use their strength at the polls to limit and even reverse the much-needed market reforms.[39]

Klaus attacked both the practicality and the merit of what he termed Havel's "small is beautiful" thinking. Decentralization is not feasible because in the Czech lands, "there has not been—in a long, long time, if ever—a strong, genuine regional identity, and I doubt that the new fashionable (among leftist intellectuals) regionalist idea, based on civil society or governance is strong enough to be taken seriously." In the Czech Republic, Klaus concluded, attachment to the nation-state was much stronger than that to the regions and was therefore more "authentic."

Klaus thought that regionalism was little more than a short-term political strategy fostered by left-wing parties who were unhappy with the results of the general elections that had brought Klaus's party to power. "The opposition wants ... a new political arena," Klaus stated while still prime minister, so that "if it does not succeed in general elections, it still can thrive in fourteen smaller parliaments." But a decentralized political system would be a "dangerous blow to the unity of the country" and "most disastrous for this country" because, in Klaus's view, it would make implementing government policies impossible and eventually result in the disintegration of the nation.

Klaus also criticized Havel's decentralization schemes as little more than wishful thinking. Havel could offer no objective evidence to support the argument that decentralization was necessary for democracy. Havel simply assumed a priori that smaller government was beneficial. However, according to Klaus, all social actions must be judged by strict measures of cost and benefit. If a political association leads to greater "well-being or happiness of the individual members of that collectivity," it should be deemed good. No association ought to be granted special status, for "the individual has the primary position; any collectivity's position is, therefore, secondary because all collectivities are only derivatives."[40]

Most important, Klaus held that inaugurating a free-market system would also result in the creation of a civil society. A civil society rests on a strong middle class who is independent of the state and who is not made up of bureaucrats whose livelihood relies on the continuation of state-sponsored programs. Market transactions would induce the middle class to become rational actors. Not only would they learn to manage their own economic affairs, but they would also carry over their new values and obligations into political life. While regionalism could make people provincial and protective of narrow parochial interests, the free market would expose people to competition from around the world and have the effect of making people sophisticated, cosmopolitan, and tolerant. People directed by consumer sovereignty would realize the need to accept the rule of law; the need for high levels of information about public affairs; the need for active participation in the political process; the value of an independent press and a free intellectual and cultural realm; and the benefits of religious, cultural, and ethnic tolerance. In effect, Klaus reasoned that voluntary economic transactions would teach people to become good citizens. In that sense, Klaus and Havel sought the same goal. They both desired that people be free to choose their own fates and control their own futures in a complex and diverse society.

HAVEL: CIVIL SOCIETY AND THE POSTMODERN WORLD

By the time the Klaus government fell, in 1997, Havel alleged that economic reforms had not been implemented fully enough. Although Havel favored a transition to the free market, he rejected the notion that human behavior can be reduced to a single cause, the rational pursuit of material well-being. Such a proposition ignores the testimony of everyday experience. After all, in a free society, where the force of the state is negligible, citizens voluntarily undertake all sorts of actions that run counter to personal self-interest. If people did not feel some attachment to the community, they would not pay their taxes, serve in the army, or obey the law; yet, it is universally true that citizens accept these responsibilities out of a sense of duty rather than a fear of punishment. There is abundant evidence, Havel claims, that human beings want to be

> anchored in one way or another to the world that surrounds us. Our family, our friends, the spiritual and social environment we are associated with, the community, town or region where we grew up and lived, and to which we accustomed ourselves, our country, our nation, our home in the broadest sense of the word all these are our anchors in this world, and more: they are integral components of our identity, indeed, they are part of ourselves. We have taken roots in our home, and our home has taken roots in us.[41]

Havel asks, if there is more to human beings than the profit motive, then "haven't we committed a colossal error" by viewing "man as a mere profit-maker and expecting that private initiative will automatically lead to public benefit?" According to Havel, people are more complex than the rational choice model would suggest, both for better and for worse. Some people "would willingly exchange three privatization funds for one kindly smile or loving touch," while others would flout "all standards, directives, and rules . . . pursuing no other aim but to cheat and rob."[42]

Of course, a truly consumer-oriented society has been created, one free of the normal obligations of citizenship and one dedicated solely to the satisfaction of material interests. This is the global civilization—familiar to anyone who has traveled—composed of Coca-Cola, McDonald's, blue jeans, MasterCard, multinational corporations, *Baywatch* reruns, CNN, and MTV. While the mass culture is surely alluring, especially to the young, it is little more than "a thin and recent veneer." Havel observes that beneath the conformity of the universal society "we find multiple layers of diverse cultural, social, and political traditions formed in different areas in the thousands of years when those different worlds lived separately or when their contacts were minimal." There are, in fact, two tendencies in the world. The first is the homogenizing effect of mass consumerism; the second is an awakening of "nations and whole regions" that have begun to assert, "often quite aggressively, their own ways of life, their unique identity, their traditions, their history, their deities, their habits, their cultures."[43] For Havel, a universal civilization is neither possible nor desirable. It is not engaging, because a world with one culture would be a dull place; all the colors mixed together would turn into a gray mass. It is not possible, because human beings need to attach themselves to something to make themselves feel needed, valued, and distinctive.[44]

If we investigate the origin of the human longing for distinction, we will be able to comprehend why people are motivated by more than the desire for material well-being. In a speech given at the Future of Hope Conference in Hiroshima, Japan, Havel reflects on the awareness of death in the human psyche. "With a little exaggeration we might say that death, or the awareness of death, is the most extraordinary dimension of man's stay on this Earth, one that inspires dread, fear, and awe and is at the same time a key to the fulfillment of human life in the best sense of the word." Because we are aware of death, we need something that transcends mere existence, something that gives meaning to life. The economic view of human beings as rational actors cannot be wholly true because we cannot live forever. No matter how much we accumulate to provide for the necessities of life and to live comfortably, we cannot escape our fate. Thus we need more than material possessions to give purpose to our lives. The traditional explanation of Being is supplied by religion. According to Havel, another method of justifying existence is the act of committing ourselves to a cause, principle, or group that we believe is greater than ourselves.[45]

Although we cannot conquer death, we can act as if death had no hold on us. After all, a group lives on after us. Our willingness to sacrifice for the group, perhaps even risking our own lives, indicates our contempt for death's inevitability. This strange human capacity for self-sacrifice reveals that, although there are selfish motives, not all motives can be reduced to the yearning for physical comfort and safety. This spiritedness, as it was called by the classical Greeks, often motivates us to act in ways that seem counter to our interests. There is clearly something inconsistent about intense public spiritedness. Why, after all, are people willing to fight and perhaps die in defense of their family, friends, nation, or property if there is little hope of enjoying those things in the future? Yet that is the kind of self-sacrifice that political passions can elicit. Catherine Zuckert attempts to explain this phenomenon:

> Political order does not emerge directly from the requirements of self-preservation but indirectly from the need people experience to defend

their lives, land and liberty. . . . The psychological source of political order is not to be found in either the desires or reason, therefore, but in the phenomenon [of] spiritedness.

In its origins, we find some of the reasons political life is so difficult to understand. People would not fight to defend their lives, lands, and liberties if they were not extremely attached to them. Spiritedness is thus rooted in love of one's own; yet we observe that in fighting to defend them, the warrior risks the very life, land, and property he is presumably struggling to preserve.[46]

"Love of one's own," as it might be called, is a key element in human behavior because it seems to evoke the political spirit. Thus it transforms itself into more than mere selfishness. In fact, it overcomes our egotism and draws us together into political communities. As such, it can be the source of good citizenship and devotion to community or country. However, if we dedicate ourselves to our own group, we often exclude the "other," who is outside our group, since the range of human attachments does not seem to be boundless. Other people sacrifice for their communities, and because the interests or principles of collectives are sometimes at odds, conflict seems to be inevitable. Thus members of one group or country may be aroused by their public spirit to strike out against the "other." Indeed, it is often the fear of a common enemy that is the most powerful force binding a group together.

Havel explains that "'otherness' is truly collective. And it is quite understandable that the 'otherness' of one group can make it seem, to the group we belong to, surprising, alien, and even ridiculous." Outsiders can sometimes become objects of scorn and loathing. People who hate, Havel wrote, "are never hollow, empty, passive, indifferent, apathetic people. Their hatred always seems to me the expression of a large and unquenchable longing, a permanently unfulfilled and unfulfillable desire, a kind of desperate ambition." Hatred of others "creates a strange brotherhood" and "a sense of togetherness." Even further, "collective hatred eliminates loneliness, weakness, powerlessness, a sense of being ignored or abandoned. This, of course, helps people deal with lack of recognition." Hatred of others provides a project, a reason for existence, and a hope of overcoming the anxiety created by the awareness of our mortality. "In hatred just as in unhappy love there is a desperate kind of transcendentalism. People who hate wish to attain the unattainable and are consumed by the impossibility."[47]

For Havel, the fundamental political problem is not related to economics. Rather, it arises because human beings are prompted by their apprehension of death to join social groups that give them a sense of solidarity and completion. Their efforts on behalf of the group offer them the opportunity to be recognized by others who share similar loyalties. "The situation is made more complicated because the need for self-affirmation is not essentially reprehensible. It is intrinsically human, and I can hardly imagine a human being who does not long for recognition, affirmation, and a visible manifestation of his own being."[48] Recognition is gained through sacrifice on behalf of the common good. However, this dedication is often turned against outsiders who might threaten the group's safety or honor. Thus, good citizenship arises from the very same source as do hatred and even violence, as the statues that nations erect to honor their soldiers can attest. Havel clarifies the vexing problem as follows:

> Reality is ambiguous. It is indeed tremendously difficult to discern the boundary between a moving, uplifting, sympathetic and thoroughly natural solidarity within a certain community, such as a nation, and a pack mentality that allows thousands, or millions, of cowardly and immature individuals to hide behind a "we" that automatically relieves them of any personal liability. Where does patriotism end and nationalism and chauvinism begin? Where is the line between civic solidarity and tribal passion?[49]

It is almost accurate to say that Havel sees a war being waged between the global civilization and the particular cultures of everyday life. The technological and communication revolutions have thrown together cultures that, for most of their histories, were blissfully unaware of each other. "Mutual differences . . . of their own particular 'otherness'" have now become apparent. Havel compares the situation to "life in a prison cell, in which the inmates get on each other's nerves far more than if they saw each other only occasionally."[50] Havel argues that while cultures sometimes fight each other, many are engaged in a struggle against the global civilization. He states:

> Within a fairly brief period of time no more than a fraction of human history a global civilization has come into being and spread around the whole planet, linking the different parts of it together, absorbing cultures or spheres of civilization which had for so long developed as autonomous units, and forcing them to adjust. A great many of the conflicts or problems in our world today, it seems to me, can be attributed to this new reality. They can be explained as struggles of different cultural identities, not with this civilization, but within themselves, for the survival or enhancement of what they are. . . . This desire for independence is an understandable reaction to the pressure to integrate and unify exerted by our civilization. Cultural entities shaped by thousands of years

of history are resisting this, for fear that within a few years they might dissolve in some global cultural neutrality.[51]

According in Havel, the crisis of our time is twofold. On the one hand, it is necessary to avoid the homogenizing and stultifying blandness of what Alexandre Kojève has termed the "universal homogeneous state."[52] On the other, it is necessary to avoid the clash of cultures that may result in new and even more fearsome ethnic conflagrations than those that took place in Bosnia and Kosovo.

Havel's project is no less than to reform the characteristic nature of political life. He is attempting to work out the problem of the general and the particular. The general is either so bland that it becomes odious to those with any spirit or so ineffective in holding people's loyalties that it does not satisfy their desire for distinctiveness and recognition. Yet, deeply held beliefs can be equally dangerous because they often result in self-righteousness and conflict. Havel hopes to make it possible for the parts to live peacefully with the whole, for cultures to remain distinct yet respectful of each other's differences, and for the good man also to be a good citizen. The playwright aims at nothing less than the transformation of human civilization.

What makes Havel believe that such a profound undertaking is possible? He sees a number of hopeful signs. First, many organizations are dedicated to integrating nation-states into a global association: the European Union, the International Monetary Fund, the World Bank, and the United Nations. Second, the world has begun to accept what Havel terms the postmodern mode of thought.[53]

> Today, this state of mind or of the human world is called post-modernism. For me, a symbol of that state is a Bedouin mounted on a camel and clad in traditional robes under which he is wearing jeans, with a transistor radio in his hands and an ad for Coca-Cola on the camel's back. I am not ridiculing this, nor am I shedding an intellectual tear over the commercial expansion of the West that destroys alien cultures. I see it rather as a typical expression of this multicultural era, a signal that an amalgamation of cultures is taking place. I see it as proof that something is happening, something is being born, that we are in a phase when one age is succeeding another, when everything is possible.[54]

The same global culture that represents a threat to human dignity may also provide an opportunity for fundamental change. Havel aspires to achieve a postmodern state both by decentralizing administration to localities throughout the world and by building up international organizations that will peacefully hold the world together. Civil society will take on many of the tasks that are local by nature, and nation-states will relinquish functions to various regional transnational organizations. In the same way that the local citizens in the Czech Republic will feel better about their country when they gain local control of their political lives, Havel is optimistic that various peoples and cultures will come to respect the other members of the international community once they feel they have control over their own destinies. "I believe," Havel explains, "that in the coming century most states will begin to transform from cult-like objects, which are charged with emotional contents, into much simpler and more civil administrative units, which will be less powerful and, especially, more rational and will constitute merely one of the levels in a complex and stratified planetary societal self-organization."[55]

The final tendency that encourages Havel to be optimistic is once again a double-edged sword. Havel believes that the principles on which the modern world is based have been exhausted. A contemporary theory is that the only way to avoid the kind of religious conflicts once so common in Europe and elsewhere is to abjure expressing any preference for spiritual principles at all. We live in "the first atheistic civilization in the history of humankind," he contends.[56] Rather than reflections on the spiritual aspects of Being, the contemporary ethos is founded on the supposition that the discoveries of science can provide us with not only enough material possessions to make us happy but also sufficient knowledge to make us wise. "The modern era," Havel writes,

> has been dominated by the culminating belief, expressed in different forms, that the world and Being as such is a wholly knowable system governed by a finite number of universal laws that man can grasp and rationally direct for his own benefit. This era, beginning in the Renaissance and developing from the Enlightenment to socialism, from positivism to scientism, from the Industrial Revolution to the information revolution, was characterized by rapid advances in rational, cognitive thinking. This, in turn, gave rise to the proud belief that man, as the pinnacle of everything that exists, was capable of objectively describing, explaining and controlling everything that exists, and of possessing the one and only truth about the world. It was an era in which there was a cult of depersonalized objectivity, an era in which objective knowledge was accumulated and technologically exploited, an era of belief in automatic progress brokered by the scientific method. It was an era of ideologies, doctrines, interpretations of reality, an era when the goal was to find a universal theory of the world, and thus a universal key to unlock its prosperity.[57]

Because "modern man thinks of himself as the lord of creation," he does not accept the authority of any authority beyond himself. But without some authority shared by people, private concerns come to supersede dedication to the common good.[58] Lack of a spiritual center leads to "moral relativism, materialism, the denial of any kind of spirituality, a proud disdain for everything supra-personal, a profound crisis of authority and the resulting general decay, a frenzied consumerism, a lack of solidarity, the selfish cult of material success, the absence of faith in a higher order of things or simply in eternity, an expansionist mentality that holds in contempt everything that in any way resists the dreary standardization and rationalism of technical civilization."[59]

Modern science has also had a destabilizing effect on the human psyche. "Classical modern science described only the surface of things, a single dimension of reality. And the more dogmatically science treated it as the only dimension, as the very essence of reality, the more misleading it became." The more we study the world, the less we know of ourselves. The greater our scientific objectivity, the less we understand our subjective selves. The more we control nature, the less sure we are of what to do with the power and freedom. We "find ourselves in a paradoxical situation," Havel explains. "We enjoy all the achievements of modern civilization that have made our physical existence on this earth easier in so many important ways. Yet we do not know exactly what to do with ourselves, where to turn."[60]

Humans are finite beings who can imagine the infinite. They will never be content with any explanation of Being that does not reach beyond their finitude. Havel insists that, since the modern scientific view of the human condition is incomplete, there is an opportunity, even a likelihood, that a new and more transcendent principle will take its place. For the first time in history, modern communications make it possible for the various religions of the world to recognize that they share comprehension of Being. They all accept a higher authority than the human will and "take the infinite and the eternal as the ultimate measures of human affairs."[61] A truly global civil society is now possible.

CONCLUSION AND APPRAISAL

There is little question that Havel's analysis of the political and spiritual condition of modern life is deeper and more penetrating than Klaus's. Klaus even admitted that he did not "understand his civil society. For me it is an empty phrase."[62] Of course, Klaus's profession of ignorance does not make Havel correct. It is difficult to test the principles of either man, since the

Czechs have instituted neither a fully transparent and free-market economy nor a decentralized political system.

Although the Czech parliament enacted a law creating new regional districts, there has been little effort to build the kind of local governments that Havel proposed. As Klaus had predicted, the Czechs have little experience with regional government, and no popular cry has demanded that authority devolve to self-governing local entities. There are local elections, but the nation is far from instituting a participatory democracy of the kind that shapes people's characters.

Which policy, if implemented, would be more likely to establish a civil society? That question is difficult to answer, a bit like asking which should come first, the chicken or the egg. I initially became interested in the question of Czech "regionalism" when I used the issue as a means of explaining the Alexander Hamilton–Thomas Jefferson debate to Charles University students enrolled in my American political thought course. There are striking similarities between Klaus and Hamilton, as there are between Havel and Jefferson.

Klaus and Hamilton each argue that it is possible to combine personal interest and civic responsibility. Each maintains that his nation can either employ the restless human spirit in the conquest of the material world or turn that passion inward and expend it on petty quarrels, internal disputes, and civil discord. The key for both is to give the commercial spirit free reign. Citizens could then pursue those professions for which they are best suited. They could follow their ambitions to the fullest. The talented could add to the wealth of the nation by creating and managing productive businesses. Greater productivity would lead to more wealth and result in more opportunity for all. Since people would be generally satisfied with their material conditions, they would see an interest in supporting the laws and the form of government that provide the preconditions for their pursuit of wealth. Finally, a commercial society would give rise to diversity since the freedom on which it rests would encourage the development of a multiplicity of human talents.

Conversely, Havel and Jefferson each believe that the pursuit of wealth sometimes makes people not high-minded but selfish. They maintain that the size and complexity of government should be limited and that power should be jealously guarded by keeping government small and close to the people. People's loyalties are best secured through allegiance to their communities and their neighbors. Civic spirit must be rooted in the soil, so to speak. Both favor a decentralized system of government in which people come to know and care about one another. Under the right social conditions, and imbued with the requisite character, people voluntarily perform their public duties—obeying the law, for example—obviating the need for strong central government and fostering individual autonomy. Moreover, Havel and Jefferson reason that the type of society favored by Klaus and Hamilton might eventually remove decision making from the people altogether, placing it in the hands of anonymous business executives and far-off government officials. With no public responsibilities, citizens would supinely accept the dictates of a well-organized, wealthy elite concentrated in the large commercial centers; true democracy might be lost.[63]

Tocqueville reminds us that America created a civil society by combining the strengths of a complex commercial society with the virtues of a decentralized political system. Perhaps by chance, the principles of Hamilton and Jefferson were both adopted, and the resulting synthesis helped form an energetic and civic-minded people.

In contrast, the Czechs after 1989 neither were able to implement a true free-market economy nor were they capable of fostering a strong sense of local responsibility. Perhaps as a result of not fully pursuing the policies of either Klaus or Havel, the Czechs were unable to adequately establish a civil society, one in which people voluntarily obeyed the law. The bitter truth of the shortcomings of the Czech transformation came to light after 1995, when stories of corruption, misuse of government funds, and misappropriation of private assets filled the media. A significant segment of the population lost faith in the political and economic reforms and felt little obligation to adhere to the kind of civic responsibility that Havel extolled. Anyone who hired a cab in Prague or who compared prices on the English-language menus to those written in Czech at tourist restaurants knows too that Klaus's principle of fair and open free-market exchanges—what Tocqueville calls "self-interest properly understood"—did not readily take hold.

As I write this chapter, almost fifteen years after the Velvet Revolution, small but significant improvements are visible in the Czech economy. The coalition government, led by the Social Democrat prime minister Vladimir Spidla, has begun the difficult task of eradicating the widespread corruption that his predecessors ignored. Moreover, the Czech Republic's entry into the European Union has forced business leaders and government officials to adopt greater transparency and responsibility.

In 1989, most commentators believed that the transition from a command- to a market-oriented economy, and from Communist Party rule to a liberal democracy, would take no more than a decade. After all, the Eastern European nations were far from underdeveloped. Their populations were highly educated, technically advanced, and culturally sophisticated. But despite these advantages, progress has been slow. The legacy of Communism looms larger than most people had originally realized. As Slavenka Drakulic argues, Communism has crept into the way many Central and Eastern Europeans think, preventing them from appreciating the responsibilities of citizenship.[64] To overcome the impediments of the past, Czech policy makers might consider pursuing the goals of both Havel and Klaus, a combination of a market economy and a local self-government.

Havel would add one more important criticism of industrial societies that Jefferson did not make, one gained by his superior vantage point in history. Materialism does not lead to true diversity. It is true that free-market systems foster greater opportunity for individual fulfillment, but they also create mass-based consumer societies in which products that gratify the most common desires are the most profitable (with "common" meaning both "broadly held" and "lowest"). If pursued to the exclusion of other ends, wealth homogenizes human beings. Not only does the goal of satisfying bodily comforts predominate, but it comes to smother the more subtle spiritual requirements. What Havel fears and counsels against is the threat of a global society constituted to gratify only the material desires in humans.

There are many questions raised by Havel's advice to reconstitute political communities. Will people reject materialism in favor of a kind of political arrangement that has existed only for brief periods? If political power is decentralized, will the distinct communities be able to avoid those violent clashes that fill the annals of history? If confrontation and war can be overcome, will citizens lose their political spirit? Will people be content to live in small communities in which their lives are fulfilled through civic activity, or does the human spirit transcend the political and long for some sort of personal salvation?

It is difficult to agree with Havel that materialism has run its course. People seem as greedy and grasping as they did at the beginning of the secular era. True, much lip service is paid to spiritualism, but pursuit of the technological and scientific way of life seems undeterred. Many people profess to want a simpler life, a more enriching life, but few actually seem to be pursuing those goals. Since the fall of Communism, the pace of the material conquest of the globe has actually quickened. Perhaps the post-Communist era proves that Klaus is correct after all—that the strongest human motive is "the uniform, constant, and uninterrupted effort of every individual man to better his condition."

Even a cursory survey of history indicates that Havel is overly optimistic about the possibility of constituting small republics that will remain at peace with one another. First, small republics have had little success. As Alexander Hamilton explains, it is impossible to read the history of the petty republics of Greece and Italy without feeling sensations of horror and disgust at the distractions with which they were continually agitated, and at the rapid succession of revolutions by which they were kept in a state of perpetual vibration between the extremes of tyranny and anarchy. If they exhibit occasional calms, these only serve as short-lived contrast to the furious storms that are to succeed. If now and then intervals of felicity open to view, we behold them with a mixture of regret, arising from the reflection that the pleasing scenes before us are soon to be overwhelmed by the tempestuous waves of sedition and party rage. If momentary rays of glory break forth from the gloom, while they dazzle us with a transient and fleeting brilliancy, they at the same time admonish us to lament that the vices of government should pervert the direction and tarnish the lustre of those bright talents and exalted endowments for which the favored soils that produced them have been so justly celebrated.[65]

Small republics have either destroyed themselves through domestic chaos or have been swallowed by larger, more powerful political entities.

Political societies are often kept together by differentiating themselves from the "other." The very political spirit that Havel sees as natural to human beings is grounded in love and in protection of one's own from outside threats. Public spiritedness seems inevitably linked to duty, honor, country—in other words, military prowess. Spiritedness is not entirely rational, since it seeks to gain individual honor through personal sacrifice. It is difficult to imagine that a world made up of small, semi-independent societies could translate the combative element in the human soul into universal social responsibility.[66]

Furthermore, if somehow peace and order could be achieved among all the people in the world, would that indicate that the political spirit had disappeared? Would not worldwide harmony further unleash the material motives in people? Would not universal peace inevitably lead to the homogenization of humankind? If one of the most ethnically diverse nations on Earth—the United States—is any indication, then tolerance and acceptance of the "other" lead to the breakdown of insular and distinct groups and to the amalgamation of differences.

Finally, can human beings be content with a political solution to their longing for completion? It is unlikely that ambitious human beings will find satisfaction in deliberating on the petty tasks of local government, such as trash collection or zoning ordinances. Moreover, mass communication and the ideas of Christianity and the Enlightenment have created a kind of universal horizon in which human beings no longer understand themselves as mere citizens. Social organizations, however deliberative and well constructed, cannot make our personal tragedies less challenging and our anxiety over death less troubling. As the result of the universal understanding of our condition, we have moved beyond political solutions to life's problems and now seek metaphysical explanations for life's mysteries.

For all that can be said against his position, Havel's vision of a future is surely an attractive one: it is one in which the deadening conformity of mass culture is overcome by the celebration of true diversity, and it is one in which people control their own destinies through active participation in social life. Havel is aware that prudence and the lessons of history weigh against his position, and he knows that political associations can only meliorate our existential anxiety. He maintains that the human race has a choice: either it can establish a form of political association in which individuals gain some control over their lives, or they can allow the centralizing tendencies of the mass technological society to rob everyone of independence and dignity. He writes that "the central political task" of our age "is the creation of a new model of coexistence among the various cultures, peoples, races, and religious spheres within a single interconnected civilization. This task is all the more urgent because other threats to contemporary humanity brought about by one-dimensional development of civilization are growing more serious all the time."[67]

In his high-profile disagreement with Milan Kundera, Havel insisted that virtuous actions ("living in the truth") were worthwhile even in the most forlorn circumstances. Havel countered Kundera's historical pessimism, arguing that human beings can control events. In the darkest days of the Czechoslovak era of normalization, Havel proclaimed that "hope is definitely not the same thing as optimism." Hope is "not essentially dependent on some particular observation of the world.... It transcends the world that is immediately experienced, and is anchored somewhere beyond its horizons."[68] He counsels us not to give up a moral stance, even with full knowledge that our fervent efforts may not succeed. He declares,

> I know that what I am saying here may seem like a mere pipe dream. Yes, as long as the world lasts, humanity will be tossed and torn by conflict of all kinds, and as long as people remain people, their bad as well as their good qualities will seek outlets. People will never be angels, and evil will never disappear from the world, but this does not mean that we are not duty bound again and again to come up with ways to make the world better, and to articulate again and again certain ideals, to set our sights on them, and to act in their spirit.[69]

NOTES

1. Richard Allen Greene, "Havel, Klaus Come to Verbal Blows," *Prague Post*, online, December 17, 1997.
2. Václav Klaus, *The Ten Commandments of Systemic Reform* (Washington, D.C.: Group of Thirty, 1993).
3. Klaus, *Ten Commandments*, 3, 4, 8.
4. Václav Klaus, *Renaissance: The Rebirth of Liberty in the Heart of Europe* (Washington, D.C.: Cato Institute, 1997), 82, 152.
5. Klaus, *Renaissance*, 27.
6. Klaus, *Renaissance*, 29.
7. Václav Havel, *Summer Meditations*, trans. Paul Wilson (New York: Vintage Books, 1993), 61–62.
8. Havel, *Summer Meditations*, 61–62.
9. Havel, *Summer Meditations*, 62; see also, *Disturbing the Peace*, 13–14 (see chap. 1, n. 4).
10. Havel, *Summer Meditations*, 67.
11. Václav Havel, "Address before the Members of Parliament," Prague, December 9, 1997.
12. Havel, *Summer Meditations*, 18.
13. Adam Ferguson, *An Essay on the History of Civil Society* (New Brunswick, N.J.: Transaction Books, 1980, first published in 1767).
14. Alexis de Tocqueville, *Democracy in America*, trans. George Lawrence (Garden City, N.Y.: Doubleday, Anchor, 1968).
15. Václav Havel, "Speech on the Occasion of 'Václav Havel's Civil Society Symposium,'" Macalester College, Minneapolis/St. Paul, Minnesota, April 26, 1999.
16. Havel, "Address before the Members of Parliament," Prague, December 9, 1997.
17. Václav Havel, "Address at George Washington University," Washington, D.C., April 22, 1993.
18. Havel, *Summer Meditations*, 4.
19. Václav Havel, "New Year's Address to the Nation," Prague, January 1, 1990.
20. Havel, "Address at George Washington University," Washington, D.C., April 22, 1993.
21. Havel, "Speech on the Occasion of 'Václav Havel's Civil Society Symposium,'" Macalester College, April 26, 1999.
22. Václav Havel, "Address at Asahi Hall," Tokyo, April 23, 1992.
23. Havel, "Address at George Washington University," Washington, D.C., April 22, 1993.
24. Václav Havel, "Transcript of an Interview for the Czech Radio," trans. Viktor Janis, November 2, 1993.
25. Havel, "Address before the Members of Parliament," Prague, December 9, 1997.

26. James S. Coleman, "Social Capital in the Creation of Human Capital," *American Journal of Sociology* 94 (1988): S95–S120; James S. Coleman, *Foundations of Social Theory* (Cambridge, Mass.: Harvard University Press, 1990); Pierre Bourdieu, "Forms of Capital," in *Handbook of Theory and Research for Sociology Education*, ed. John G. Richardson (New York: Greenwood Press, 1983); Glenn Loury, "A Dynamic of Racial Income Differences," in *Women, Minorities, and Employment Discrimination*, ed. P. A. Wallace and A. LeMund (Lexington, Mass.: Lexington Books, 1977); Michael Woolcock, "Social Capital and Economic Development: Toward a Theoretical Synthesis and Policy Framework," *Theory and Practice* 27 (1998): 151–208; Robert D. Putnam, *Bowling Alone: The Collapse and Revival of American Community* (New York: Simon & Schuster, 2000); Robert D. Putnam, ed., *Democracies in Flux: The Evolution of Social Capital in Contemporary Society* (Oxford: Oxford University Press, 2002).

27. Coleman, "Social Capital in the Creation of Human Capital," S100–S101.

28. Václav Havel, "New Year's Address to the Nation," Prague, January 1, 1994.

29. James Q. Wilson, *Moral Sense* (New York: Free Press, 1993), 49.

30. Václav Havel, *The Art of the Impossible*, trans. Paul Wilson and others (New York: Alfred A. Knopf, 1997), 147.

31. Václav Havel, "Substantial Extracts from a Speech to Mayors at the Occasion of the End of Their Mandate," trans. Viktor Janis, November 3, 1994.

32. Havel, "Speech on the Occasion of 'Václav Havel's Civil Society Symposium,'" Macalester College, April 26, 1999.

33. Havel, "Address before the Members of Parliament," Prague, December 9, 1997.

34. Václav Havel, "Speech upon Receiving the Onassis Prize for Man and Mankind," Athens, May 24, 1993.

35. Havel, "Speech on the Occasion of 'Václav Havel's Civil Society Symposium,'" Macalester College, April 26, 1999.

36. Havel, "Speech upon Receiving the Onassis Prize for Man and Mankind," Athens, May 24, 1993.

37. In a 1975 interview with Jiří Lederer, Havel claimed to be a socialist (Havel, "It Always Makes Sense to Tell the Truth," *Open Letters*, 97 [see chap. 1, n. 13]). By 1991, Havel's "heart" was "slightly left of center" (Havel, *Summer Meditations*, 61).

38. Greene, Richard Allen. 17 December 1997. "Havel, Klaus Come to Verbal Blows," *Prague PostOnline*. www.praguepost.cz/index.html.

39. Václav Klaus, "Interview on HTV," in *Nado raz* (To the hilt), by Jana Klusakova, trans. Viktor Janis, November 1997.

40. Klaus, *Renaissance*, 101–103.

41. Václav Havel, "Speech on National Day of the Czech Republic," Prague, October 28, 1995.

42. Václav Havel, "New Year's Message of Greetings," Prague, January 1, 1997.

43. Václav Havel, "Speech to the Latin American Parliament," Sao Paulo, Brazil, September 19, 1996.

44. Václav Havel, "Speech to the National Press Club," Canberra, Australia, March 29, 1995.

45. Václav Havel, "Speech at the Future of Hope Conference," Hiroshima, December 5, 1995.

46. Catherine H. Zuckert, *Understanding the Political Spirit: Philosophic Investigations from Socrates to Nietzsche* (New Haven, Conn.: Yale University Press, 1988), 4.

47. Václav Havel, "Speech at the Oslo Conference on 'The Anatomy of Hate,'" Oslo, August 28, 1990.

48. Václav Havel, "Speech upon Receiving the Sonning Prize," Copenhagen, May 28, 1991.

49. Václav Havel, "Address in Acceptance of 'Open Society' Prize," Budapest, June 24, 1999.

50. Václav Havel, "Speech upon Receiving the Jackson H. Ralston Prize," Stanford University, September 29, 1994.

51. Havel, "Speech to the National Press Club," Canberra, Australia, March 29, 1995.

52. Alexandre Kojève, *Introduction to the Reading of Hegel*, assembled by Raymond Queneau, ed. Allan Bloom, trans. James H. Nichols Jr. (Ithaca, N.Y.: Cornell University Press, 1980).

53. Václav Havel, "Speech at Chulalongkorn University," Bangkok, February 12, 1994.

54. Václav Havel, "Address to the Senate and the House of Commons of the Parliament of Canada," Parliament Hill, Ottawa, April 29, 1999.

55. Havel, "Address to the Senate and the House of Commons of the Parliament of Canada," Ottawa, April 29, 1999.

56. Václav Havel, "Address to FORUM 2000 Conference," Prague, September 4, 1997.

57. Václav Havel, "Address to World Economic Forum," Davos, Switzerland, February 4, 1992.

58. Havel, "Address at George Washington University," Washington, D.C., April 22, 1993.

59. Havel, "Speech upon Receiving the Jackson H. Ralston Prize," Stanford University, September 29, 1994.

60. Václav Havel, "Speech upon Receiving the Philadelphia Liberty Medal," Philadelphia, July 4, 1994.

61. Havel, "Speech at the Future of Hope Conference," Hiroshima, December 5, 1995.

62. Quoted in David Remnick's "Exit Havel," *New Yorker*, February 17 and 24, 2003, 96.

63. James F. Pontuso, "Political Passions and the Creation of the American National Community: The Case of Alexander Hamilton," in *Perspectives on Political Science* 22 (Spring 1993): 70–83.

64. Slavenka Drakulic, *Café Europa: Life after Communism* (New York: W.W. Norton, 1997).

65. Alexander Hamilton, John Jay, James Madison, *The Federalist Papers*, online (http://libertyonline.hypermall.com/Federalist).

66. For a different view of the possibility of a worldwide transformation, see Martin J. Matuštík's *Postnational Identity* (New York: Guilford Press, 1993), 187–229. For an examination of Havel's view of social responsibility, see Jean Bethke Elshtain's "The Performer of Political Thought: Václav Havel on Freedom and Responsibility," in *Theory and Practice*, ed. Ian Shapiro and Judith Wagner DeCew (New York: New York University Press, 1995), 464–482.

67. Havel, "Speech upon Receiving the Philadelphia Liberty Medal," Philadelphia, July 4, 1994.

68. Havel, *Disturbing the Peace*, 181.

69. Havel, "Speech at Chulalongkorn University," Bangkok, February 12, 1994.

6

AN "UNTACTICAL" PRESIDENT

HAVEL NA HRAD

Perhaps if Havel had known all the trouble that the office would cause him, he might have been even more reluctant to enter a profession he had always criticized.[1] There were surely many times during his thirteen-year presidency when he would have enjoyed returning to his first love, the theater. But, whatever personal goals or political ambitions Havel may have harbored, he saw his time as president more as a civic duty than a personal achievement. "The true test of a man," Havel has often said, paraphrasing Patočka, "is not how well he plays the role he has invented for himself, but how well he plays the role that destiny has assigned him."[2]

It is not the focus of this book to delve into the day-to-day policy decisions of Havel's thirteen years as Czech president. We must, however, review some of the criticisms of Havel's presidency, since it is now the generally accepted opinion that Havel was a political failure.

Steven Erlanger voiced disappointment with Havel in a *New York Times* article entitled "A Decade after Triumph, Havel Is Crushed Velvet." Erlanger's 1999 essay argues that, ten years after the Velvet Revolution, little had been accomplished to bring about the transition to free-market economics and a stable democracy. The economy was sluggish; the privatization process had been plagued by widespread corruption; few people had been punished for their crimes; badly needed legislation languished in the parliament; and the only point of agreement between the two leading parties was that they would not prosecute each other's members for violations of the public trust. Erlanger states:

Under Klaus and [then] Prime Minister Milos Zeman, Western diplomats say, Prague has done too little to restructure its economy, reform its judicial and legal system, crack down on corruption, build respect for the rule of law, protect outside investors and pressure politicians to act in the democratic spirit.[3]

John Keane's widely reviewed biography *Václav Havel: A Political Tragedy in Six Acts* also argues that Havel wasted his political capital and disappointed his fellow citizens.[4] Keane, who knew Havel during the embattled Czech's dissident years, helped him smuggle some writings to the West and edited Havel's *Power of the Powerless*. Keane aims to scrutinize Havel's life "without apologies, without illusions." He seems to respect Havel's courage and is sympathetic to many of his principles. However, perhaps because he has no heroes, his endeavor to be evenhanded, realistic, and dispassionate fails to adequately depict the strangeness and majesty of Havel's life.[5]

In one section about courage, Keane details an exchange between Havel and Czech writer Ludvík Vaculík, who together had signed Charter 77, demanding that the Czechoslovak government abide by its obligations as a signatory to the Helsinki Treaty on Human Rights. In 1978, Vaculík criticized fellow Chartists for risking imprisonment for actions that had no prospect of changing government policy. Confrontation with a powerful and ruthless government dragged friends, family, and coworkers into a dangerous situation, he argued. He saw the intransigence of the Chartists as little more than self-righteous moralizing, an effort to demonstrate their superiority over average citizens who lived decent lives but did not challenge the status quo. Havel responded by arguing that Vaculík's position was a retreat from the principles of the charter. Havel admitted that facing down a totalitarian state was risky business, but he believed that not opposing the government legitimized the party's rule and contributed to perpetuating the Communist dictatorship.[6]

Keane uses this incident as one of the *tableaux vivants* that, he claims, help illuminate Havel's life. Havel's sentiments were "almost classical," Keane contends; Havel believed as an ancient Greek or Roman believed: that courage was a precondition of citizenship.[7] Yet this *tableau vivant* almost makes us believe that Havel's courage consisted only of writing harsh letters to his associates. In fact, Havel spent most of his life in open opposition to one of the most repressive regimes in history. When Havel was not imprisoned for his defiance, he was hounded by the authorities. He underwent long and difficult interrogations by StB agents. He was continually followed. His life was threatened regularly in "anonymous" telephone calls. His apartment was broken into; his papers were stolen; and his friend and teacher Jan Patočka was interrogated so relentlessly that he suffered a fatal stroke.[8] Although Edá Kriseová's *Václav Havel: The Authorized Biography* has been criticized for lionizing Havel, her work is a more poignant and accurate portrait of Havel's courage in the face of evil.[9]

Keane's analysis fails to convey the drama of Havel's resistance. Other people of conscience, such as Nelson Mandela and Aleksandr Solzhenitsyn, would have been imprisoned no matter what stance they took toward the authorities. Mandela could do nothing about being black, and his freedom frightened South Africa's apartheid government. Solzhenitsyn had even less influence over Stalin's cruel megalomania. Havel could have left prison any time he wanted; he had merely to "write a single sentence asking for a pardon" and backhandedly renounce his "anti-socialist activities."[10] The Communist leadership would have loved for the internationally famous playwright to forswear his opposition. Think, then, of the enormous act of will Havel must have exerted to remain in jail knowing that he was the agent of his own incarceration. Just a few words repudiating Charter 77 would have secured his freedom. Regardless of whether he was ill, depressed, or frightened, Havel had to struggle not to submit. Summoning the courage to hold fast to his principles required a never-ending battle against himself.[11] Can a dry comparison to classical literature really do justice to such fortitude?

Keane repeats Stanislav Milota's rebuke of Havel that, once in office, Havel came to appreciate the perks of office too much and refused to listen to opinions contrary to his own, especially those of his former dissident friends. Milota chides Havel for riding in "chauffeur-driven limos" instead of "catching a tram up to the Castle [the seat of government]."[12] Keane fails to include Havel's quite sensible response: "It would certainly not make sense for a politician to miss an important state meeting with a foreign partner simply because he has been held up by the vagaries of public transport, so he has a government car and a chauffeur."[13] Perhaps Havel stopped listening to his former dissident allies because their very steadfastness made them poor politicians under democratic rule, where compromise and moderation are required. "The evolution of democracy," Havel muses, "often pushes [dissidents] out of politics altogether to make way for people who . . . are more realistic and thus more adaptable in everyday practical politics."[14] Keane's accusation that Havel somehow abused his power and displayed great hubris is surely overstated. What abuses of power? Havel never suspended the rule of law, ruled arbitrarily, or gained financially from his public service.[15] In fact, much of Havel's fortune goes to support foundations established by his former wife Olga.[16]

Keane maintains that Havel is a tragic failure primarily because he became unpopular with the Czech people.[17] There are many reasons for this disaffection, some trivial, some serious. Much public criticism was aimed at Havel's second wife, Dagmar. Olga was popular, and Dagmar—who married Havel less than a year after Olga's death—was considered something of an interloper. Olga created a medical foundation; Dagmar was an actress who once starred in a risqué movie. Over many years, Olga learned how to behave as the wife of a great man. Dagmar, more used to celebrity than fame, misunderstood her place at the side of the nation's leader.[18]

Keane echoes Erlanger's charge that Havel was unable to guide the nation successfully through the difficult post-Communist transition. To present a true picture of Havel, however, Keane might have dug a little deeper into Czech politics. Had he done so, he would have understood that the Czech people's impatience with their political leadership was inevitable. Surmounting forty years of disastrous Communist rule has been more difficult than anyone imagined. As Slavenka Drakulic argues, Communism poisoned the thinking of many Central and Eastern Europeans, preventing them from becoming self-activated citizens or entrepreneurs.[19]

Why should Havel be held responsible for the lack of economic progress? As Havel explains, "The authority of the [Czech] President [is] more statesmanlike than political," for he wields little actual power. Traditionally, the president of the Czech Republic is above party affiliation and acts more as a referee between competing party blocs. Elected by the legislature, the president is more a symbol of the nation than a true executive, for the Czech Republic is a parliamentary democracy where the prime minister wields the actual decision-making authority.[20] To paraphrase Alexander Hamilton, one of the architects of the strong American presidency, for the executive branch of government to be powerful, it must have adequate constitutional provision and sufficient electoral means. Because the Czech president has neither, Havel can hardly be blamed for the failed policies of the true political leadership.

Much of the Czech people's cynicism toward politics was created by the ebullient former prime minister Václav Klaus, who promised in 1992 that the transition to a prosperous free-market economy would be completed in five years. However, the Czech gross domestic product actually contracted in 1997 and remained flat for three years thereafter. The reasons for the failure of Klaus's approach are complex. Coupon privatization dispersed responsibility for the management of companies almost as broadly as Communism did. The investment firms that purchased the privatization coupons were more interested in quick returns than in restructuring companies, and managers had no real incentive to modernize industries. The *Prague Post* reported that

> investment funds quickly emerged with promises of high returns on the newly acquired shares. Many fund managers soon found themselves in control of large segments of Czech industry without even having to purchase stock themselves. They also found that nothing in the law prevented them from simply transferring a company's assets wherever they pleased.[21]

With little supervision from stockholders, managers were free to "tunnel" companies, selling off lucrative assets and pocketing the profits.

After the initial euphoria associated with the Czech "miracle"—as the early years of the Klaus government were called—investors lost faith in the reliability of Czech companies, and capital evaporated. Moreover, Klaus failed to privatize the banks. When inefficient companies came looking for loans, the government—fearing the political costs of high unemployment—allowed, and perhaps encouraged, banks to prop up industries that could not be competitive in the world market. Under mounting debt, the banks nearly collapsed, and the flaws of Klaus's policies were revealed. The Czech Republic faced the same painful reality of plant closings and unemployment that had afflicted Poland and Hungary earlier in the decade. It is little wonder that Czechs—numbed by their Communist bosses' false promises of a better future—cast a skeptical eye at all their leaders, including Havel.[22]

EXISTENTIAL REVOLUTION

Aviezer Tucker levels more sophisticated and serious charges against Havel. Tucker shows in great detail how the lofty hopes of the Velvet Revolution became the disappointing realities of the "Velvet Corruption." The post-Communist era was hijacked by the Communist *nomenklatura* elite, who, in contradiction to every one of their Marxist principles, became a self-seeking, dishonest, but financially successful ruling class who then used their ill-gotten gains to corrupt the political system. Under Communism, the *nomenklatura* claimed to despise capitalism, yet they undoubtedly prepared themselves well for its arrival. The three greatest advantages the *nomenklatura* had over their fellow citizens were capital, human capital, and connections. They either stole the capital from the state under Communism or pilfered it from state-owned industries during the transition. They acquired human capital not only by ensuring that the participants received the best education for themselves and their offspring but also by becoming fluent in English, the language of commerce. Only trusted party members were allowed to have top educational, managerial, and government posts; therefore, the *nomenklatura* had the advantage of knowing how things worked and how things could be manipulated. They held membership in the array of organizations and clubs instituted under Communist rule. They knew each other and used these associations and networks to plot how best to take advantage of opportunities and how to avoid being caught or punished for their nefarious activities.[23]

Havel took no part in these disreputable activities; in fact, he vigorously objected to them. He complained that

> in the course of the past ten years of our economic transformation, hundreds of billions have unaccountably disappeared from many banks and companies; billions have not been paid in taxes; and—worst of all—it seems as if only very few have been brought to justice for such offences; who knows whether some of those who managed to transfer money to tax havens do not even enjoy the silent admiration of the people around them. Who does not repay his debts here and who hires assassins to get rid of his creditors? And who among those who should serve as models for others, that is, among the leaders of political parties, denies his own financial machinations with a casual smile?[24]

Tucker blames Havel for not doing enough to stop corruption. Tucker argues that Havel's philosophic principles led him to hope for an "existential revolution" that would recast the way human beings related to each other and society, making the grimy aspects of politics unnecessary. Even after entering office, Tucker contends, Havel continued to believe the naïve notion of "non-political politics," and he resisted calls to form a political party that might have challenged the power of the *nomenklatura*. Havel failed to punish the former Communist leadership for their brutal tyranny, and by doing so, he opened the door for the networks established by the StB to reestablish themselves after the fall of Communism, but now with the intent of enriching their members and undermining the efforts to establish a liberal democracy. By refusing to take direct action, Tucker concludes, Havel was reduced to making rhetorical appeals in favor of responsibility, which in the face of the rampant corruption, seemed to many Czechs like the reproaches of an ineffectual moralizer.

Tucker's arguments are worthy of consideration, even if they are not always persuasive. First, we should remember how much Havel actually achieved. He oversaw the creation of a constitutional democracy, helped expel Warsaw Pact troops from his country, and pushed the Czech Republic toward Europe by overseeing negotiations for entry into NATO and the European Union. Through his friendship with Madeline Albright, he strongly influenced President Bill Clinton to end the wars in Bosnia and Kosovo, and, more than anyone else, he established—or perhaps reestablished—the international perception that the Czech Republic was a center of cultural and artistic activities.

Yet for all he accomplished, Havel did not want to be a leader who did everything for his people. After forty years of living under Communism, where the government made choices for everybody, he preferred that people begin to do things for themselves. Like Thomas Jefferson, another champion of civil society, Havel believed that self-government is best learned by the practice of governing oneself. Like Jefferson, he attempted to vest power and responsibility in the people. Believing that the rule of law was more important than the policies of one man, Havel acted within the confines of the law, recommending his ideas to the legislature rather than merely implementing them by executive fiat. Many of his proposals were rejected by the parliament.[25]

Tucker argues that Havel's inability to influence policy is a sign of weakness, one that could have been remedied had Havel organized a political base that would have supported his legislation. What if Havel had led a political party? How long would Havel's political party have survived? The transition to a free-market economy in former Communist countries was complex and difficult, not simply because it involved a change from one set of economic principles and policies to another, but because what was required was a conversion from a failed economic system to one to which most people were unaccustomed. Every post-Communist country experienced hardship, high unemployment, inflation, reduced purchasing power (especially among pensioners), and a terrifying uncertainty virtually unknown in the time when full employment was guaranteed and all economic activity was planned.

Voters in every country who suffered through these painful changes took their frustration and unease out on elected officials. The initial post-Communist, dissident-led governments were all voted out of office. Hungary, Romania, Bulgaria, Serbia, and Poland—the last of which was perhaps the most staunchly anti-Communist of all—elected reform Communist parties. The *nomenklatura* have flourished everywhere. If Havel had not stayed above politics to the degree that he did, and had he founded a political party, his influence might have been weaker than it actually was. As the head of a party, he would have been held responsible by voters for the pain and suffering of transition. Like other dissident leaders, such as Lech Walesa, he probably would have been considered politically irrelevant once his party inevitably fell from power. Is it not more likely that Havel, of all the dissident leaders, lasted longest exactly because he was a moral figure, not a political one? Whatever influence he had was the result of his remaining above day-to-day policy decisions—and who knows how important a moral figure may be in setting the tone for Czech civic culture?

Tucker argues that Havel should have used his political clout to punish former Communists. In a population of fifteen million, the Czechoslovakian Communist party recruited 2.5 million members. With such a large proportion of the population complicit in the workings of the regime, how could responsibility for the misdeeds of Communism have been allocated? Where would the line have been drawn for those determined to be legally accountable? Bringing the top 1 percent of the *nomenklatura* to justice would have required twenty-five thousand trials. Would the stability of the new democratic government of Czechoslovakia have been enhanced by the spectacle of so many people being rounded up and prosecuted? Moreover, what evidence could be used to establish legal culpability? Of course, the Communists had ruined the thriving pre–World War II economy and had devastated the environment in the process. But can bad economic and ecological policies be punished in criminal court? Communists had tyrannized the country, but they had operated under a legal system that permitted them to do so. True, the "invitation" to allow Warsaw Pact troops to invade Czechoslovakia in 1968 was treason, but the principle of the "leading role of the Communist Party," written into the constitution, actually might have legally exonerated those Communist leaders responsible for the invasion. Should the post-Communist government have prosecuted Communists for actions that, while morally reprehensible, had been legally sanctioned? Are ex post facto laws ever just?

Had Havel attempted to vigorously pursue former Communists in the courts, he might have been successful in thwarting the power of the *nomenklatura*, but he also risked a turned public opinion in their favor. Reprisal might have seemed heavy-handed and vindictive. Instead of being considered an ineffectual moralizer, Havel might have been criticized for using his office to settle personal grudges against his former tormentors. The problem with the kind of retribution that Tucker advocates is the number of people who took part in the crimes of Communism. It surely did not escape the ironic president that, while Communism had not been successful at distributing wealth, it had been masterful at dispersing culpability.

Havel worried that long, complicated legal proceedings might extend the Communist-era mind-set. He believed that it was better to get on with building a democracy and fixing the problems at hand than to mete out punishment for past misdeeds. Moreover, if Czechoslovaks recognized their own part in supporting an evil regime, they could begin to understand the kind of individual responsibility needed to build a civil society. He made all this clear in his first speech to the nation.

> It would be very unreasonable to understand the sad legacy of the last forty years as something alien, which some distant relative bequeathed to us. On the contrary, we have to accept this legacy as a sin we committed against ourselves. If we accept it as such, we will understand that it is up to us all, and up to us alone to do something about it. We cannot blame the previous rulers for everything, not only because it would be untrue, but also because it would blunt the duty that each of us faces today: namely, the obligation to act independently, freely, reasonably and quickly.[26]

Despite what Tucker suggests, Havel's condemnation of political parties is neither total nor rooted in the hope that an existential revolution will make them unnecessary. Rather, it is based on a critical examination of the ways that parties and party politicians sometimes behave. In 1968, Havel publicly called for the creation of a multiparty system in Czechoslovakia, a notion considered heretical even in the heady days of the Prague Spring.[27] As president, he affirmed that parties are "an integral part of modern democracy and an expression of its plurality of opinion."[28] But Havel has also presented his misgivings about parties and "put into words" his "personal 'utopia'" where a "significant shift in human consciousness" would be preferable to organizing a power-seeking political party. Havel objects to parties because they are large, often anonymous organizations in which citizens lose personal contact with their leaders. He would rather see a system "something like political clubs, where people could refine their opinions, get to know each other personally, and seek to determine who among them would be the best to administer the affairs of the *polis*."[29]

Havel also disapproves of parties on historical grounds; the "dictatorship" of party politics during the first republic divided the Czechoslovak nation along ethnic lines, left power in the hands of the party leadership rather than elected officials, and led to unstable coalitions that nearly undermined democracy. More generally, Havel complains that loyalty to the party is often stronger than loyalty to the country. Party politicians sometimes support or oppose a policy based on whether it will help them at the polls, not on whether the policy is good or bad. Parties out of power are especially irresponsible about criticizing and forestalling much-needed legislation, to make the political situation worse to enhance their chances in the next election. Ambitious politicians promote popular but unwise or impractical programs to endear themselves to the populace and advance their political careers. Parties encourage short-sightedness, selfishness, and petty bickering. They encourage political competition rather than nurturing moral responsibility. Parties may be necessary to democracy, but, as Havel argues, democracy is better served when we are attentive to the defects of parties.[30]

Havel is aware that his moral stand against parties is "an approach which, in this world, is extremely impractical to apply in daily affairs," but he adds that he knows "no better alternative."[31] As president, he wanted to maintain distance between himself and those immersed in the everydayness of practical politics. He thought it necessary to "step back and look at things from a distance and store this experience for later use."[32] He sought the "luxury of behaving untactically" so that he could remain "freer than those who cling to power."[33]

The problem with political power is its tendency to corrupt those who have it. People enter politics to promote their agendas, to satisfy their desire for recognition, and to enjoy the perks of office. Politicians are no better or worse than the rest of humanity. But their position entices them to confuse—even in their own thinking—public-spirited motives with more self-interested ones, such that "only God Himself knows whether" they are acting for the community or themselves. The situation is further complicated because self-affirmation is an intrinsically human desire and a "visible manifestation of our being." In the midst of serving the country, it becomes unclear to leaders when the perks associated with the job—including the adulation accorded to politicians—become the reason that they struggle so hard to stay in power. Havel's own experience with high office led him to wonder,

> Where do the interests of the country stop and the delight in privilege begin? Do we know, and are we at all capable of recognizing, the moment when we cease to be concerned with the interests of the country for whose sake we tolerate these privileges and start to be concerned for the advantages themselves, which we excuse by appealing to the interests of the country? Regardless of how pure his intentions may originally have been, it takes a high degree of self-awareness and critical distance for someone in power however well-meaning at the start to recognize that moment. I myself wage a constant and rather unsuccessful struggle with the advantages I enjoy, and I would not dare say that I can always identify that moment clearly. You get used to things, and gradually, without being aware of it, you may lose your sense of judgment.[34]

Havel hoped to overcome the prevalent cynicism about politicians by infusing politics with the sensibilities and critical judgment of poets and philosophers:

> Who, for that matter, is better-equipped to perceive the global context in which political actions take place, to assume a share of the responsibility for the state of the world, and to restore to political prominence values such as conscience, love for one's fellow humans, respect for nature, for the order of Being, and for the pluralism of cultures? Who else should give politics that much-needed spiritual and transcendental dimension and restore to it that dwindling supply of human perception and sensitivity? Who else is equipped to combat the growing notion that politicians are power-grabbing machines run by public relations experts and tuned to the public opinion of the moment?[35]

Tucker's most serious accusation against Havel is that the Czech president neglected practical affairs because he expected an existential revolution to fundamentally alter the character of human relationships. Tucker traces Havel's enthusiasm for an existential revolution to Heidegger, and Tucker's contention has some merit. Heidegger's philosophy deconstructs all metaphysical certainty and therefore undermines any ideology that might become tyrannical. The dissident Havel agrees with that aspect of Heidegger's thought. But Heidegger's philosophy also claims that Being reveals itself in history—and thus it can also be the source of a totalitarian temptation, the temptation to impose philosophic clarity on the practical world and adopt a fully satisfying account of Being in our daily lives. Or, after the turn, Heidegger's philosophy of waiting could be seen as a call for a kind of nihilism, of waiting for something unknown and unknowable. Heidegger deconstructs the ground from which humans make judgments.

Havel advocates an existential revolution to counteract the modern world's ill effects that stem from the arrogant efforts of human beings to control and dominate the natural world, including the destiny of the human species. In expressing this view, Havel reveals his intellectual debt to Heidegger by succinctly describing the German philosopher's stance after the "turn":

> "Only a God can save us now," Heidegger says, and he emphasizes the necessity of "a different way of thinking," that is, of a departure from what philosophy has been for centuries, and a radical change in the way in which humanity understands itself, the world, and its position in it. He knows no way out and all he can recommend is "preparing expectations."

> Various thinkers and movements feel that this as yet unknown way out might be most generally characterized as a broad "existential revolution." I share this view, and I also share the opinion that a solution cannot be sought in some technological sleight of hand, that is, in some external proposal for change, or in a revolution that is merely philosophical, merely social, merely technological, or even merely political.[36]

It is true that Havel hopes for an existential revolution that will blunt some of the deadening and alienating effects of our spiritually empty global technological society, but Tucker misunderstands what Havel means by an "existential revolution." Havel does not expect that peace and harmony will reign or that politics, for good and bad, will disappear. He emphasizes that his hopes do not blind him to the real possibilities for change.

> If I talk here about my political—or, more precisely, my civil—program, about my notion of the kind of politics and values and ideals I wish to struggle for, this is not to say that I am entertaining the naïve hope that this struggle may one day be over. A heaven on earth in which people all love each other and everyone is hard-working, well-mannered, and virtuous, in which the land flourishes and everything is sweetness and light, working harmoniously to the satisfaction of God: this will never be. On the contrary, the world has had the worst experiences with utopian thinkers who promised all that. Evil will remain with us, no one will ever eliminate human suffering, the political arena will always attract irresponsible and ambitious adventurers and charlatans. And man will not stop destroying the world. In this regard, I have no illusions.[37]

Havel specifically warns against the kind of waiting that Heidegger advocates after his "turn." Havel indicates that Heidegger's expectation of a new revelation of Being is as pointless as Samuel Beckett's characters' hope for some improbable redeemer to give meaning and identity to their lives in *Waiting for Godot*. Havel explains:

> Allow me to use this opportunity for a brief consideration of the phenomenon of waiting.... There are different ways of waiting. At one end of the great spectrum there is waiting for Godot, who embodies universal salvation. I come from a country that is full of impatient people. Perhaps they are impatient because they have waited for Godot for so long they think Godot has finally come. This is an error as profound as the one on which their waiting was based. Godot did not come. And that is just as well, because any Godot that did come would be merely the

imaginary Godot, the Communist Godot. . . . You cannot wait for Godot. Godot will not come, because he does not exist.[38]

Rather than waiting, Havel advocates that individuals act responsibly and take purposeful steps to make their own lives and the condition of their communities better. After all, to grow anything of value, people must "plant the seeds and water the ground well."[39] "In the first place," he explains,

> as I understand it, spiritual renewal (I once called it an "existential revolution") is not something that one day will drop out of heaven into our laps, or be ushered in by a new messiah. It is a task that confronts us all, every moment of our existence. We all can and must "do something about it," and we can do it here and now. No one else can do it for us, and therefore we can't wait for anyone else.[40]

The difference between Havel's hope for improvement in the human condition and Heidegger's resigned anticipation that a new revelation of Being will save us can be traced to their different conceptions of existence. For Heidegger, the truth discloses itself in a revelation of Being; for Havel, the truth is already present in the world and communicates itself in our observations of everyday life. Those observations include the way we react to our lives, including, of course, judgments about the meaning and value of experience. From the facts that we experience, we make value judgments about how to live. The natural world ultimately dictates what we see and what we value. Havel maintains that "an existential revolution" must have an "intrinsic *locus*" rooted in the particulars of "human existence." "It is only from that basis that it can become a generally ethical—and, of course, ultimately a political—reconstitution of society."[41] The locus that Havel favors is a rootedness derived from a participation in, and a governing of, one's local community.

Finally—unlike Heidegger's revelation of Being, which could be philosophically anything since it establishes what is true and worthwhile—Havel's existential revolution is based on the natural world and is therefore limited by what it prescribes and proscribes: "We must honor with the humility of the wise the limits of that natural world and the mystery which lies beyond them."[42]

We can perceive Havel and Heidegger's difference and judge the relative value of their theories by assessing how they attempted to put their theories into practice. We can also comprehend their differing views on the relationship between philosophy and politics. Heidegger overestimated the practical value of philosophy in political life. He stated that, in 1933, he "expected from National Socialism a spiritual rejuvenation of all life, a reconciliation of social antagonisms, and the rescue of Western existence from the danger of communism."[43] Karl Jaspers believes that Heidegger wanted to become leader of the Nazi movement—or, at the very least, the *Führer's führer*.[44] Rorty argues that Heidegger believed that his philosophy alone could bring the destiny of the German people to fruition.[45]

But why would Heidegger believe that his ideas were so crucial to rescuing the human race? What led him to such "stark political naiveté" and "lack of modesty"?[46] Why would he associate his great mind with a vicious and bigoted doctrine, even for a short time? Heidegger believed that, by having no core, Being could be manifest or revealed in his philosophy. Heidegger wanted to make philosophy into politics. He wanted politics to have the certainty of a philosophic revelation of Being.

Havel, who did eventually become leader of his country, did not attempt to bring about a new revelation of Being, even if, as Tucker suggests, he might have been hoping for some critical change in the course of Western civilization after the collapse of Communism. Havel was not immoderate in what he expected from politics, because the order of Being—that is, the natural world—establishes principles and practices that the human mind can perceive as good or bad, noble or base, loving or hateful. Therefore, the order of Being limits what we should do in political life. No revelation of Being can alter or transform life entirely.[47]

Of course, Havel had the wisdom of hindsight. He had studied Heidegger's mistake, and he knew the disastrous result of attempting to marry philosophy and politics. Instead, he wanted to make philosophy and abstract ethical ideas into symbols or goals, the never-quite-achieved standards of human conduct. He also attempted to act as a moral example. He did not seek power by forming a political party or social movement, a decision that disappointed Czechs who were looking to him for solutions to particularly pressing political problems—hence, the charge that he was too abstract, impractical, and preachy. Havel maintained a distance from politics and specific political programs because he wanted to establish his moral independence. He did not attempt to make politics wholly "moral" by putting philosophic theory into practice, as Heidegger had tried to do; but neither did he abandon philosophy or moral theory in the day-to-day political battles over policy.[48]

Tucker believes that Havel's reliance on the transcendent realm is dangerous because belief in the transcendent makes people parochial, ethnocentric, and violent. Havel actually agrees with this view, as his "Anatomy of Hate" speech shows.[49] However, Havel is also aware that history demonstrates the rank viciousness of atheist doctrines such as Communism and Nazism. Tucker and Havel are both humanists—in that they both value human life and dignity—but unlike Tucker, Havel attempts to explain why his brand of humanism is superior to Communism, Nazism, or any of the other barbaric doctrines. Tucker assumes that humanism is true, but he gives no account of why it is true. Havel tries to establish that humanism is part of the natural world constructed by the transcendent order of Being—and he does so to avoid the catastrophic social doctrines such as Communism and Nazism.

RESPONSIBILITY

Havel is often reproached for using the presidential office to preach and scold his fellow citizens, and it is true that most of the time he preached about responsibility. Given the difficult transition from a political system where responsibility resided in the state rather than in each individual, perhaps Havel had good reason to continually revisit the topic. But to understand why Havel raised the issue, it is necessary to understand what he means by responsibility.

It was in prison that Havel grappled most intensely with the issue of responsibility. Havel had to ask himself whether his time in prison had a purpose. What was he trying to accomplish? Could his act of defiance effect a change in the sluggish Czechoslovak regime? If his actions were unlikely to have practical results, why undertake them? From these considerations Havel raised the question of whether a proper standard of conduct can be identified—with the standard being what he called "responsibility." What exactly was that standard of conduct, and how was it known? How should it be applied to practical decisions in everyday life?[50]

Responsibility means first and foremost that we make our own choices and decisions. We cannot shift the blame or pass the buck for our actions. We alone are accountable for what we do. We behave responsibly when we understand that we are free to go beyond or transcend factors in the environment that help define us. Thus our freedom depends on making choices for ourselves, as the existentialists argue. But maintaining our freedom entails acting sensibly, not behaving impulsively or letting our passions control us. Havel knew that when we become too passionate, we lose control. Thus we can be responsible only if we have freedom of choice, and we can have true freedom of choice only if we remain responsible. Responsible behavior is not a function of our corporeal bodies and is therefore not part of our physical nature. However, the fact that we experience shame, sorrow, and empathy proves that elements of our being transcend the physical. Responsibility is not natural in the same way that the laws of physics, chemistry, and biology are natural; in fact, if it were, we would merely follow the laws of nature or instinct and have no responsibility—just as the rest of the material world does. But since we constantly make judgments about the value of our actions, there can be no doubt that a sense of responsibility is innate.

We know we are social beings because we experience loneliness. We could not be truly free if we lived without society, since we would spend all our time trying to sustain our physical existence. Because society is the place where we satisfy our physical desires and our need to belong—a "home," it might be said, for our psychological needs—we therefore feel a sense of responsibility to and for the community.[51] It is possible for us to neglect our responsibilities to the community, but when too many people act selfishly, social life becomes unworkable. When society is composed only of self-interested people, we become "estranged," and we experience "a special kind of animosity; ill will; egoism; disrespect for both legal and moral rules; greed; skepticism; maybe even cynicism."[52]

If we selfishly destroy social life, we also destroy our freedom and perhaps even risk our lives. Since responsibility cannot be selfish, the rules that guide it must not derive exclusively from our wills or choices. There must be something higher, beyond the will, that dictates the nature of responsible behavior. Because we are all aware of what selfishness is—although we may differ on whether a particular act is selfish—there must exist "somewhere" an idea or a standard that informs our judgment. Havel argues that responsibility is part of the natural world and emanates from the order of Being, although he can never quite prove this position—because such a proof would rob us of our freedom and dignity.[53]

Responsibility is the key to our identity because we are defined by what we think we should do and how we behave toward ourselves and others. If we throw ourselves into a social movement based on an ideology, or derive all our judgments from a spiritual doctrine that purports to know the whole truth, we abrogate our free will, our responsibility, and our identity. If we try to lose ourselves in everydayness, think only of ourselves, and neglect our civic duties, we may be able to survive, but we do so by encouraging—or even allowing—others to take responsibility for deciding our fate. When others decide for us, we lose part of our identity.[54]

Ignoring our responsibilities can be quite dangerous to others. For example, if we abuse our children, abandon our elderly parents, drive an automobile while drunk, wantonly pollute the environment, do shoddy work while constructing a building, or mistreat a patient in a hospital, we jeopardize the lives and well-being of others. Although many people do act irresponsibly, no one wants to admit to being irresponsible, for to do so would undermine the sense of identity. Who, for example, could relish the idea of the following epitaph: Here lies a man who hurt his family, recklessly killed his neighbors, and injured others because of his careless work?

It is hard to make responsible decisions. After all, what defines "responsible behavior" to our families, job, and community? Jean Bethke Elshtain is correct to argue that, for Havel, moral choice is a middle ground between certainty and doubt, convention and freedom, discipline and spontaneity.[55] If we tip the scale in either direction and become, say, too dogmatic or too resigned, we risk abandoning responsible behavior and forgetting our truly human identity. The human condition is such that we can never be certain that our actions will have a positive result. We can never even be fully confident that there is such a thing as the "human good." But human affairs can never work out for the good if we ignore our responsibilities and deny that moral standards exist. Havel explains that "if there is to be any chance at all of success, there is only one way to strive for decency, reason, responsibility, sincerity, civility, and tolerance, and that is decently, reasonably, responsibly, sincerely, civilly, and tolerantly."[56]

Perhaps Havel is too hopeful about the fate of the human race. But miracles do happen. Who, after all, would have imagined during the height of the Cold War that the author of surrealist plays who had spent most of his adult life as a political recreant and social outcast would become one of the most articulate political leaders of his generation, leading a nation that Neville Chamberlain once called a "country far away and a people about whom we know very little"?

NOTES

1. Havel, *Summer Meditations*, xv (see chap. 5, n. 7); Michael Simmons, *The Reluctant President* (London: Methuen, 1991).

2. Havel, *Disturbing the Peace*, 72 (see chap. 1, n. 4).

3. Steve Erlanger, "A Decade after Triumph, Havel Is Crushed Velvet," *New York Times,* online, November 4, 1999.

4. Keane, *Political Tragedy in Six Acts*, 1–16, 410–505 (see chap. 4, n. 94); Richard Allen Greene, "Backstage Man," *Prague Post,* online, October 20, 1999; Gregg Easterbrook, "Review of *Václav Havel: A Political Tragedy in Six Acts*," *Washington Monthly* 32, no. 9 (September 2000): 48; Slavoj Zizek, "Attempts to Escape the Logic of Capitalism," *London Book Review*, online, September 6, 2000; Stephen Winterstein, "Review of *Václav Havel: A Political Tragedy in Six Acts* and *Post–Cold War Europe Up Close and Personal*," *ORBIS* 45, no. 4 (Fall 2001): 648. See Keane's defense of his book in John Keane's "Too Clever by Half," *Central European Review* (online) 1, no. 24 (December 6, 1999).

5. Keane, *A Political Tragedy in Six Acts*, 11, 12.

6. Keane, *A Political Tragedy in Six Acts*, 258–266.

7. Keane, *A Political Tragedy in Six Acts*, 265.

8. For details of the harassment that Havel suffered, see Václav Havel's "Reports of My House Arrest," *Open Letters*, 215–229 (see chap. 1, n. 13).

9. Kriseová, *The Authorized Biography*, 154–161 (see chap. 1, n. 8).

10. Havel, *Letters to Olga*, 19, 33, 38 (see chap. 1, n. 19); *Disturbing the Peace*, 158–159.

11. "One can therefore defend one's dignity anywhere, at any time; it is not a onetime decision, but a daily and rather demanding 'existential praxis'" (Havel, *Letters to Olga*, 302).

12. Keane, *A Political Tragedy in Six Acts*, 411.

13. Václav Havel, "Address upon Receiving the Sonning Prize," Copenhagen, May 28, 1991.

14. Václav Havel, "Address at Wroclaw University," Wroclaw, Poland, December 21, 1992.

15. There were difficulties over the sale of Havel family property. See "Havel in Family Feud over Multi-million Crown Palace," *CTK* Czech News Agency, Prague, online, March 3, 1997.

16. "Havel's property basic fund of Václav and Olga Havel Foundation," *CTK* Czech News Agency, Prague, online, January 4, 1997.

17. Keane, *A Political Tragedy in Six Acts*, 407–510.

18. "Dagmar Veskrnova: The Ninth First Lady," *CTK* Czech News Agency, Prague, online, January 4, 1997; "New Role of Dagmar Veskrnova, with Václav Havel as Her Partner," *CTK* Czech News Agency, Prague, online, January 4, 1997; Erlanger, "A Decade after Triumph, Havel Is Crushed Velvet," *CTK* Czech News Agency, Prague, online, January 4, 1997.

19. Slavenka Drakulic, *Café Europa: Life after Communism* (New York: W.W. Norton, 1997).

20. Václav Havel, "The Role of the Czech President," trans. Paul Wilson, in *Critical Essays on Václav Havel*, ed. Maketa Goetz-Stankiewicz and Phyllis Carey (New York: G. K. Hall, 1999), 261.

21. Ondrej Benda, "Privatization Guru Foresaw Tunneling," *Prague Post,* online, January 6, 1999.

22. Jan Stojaspal, "Nothing to Toast About: Czechs Struggle to Mend the Tattered Remnants of Their 'Velvet Revolution,'" *Time International*, March 15, 1999, 18.

23. Tucker, *The Philosophy and Politics of Czech Dissidence*, 209–241 (see chap. 2, n. 10).

24. Václav Havel, "National Day Address," Prague, October 10, 2000. Havel has been accused of dealing with Marian Calfa, his first prime minister and a former Communist, and of an association with Václav Junek, a reputed StB agent who was dismissed as president of the Chemapol Group in 1999 for questionable financial dealing. Havel sold his share of the Lucerna Palace complex to a business group headed by Junek. Havel donated most of the assets from the sale to charity. See Siegfried Mortkowitz, "Junek Ousted as Chemapol Head," *Prague Post,* online, February 10, 1999.

25. Rick Fawn, "Symbolism in the Diplomacy of Czech President Václav Havel," *East European Quarterly*, electronic collection: A54297060, 33 (Spring 1999): 1; Havel, *Summer Meditations*, 59.

26. Václav Havel, "New Year's Address to the Nation" Prague, January 1, 1990.

27. Václav Havel, "On the Theme of an Opposition," *Open Letters*, 25–35; *Disturbing the Peace*, 98–99.

28. Havel, *Summer Meditations*, 53.

29. Havel, *Disturbing the Peace,* 17.

30. Havel, *Summer Meditations*, 54–55.

31. Havel, "Politics and Conscience," *Open Letters*, 269.

32. Erlanger, "A Decade after Triumph, Havel Is Crushed Velvet."

33. Havel, *Summer Meditations*, 8.

34. Havel, "Address upon Receiving the Sonning Prize," Copenhagen, May 28, 1991.

35. Havel, "Address at Asahi Hall," Tokyo, April 23, 1992.

36. Havel, "The Power of the Powerless," *Open Letters*, 206–207.

37. Havel, *Summer Meditations*, 16.

38. Václav Havel, "Speech to the Academy of Humanities and Political Sciences," Paris, October 27, 1992.

39. Havel, "Speech to the Academy of Humanities and Political Sciences," Paris, October 27, 1992.

40. Havel, *Disturbing the Peace*, 12.

41. Havel, "The Power of the Powerless," *Open Letters*, 206–207.

42. Havel, "Politics and Conscience," *Open Letters*, 267.

43. Quoted in Thiele, *Timely Meditations*, 133n (see chap. 2, n. 31).

44. Dallmayr, *The Other Heidegger*, 25 (see chap. 2, n. 45).

45. Richard Rorty, "Taking Philosophy Seriously," *New Republic*, April 11, 1988, 31.

46. Dallmayr, *The Other Heidegger*, 25.

47. Havel, "Address at Asahi Hall," Tokyo, April 23, 1992; *Letters to Olga*, 371.

48. Havel, "Speech to the Academy of Humanities and Political Sciences," Paris, October 27, 1992.

49. Havel, "Speech at the Oslo Conference on 'The Anatomy of Hate,'" Oslo, August 28, 1990.

50. Havel, *Letters to Olga*, 100.

51. Václav Havel, "Acceptance Remarks upon Conferment of the Grand Prix of the World Academy of Cultures," Paris, February 1, 2001; *Summer Meditations*, 31.

52. Václav Havel, "New Year's Address," Prague, January 1, 2000. Havel is speaking about his own country, but the point can be extended generally.

53. Havel, *Letters to Olga*, 147.

54. Havel, *Letters to Olga*, 145.

55. Elshtain, "Václav Havel on Freedom and Responsibility," 464–482.

56. Havel, *Summer Meditations*, 8.

INDEX

ABC Theater, 4
absurd theater, 4, 16–17, 69–76, 78, 91, 105, 113–15, 116n2, 116n3
Academy of Performing Arts, 3
Ademec, Ladislav, 8
Ambros, Veronika, 119–120n80
anti-Charter 77, 10
Aquinas, St. Thomas, 48
Aristophanes: *The Clouds* by, 66
Aristotle, 20, 43, 91, 133; *Politics* by, 91

Baranczak, Stanislaw, 70, 77, 84, 116n3
Bayard, Caroline, 17
Baywatch, 136
Beckett, Samuel: *Waiting for Godot* by, 120n80, 163–64
Berlin, 128
Bohemia, 3, 5
Bosnia, 11, 140, 158
Bourdieu, Pierre, 130
Bradbrook, M. C., 76
Brecht, Bertold, 105–107, 114–15; *The Three Penny Opera* by, 105–107
Brezhnev, Leonid, 5
Brustein, Robert, 77, 117n34
Bujak, Zbygniew, 6
Bulgaria, 158

Café Slavia, 4, 9–10
Calfa, Marian, 9, 169n24

Carey, Phyllis, 76, 120n90
Castro, Fidel, 11
Central Europe (European), 1, 5, 70, 105, 116n3, 145, 155
Chamberlain, Lesley, 77
Chamberlain, Neville, 168
Charles University, 5, 143
Charter 77, 6, 87, 153, 154
Chartist(s), 6, 153
China, 7
Civic Forum, 8
civil society, 89, 123, 125–47, 158
Clinton, Bill, 158
CNN, 136
Coca-Cola, 87, 136, 140
Cold War, 168
Coleman, James S., 130
Committee to Defend the Unjustly Prosecuted (VONS), 7
Communism, 3, 31, 33, 56, 58–60, 62, 66, 79, 85, 89–90; fall of, 7–8, 11, 34, 49, 63, 64–66; legacy of, 127–30, 144–45, 155–59, 165–66
Communist(s), 3, 7–8, 56, 85, 108, 116, 129, 134, 159
coupon privatization, 123, 127, 155
Cuba, 11
Czechoslovakia, 3, 5, 8–10, 31, 33, 58, 70–71, 84, 103, 116n2,

118n52, 128, 159–60; 1968
   invasion of, 56
Czech Republic, 32, 123, 127, 134,
   141, 144, 156–58
Czech University of Technology, 3

Dallmayr, Fred, 28
Day, Barbara, 116n2, 118n52
DeMan, Paul, 113
Descartes, Réne, 21, 24, 111
Dienstbier, Jiri, 76
Dubček, Alexander, 5, 8

Elshtain Jean Bethke, 19, 151n66
Enlightenment, 18, 65, 71, 104, 146;
   relationship between science and
   the, 12, 78, 98, 103, 141
era of normalization, 5, 62, 71, 85,
   107–108, 128, 147
Ericson, Edward E., Jr., 18
Erlanger, Steven, 152, 155
Esslin, Martin, 70, 74, 120n80
Europe (European), 7 64, 108, 134,
   141, 144, 158
European Union (EU), 140, 144
existentialism, 19, 74, 120n80, 169n11;
   and anxiety, 147; and attitude, 31,
   55; and continuity, 100; and
   doctrine, 17; and fear, 57, 109; as a
   movement, 25; as a philosophy,
   52n53; and protest, 62; and reality,
   104, 109; as a stance, 27; and
   uncertainty, 61
existentialist(s), 33, 42, 63, 166

Findlay, Edward F., 15, 43–44
Forman, Milos, 4
Foucault, Michel, 27
France, 127

Gaia principle, 19, 47–48
Gay, John, 107, 110, 112, 114–15; *The
   Beggar's Opera* by, 105–106, 109, 111

Gellner, Ernest, 64–65
Germany, 24
Gillespie, Michael Allen, 31
God, 15, 18–19, 25–26, 28, 30, 40,
   46–48, 72–73, 76, 94, 98, 161–63
Goethe, Johann Wolfgang von, 1, 102
Goetz-Stankiewicz, Marketa, 76, 78
Gorbachev, Mikhail, 7
Gott, Karel, 10

Hamilton, Alexander, 143–45, 156
Hammer, Dean C., 17
Hašek, Jaroslav, 78; *The Good Soldier
   Švejk* by, 90
Havel, Ivan, 4
Havel, Václav: and civil society, 125–33,
   138–42; and the existential
   revolution, 17, 156–66; and life,
   2–12, 154–55, 168n24; and living in
   truth, 9, 33, 65; and memory of
   Being, 15, 35, 40; and order of
   Being, 19, 34–35, 41, 44, 47–49, 55,
   61, 162, 165–67; as president, ix,
   1–3, 8–11, 15, 17, 64, 123, 152–70;
   "A Word about Words" by, 96;
   Audience by, 10, 16, 71, 76–84,
   86–87; *The Beggar's Opera* by,
   105–116; "Dear Dr. Hušak" by 6,
   56; *The Garden Party* by, 5, 70,
   92–94, 101, 119n80; *The Increased
   Difficulty of Concentration* by, 4,
   96–102; *Largo Desolato* by, 7; *Letters
   to Olga* by, 7, 15, 117n15; *The
   Memorandum* by, 4, 70, 94–96, 101;
   "Politics and Conscience" by 56;
   "Power of the Powerless" by 6, 53,
   156; *Private View* by, 78, 117n34;
   Protest by, 71, 76, 82, 88–90;
   Temptation by, 7, 101–5; *The
   Unveiling* by, 10, 71, 76–77, 85–88
Havelova, Dagmar, 155
Havelova, (Šplíchalová), Olga, 3, 7, 10,
   19, 36, 44, 100, 117n15, 154–55
Hegel, Georg, 22

Heidegger, Martin, 17, 19–36, 45, 49, 63, 73–74, 95–96, 98, 100, 104, 162–65; as antifoundational, 25–26, 34, 39, 42; *Being and Time* by, 26, 100; and change in Being, 29–30, 34, 39; and Dasein, 19, 23–24, 28–33, 52n45, 63, 65, 73, 92, 100–101; and l'*affaire*, 20, 29; and language, 23–24, 26–27, 59; and no-thing, 21, 23, 25, 28, 33, 49, 100, 114; and technology, 21–22, 25, 31; and throwness, 23, 36–38, 41–42, 87, 101; and the turn (turning), 20, 24–25, 30, 162–63
Helsinki Treaty, 153
Hiroshima, 137
Hitler, Adolf, 16, 29
Hrad, 8, 152
Hradčany, 2
Hungary, 7, 9, 156, 158
Husak, Gustav, 6

International Monetary Fund, 140
Ionesco, Eugène, 17, 74, 120n80

Japan, 137
Jefferson, Thomas, 143–45, 158
Judeo-Christian, 48

Kafka, Franz, 9, 78
Kafkaesque, 12
Keane, John, 5, 10, 118, 153–55
Khrushchev, Nikita, 56
Klaus, Václav, 10, 123–27, 130, 134–35, 141, 143–54, 153, 155, 156; *The Ten Commandments of Systemic Reform* by, 124
Kochhar-Lindgren, Gary, 83
Kohout, Pavel, 76, 78, 81, 89, 119n58
Kosovo, 11, 140, 158
Kriseová, Evá, 4, 121n99, 154
Kundera, Milan, 1, 4, 70–71, 147

Landovsky, Pavel, 76
Lawler, Peter Augustine, 18–19, 46–48

Lennon, John, 11
Loury, Glenn, 130
Lucerna Palace, 1, 169n24
Lyotard, Jean-François, 17, 26

Machiavelli, Niccolò, 71
Madison, James, 53n60
Magic Lantern, 4
Majer, Peter, 16
Mandela, Nelson, 154
Marx, Karl, 21–22, 58, 61, 75, 81, 118n46
Marxism, 22, 58, 126
Marxist(s), 31, 39, 58, 61, 65, 81, 105, 107, 114–15, 156
Masaryk, Tomaš Garrigue, 3
Masarykian humanism, 3, 38
Mastercard, 136
McDonalds, 136
Miller, Arthur, 2
Milota, Stanislav, 154
Moravia, 3
MTV, 136

National Socialism, 30, 164
National Theater, 4, 10
NATO, 158
Nazi(ism), 7, 20, 24, 28–30, 34, 165–66
New Republic, 8
New York, 77
New York Times, 152
Nietzsche, Friedrich, 20, 24, 91, 109
Nobel Prize, 4
nomenclature, 81, 94
nomenklatura, 156–59

Obie Award, 4
Opletal, Jan, 7

Pabst, G. W., 107, 115
Palach, Jan, 5, 7
paneláks, 60–61
Patočka, Jan, 4, 6, 13n16, 17, 43–46, 152, 154
Perspectives on Political Science, 19

Plato, 6, 16, 20–21, 24, 41–47, 52n46, 53n60, 73, 75, 113; *Crito* by, 6; *Gorgias* by, 47; *Lysis* by, 44; *Phaedo* by, 6; *Republic* by, 44, 47
Poland, 7, 156, 158
postmodernism, 15, 17, 25–28, 79, 83, 86, 109, 135–42
postmodernist(s), 26–27, 33, 83, 89, 104, 113
Prague, 2, 4–5, 8, 37, 58, 70, 144, 153
Prague Castle, 3, 8, 10, 32
The Prague Post, 156
Prague Spring, 56, 71, 85, 88, 107, 128, 160
Putnam, Robert D., 130

responsibility, ix, 3, 12–13n6, 16, 35, 37–38, 41–42, 55–56, 60–61, 63, 65, 90, 101, 110, 113, 128, 130–31, 144, 146, 151n66, 155, 157–62, 166–68; civic, 87, 108, 126, 143–44
Rhine River, 21, 32
Romania, 158
Rorty, Richard, 17–18, 27, 51n39, 83–4, 86–87, 118n52, 165

samizdat, 6
Sartre, Jean Paul, 25–27
secret police, 10, 57, 80–82, 84, 103, 116n3, 118n44
Seifert, Jaroslav, 4
Serbia, 158
Sire, James W., 19, 82
Slovakia, 10
Smith, Adam, 37, 124
Socrates, 16, 20, 43–45, 66, 73, 91, 113
Solidarity, 6–7
Solzhenitsyn, Aleksandr, 11, 18, 154; *Candle in the Wind* by, 92; *The Gulag Archipelago* by, 56
South Africa, 154
Soviet (Union), 5, 7, 55, 57, 66, 71
Spidla, Vladimir, 144

Stalin, Joseph, 4, 56–57, 70, 154; and labor camps, 16
Stalinist(s), 4, 56, 94
StB (secret security police), 6, 10, 108, 153, 157, 169n24
Steiner, Peter, 71, 107, 109
St. Vitus Cathedral, 32

Thatcher, Margaret, 134
Theater of the Balustrade, 4
Thiele, Leslie Paul, 25, 28, 52n46, 53n60
Thomas, Alfred, 77–78, 85
Tocqueville, Alexis de, 127, 144
Tresmontant, Claude, 48
Trojanowska, Tamara, 77, 90
Tucker, Aviezer, x, 17, 34, 156–60, 162–63, 165–66

United Nations, 140
United States, 127, 146

Vanek, Ferdinand, 73, 76–92, 118n44
Velvet Corruption, 156
Velvet Divorce, 10
Velvet Revolution, 8, 10, 64–65, 144, 152, 156
Vladivostok, 128
Vltava River, 2, 8

Walesa, Lech, 158
Warsaw Pact, 5, 56, 108, 158–59
Wenceslas Square, 2, 5, 8
Wilson, James Q., 13n6, 122n136, 131
Wilson, Paul, 57
Woolcock, Michael, 130
World Bank, 140
World War II, 20, 24, 159
Writers' Union, 4

Zappa, Frank, 11
Zeman, Milos, 153
Zuckert, Catherine, 137

ABOUT THE AUTHOR

James F. Pontuso is William W. Elliott Professor of Political Science at Hampden-Sydney College in Virginia. He is author of *Assault on Ideology: Solzhenitsyn's Political Thought* (Lexington Books, 2004), coauthor with Roger Barrus, et al., of *The Deconstitutionalization of America: The Forgotten Frailties of Democratic Rule* (Lexington Books, 2004), and editor of *Political Philosophy Comes to Rick's: Casablanca and American Civic Culture* (Lexington Books, forthcoming).